FIRST FRUITS

Presented to:

_____

From:

_____

FIRST FRUITS

"Spiritual strength requires diligence, yet patience; determination, yet waiting. That's why many believers limp instead of soar as God intends. *First Fruits* is a gift to the Body for both the strong and the weak. Encouraging, challenging, thought-provoking, wise...if you are looking to strengthen your relationship with Jesus, I highly recommend Susan's powerful book to you."

—Jeff Young
Minister of Spiritual Development
Prestonwood Baptist Church, Plano, Texas

"Congratulations to my dear friend Susan Butler for developing this remarkable book, *First Fruits!* I've always known Susan to be an exemplary wife, mother, friend and personal achiever, yet now she reveals her commitment to bless and encourage others in a fresh, new way. She inspires all of us to receive God's first and best in the person of Jesus Christ so we can experience that first-and-best life He planned for us to have. I love Susan's concept, her writing style, the practical application to life, and I like how it makes me feel when I read it. Read *First Fruits* daily! Learn from it, live out the scriptural teaching, and you'll see blessed and better days ahead."

—Dan Sampson
Sampson Resources, Dallas, Texas

"Susan and her husband, C.J., have been special friends and encouragers of our worship and missions ministry, "The Master's Music," for many years. Their desire to see Christ honored in worship is wonderfully evident in Susan's devotion book, *First Fruits,* which draws the believer in Christ into a fresh experience with Him every day. Thank you, Susan, for beautifully directing our first thoughts, our first words, and our first expressions of love to the One Who first loved us."

—Chris and Diane Machen
The Master's Music, Plano, Texas

"In *First Fruits*, Susan has captured the very essence of what we teach as prayer coaches; that from the moment we are "born again" into the family of God, we must begin to grow in our knowledge of Who He is and what He desires of us here on earth ... to intimately <u>know</u>—not just know about—the Father, Son and Holy Spirit. *First Fruits* empowers seekers to grow in their relational knowledge of the Lord through their daily meeting with God. We delight in encouraging others to add this tool to their tool belt of growth and intimacy with the blessed Trinity!

One of our favorite things to coach is to spell "intimacy" like God does: In—to—ME—see. He already knows everything about each person created (Psalm 139); the challenge we have is to see into Him. *First Fruits* does that with depth, yet practically, for the new believer as well as the one who has traveled "the way" for years. Thank you, Susan, for "coaching" all of us into a more intimate walk with our Savior. In the words of former Dallas Cowboys Head Coach, Tom Landry, the role of a coach is to "inspire others to do things they don't want to do, in order to achieve things they want to accomplish." *First Fruits* does just that!"

—**Dennis and Betty Jo Conner** have coached people for the past fifty years of their marriage—whether at the elementary school "special needs" level or the high school, university, or professional tennis coaching level, or as twenty-four year staffers with the Fellowship of Christian Athletes—they now are fulltime Prayer Coaches with Called to Serve, their prayer ministry in Dallas, Texas.

FIRST FRUITS

Giving God Your Best
365 Days of the Year

D E V O T I O N A L

SUSAN BUTLER

New York

FIRST FRUITS

Giving God Your Best 365 Days of the Year

© 2016 SUSAN BUTLER.

Unless otherwise noted, Scripture quotations are taken from the New American Standard Bible®, marked NASB, © 1976, 1978, The Moody Bible Institute of Chicago. Used by permission of The Lockman Foundation, Ryrie Study Bible.

Scripture quotations marked KJV are from the King James Version in the Public Domain.

Scripture quotations marked NKJV are taken from the New King James Version® copyright © 1982 by Thomas Nelson. Used by permission. All rights reserved.

Scripture quotations marked NIV® are from the New International Version®, © 1973, 1978, 1984, 2011 by Biblica, Inc. ™ Used by permission of Zondervan. All rights reserved worldwide. www.zondervan.com.

Scripture quotations marked NLT® are taken from the Holy Bible, New Living Translation © 1996, 2004, 2007, 2013 of Tyndale House Foundation. Used by permission of Tyndale House Publishers, Inc., Carol Stream, Illinois 60188. All rights reserved.

Scripture quotations marked TLB® are taken from The Living Bible © 1971. Used by permission of Tyndale House Publishers, Inc., Carol Stream, Illinois 60188. All rights reserved.

Scripture quotations marked THE MESSAGE © by Eugene H. Peterson 1993, 1994, 1995, 1996, 2000, 2001, 2002. Used by permission of Tyndale House Publishers, Inc., Carol Stream, Illinois 60188. All rights reserved.

Scripture quotations taken from The Voice ™ © 2008 by Ecclesia Bible Society. Used by permission. All rights reserved.

Information quoted from Easton's Bible Dictionary, included in Bible Gateway, used by permission of The Zondervan Corporation. All Rights Reserved. www.zondervan.com

Information quoted from Dictionary of Bible Themes, © 1995-2010, included in Bible Gateway, used by permission of The Zondervan Corporation. All Rights Reserved. www.zondervan.com

Information quoted from Merriam-Webster Dictionary, used by permission 2015.

Quotations from Zola Levitt are used by permission of Zola Levitt Ministries, © 2015, www.levitt.com.

"Attitudes" quote, Copyright © 1981, 1982 by Charles R. Swindoll, Inc. All rights reserved worldwide. Used by permission 2015.

Published in New York, New York, by Morgan James Publishing. Morgan James and The Entrepreneurial Publisher are trademarks of Morgan James, LLC.
www.MorganJamesPublishing.com

The Morgan James Speakers Group can bring authors to your live event. For more information or to book an event visit The Morgan James Speakers Group at www.TheMorganJamesSpeakersGroup.com.

Shelfie

A **free** eBook edition is available with the purchase of this print book.

CLEARLY PRINT YOUR NAME ABOVE IN UPPER CASE

Instructions to claim your free eBook edition:
1. Download the Shelfie app for Android or iOS
2. Write your name in **UPPER CASE** above
3. Use the Shelfie app to submit a photo
4. Download your eBook to any device

ISBN 978-1-63047-746-2 paperback
ISBN 978-1-63047-747-9 eBook
ISBN 978-1-63047-748-6 hardcover
Library of Congress Control Number:
2015914085

Cover Design by:
Rachel Lopez
www.r2cdesign.com

Cover Design by:
Bonnie Bushman
The Whole Caboodle Graphic Design

In an effort to support local communities and raise awareness and funds, Morgan James Publishing donates a percentage of all book sales for the life of each book to Habitat for Humanity Peninsula and Greater Williamsburg.

Get involved today, visit
www.MorganJamesBuilds.com

Habitat
for Humanity®
Peninsula and
Greater Williamsburg
Building Partner

To the LORD God Almighty
"Not to us, O LORD, not to us,
But to Your name give glory,
Because of Your lovingkindness,
Because of Your truth."

Psalm 115:1 (NASB)

CONTENTS

ACKNOWLEDGEMENTS

My gratitude goes first to my husband, C.J. Butler, who has patiently supported me for over three years during the writing of *First Fruits*. He has been invaluable in his suggestions and "broad stroke" mentality, as well as an encourager during the final stretch.

Ashlea Palladino, our daughter, has been my editor during this journey, doing an excellent job of keen-eyed marksmanship on any verb, tense or comma inserted at the wrong juncture, always with perfectly timed humor! Her investment in the project cannot be overstated.

On a creative note, my granddaughter, Caroline Palladino, is responsible for painstaking attempts to put her grandmother in the most attractive light possible for the author's photograph. I think she has a future!

Other family members who have encouraged me to press on are my son, Bart Butler; my sister, Lori Taylor; my brother, David Hanson; my Aunt Eloise Whittlesey (a writer herself); and my Aunt Mae Potter. In addition, a group of good friends who have walked along side me are Della and Bob Best, Dianne and Bob Fenimore, Terri and Mack Holmes, Claudia and Howard Nelson, Cheryl and Waylon McMullen, Sue and Tim Kirchner, Jeanne Grubbs, Sondra Saunders, Mary Jane Phillips, Shirley Bobbitt, Rhonda Parker, Linda Eiland,

Gretchen Sampson, Brenda Gaustad, Janice Pitts, Sherry Scammahorn, Camille Dillard, Judie Cline, Patti Thomas, Louise Dillard, Karen Singleterry, Betty Jo Connor, Gerry Roy, and Angel Hadley. If encouragement were a jewel, I'd be decked out.

I want to thank a group of particularly special friends and spiritual advocates who provided first-draft mentoring. My mother, Lou Hanson; my sister, Bonnie Walker; my brother-in-law, David Walker; my nephew, Jason Taylor; my ministers at Prestonwood Baptist Church, Neal Jeffrey, Jeff Young, Jarrett Stephens, and Dan Sampson; and very special friends, Connie Howard, Mary Tinsley, Cheryl Murff and Virginia Grounds. Their comments and suggestions inspired me to forge ahead and continue trusting in God's strong lead to this long-awaited finish line.

Finally, my publishing team at Morgan James Publishing is responsible for the beautiful physical product we call *First Fruits*. My time spent with Terry Whalin, Acquisitions Editor, was key in developing an understanding of the publishing world and the expectations of their team for the author. Keri Wilson, my Managing Editor, brought further understanding of the processes for moving *First Fruits* from manuscript to final book form. She has been an encouraging, enthusiastic and responsive partner—the perfect complement to this rookie author! Jim Howard, Publishing Director, gave leadership to the specific consequential direction of *First Fruits* from the title to the back cover, and did it with a knowledgeable, yet comfortable style; a man of grace. Rachel Lopez, my talented and perceptive designer, is responsible for the beautiful book cover. Last, David Hancock, Founder of Morgan James Publishing, who worked with me in moving beyond their standard book length to accommodate the daily devotional format of *First Fruits*. He has built a company with high standards in every area; I am so pleased to be on board with Morgan James.

FIRST FRUITS
Introduction

When I had my first conversation with God about writing *First Fruits*, the book had no name nor content. I simply shared with Him my desire to write a book. Within minutes, He impressed me with the thought that He would help me, and that my first writing project needed to be for Him. He then gave me the format of a perpetual calendar devotional, and the title, "First Fruits." It would signify my first effort to write for Him, and encourage readers to give the Lord the first portion of each day to meditate on His Word.

Two years into the writing project, when my friend, Betty Jo Connor, found out the name of my book, she encouraged me to read what Zola Levitt, a Jewish convert to Christianity, had to say about first fruits. In his book entitled *The Seven Feasts of Israel*[1] he explains the significance of the third feast, "First Fruits."

Leviticus 23:10–11(KJV) instructed: "Speak unto the children of Israel, and say unto them, When ye be come into the land which I give unto you, and shall reap the harvest thereof, then ye shall bring a sheaf of the first fruits of

---

1   Zola Levitt Ministries, © 2015, www.levitt.com. *The Seven Feasts of Israel*, p.6–8. *The Miracle of Passover*, p. 17.

your harvest unto the priest: And he shall wave the sheaf before the Lord, to be accepted for you; on the morrow after the Sabbath the priest shall wave it."

I had marked the above scripture early on in my writing as an encouragement concerning God's gift of the title *First Fruits*. But what I learned from Levitt's book and want to share with you was both astounding and thrilling, confirming to me that the title God had impressed upon me was for a purpose beyond my original understanding.

The First Fruits Feast is always the Sunday following the week of the Feast of Unleavened Bread, held in the spring each year. This day has eventually become known as Easter among Christians. But what many do not realize is that the name Easter was derived from the Babylonian pagan goddess of fertility, "Ishtar". Zola explains that "we miss a very important Biblical truth by not using the term 'First Fruits' as the name of this feast, because "first" implies a second, a third, and so on, and that is the real meaning of the feast. We do not merely celebrate the resurrection of the Lord on First Fruits (Easter), on which it indeed occurred, but even more so, the resurrection of the entire Church!"

In 1 Corinthians 15:23 (KJV) Paul states "For as in Adam all die, even so in Christ shall all be made alive. But every man in his own order: Christ the first fruits; afterward they that are Christ's at his coming." Zola continues, "Jesus celebrated the Sunday of the week of His crucifixion by rising from the dead. It was not some other day He chose but the very day of First Fruits … Jesus even presented His proper First Fruits offering to the Father. Graves were opened and dead people rose and were seen after His resurrection in Jerusalem. Matthew 27:53 (KJV). First Fruits was the last of the feasts that The Lord was seen personally fulfilling on earth."

First Fruits, therefore, represents not only our gifts to God, but more importantly, His First Fruits Gift to us in the person of Jesus Christ—He is the Hope of our own resurrection!

Week One

INTRODUCTION
TO PRECEPTS

I believe the Bible is the Word of God, inspired by God, and written by individuals He selected. Second Timothy 3:16–17 (NASB) states "All Scripture is inspired by God and profitable for teaching, for reproof, for correction, for training in righteousness; so that the man of God may be adequate, equipped for every good work."

As you begin this devotional book, you will see a precept (a principle leading to some form of action) assigned to each scripture, in addition to the message for that day. In most cases, the precept is a positive action such as Love, Hope or Obedience. In a few instances, however, the precept is a negative action such as Unbelief, Worry or Suffering. Ultimately, the scripture and message assigned to each precept will guide you to positive action. To give you greater insight and understanding, there is a page dedicated to each of the 51 precepts used throughout the book. Look for a different precept page at the beginning of each week.

This devotional book was written using 365 of my favorite scripture passages with the hope and purpose of leading you to a better understanding of God and His purpose for your life. As you read the scripture and the message that follows, my prayer is that God will speak to you, just as He spoke to me during the writing process. He inspired me to write in the first person of God. Each writing session began with a prayer that I would be filled with His Holy Spirit. I asked that His Word would be interpreted clearly, and to get me out of the way so that His message would touch the hearts of seekers. Each session ended with thanksgiving as He taught me much about "being still and knowing He is God." Psalm 46:10 (KJV).

Reflections:

_____

_____

SALVATION

"For God so loved the world that He gave His only begotten Son, that whoever believes in Him should not perish, but have eternal life. For God did not send the Son into the world to judge the world, but that the world should be saved through Him." John 3:16–17 (NASB)

I love you. I give you a new day—a new Beginning. Because I created you, I want you to love me, learn my ways and spend eternity with me. Think of a parent's love for a child. I sent my only Son to earth to show you what perfect love is. He suffered and died for you—to save you, not to judge you. Jesus died a painful, brutal, humiliating and lonely death on a cross—for you. That is our great love for you, so that you can be saved from an eternity without us. Accept this free Gift, and walk with us. We will teach you great and mighty things.

GRACE

"In Him we have redemption through His blood, the forgiveness of our trespasses, according to the riches of His grace, which He lavished upon us. In all wisdom and insight He made known to us the mystery of His will, according to His kind intention which He purposed in Him."
Ephesians 1:7–9 (NASB)

Redemption—Grace—Purpose. These are powerful words, and they all apply to you. The mystery of my purpose, my will, is that Christ's blood can redeem and forgive you for all your sin. His sacrifice cleanses you from your unrighteousness. Though you cannot fully comprehend the magnitude of His Grace so richly lavished upon you, accept this great gift of Redemption through Christ's blood on the cross. He died for *you*.

GRACE

"For as through the one man's disobedience the many were made sinners, even so through the obedience of the One the many will be made righteous. And the Law came in that the transgression might increase; but where sin increased, grace abounded all the more."
Romans 5:19-20 (NASB)

When Adam disobeyed me in the garden, he determined the fate of all mankind to be sinners. But through the obedience of My Son Jesus, many will come into right favor with me. Though the Law has come to point out the sins of mankind, His grace has come to cover your sins like soft rain on parched petals. Give praise to Jesus for His victory over sin and death.

FAITH

"Your faith should not rest on the wisdom of men, but on the power of God." 1 Corinthians 2:5 (NASB)

No matter what you are dealing with, your first Counsel should always be me. There is no challenge too great, no enemy too strong, no circumstance too complicated for us to overcome together. So be wise in your faith—seek My Wisdom, read My Word and get alone so you can hear My Answer. My Power is all you need.

FAITH

"And without faith it is impossible to please Him, for he who comes to God must believe that He is, and that He is a rewarder of those who seek Him." Hebrews 11:6 (NASB)

Faith—it is unseen and yet can be strong enough to elicit My Power to heal the dying child, or change the course of history. That is why you must believe with your whole heart that I am who I say that I am, and I will do what I say I will do. Without faith, it is impossible to please me. There is power in My Name. I reward those who seek me.

FAITH

"Even so faith, if it has no works, is dead, being by itself. But someone may well say, 'You have faith, and I have works; show me your faith without the works, and I will show you my faith by my works.' … You see that a man is justified by works, and not by faith alone."
James 2:17, 18, 24 (NASB)

Through faith comes salvation—and through faith come good works. If you have the faith to believe in the redemption of sins through My Son Jesus Christ, then the outward proof of this faith is your desire to give of yourself as Christ did. Jesus sacrificed Himself on the cross for all who would believe. You are to sacrifice in other ways, following Jesus' actions during His earthly ministry. Your ministry to those in need is an outward expression of inner faith. Because I know your heart, you are justified by this demonstration of faith.

SOVEREIGNTY

"Daniel answered and said, 'Let the name of God be blessed forever and ever, for wisdom and power belong to Him. And it is He who changes the times and the epochs; He removes kings and establishes kings; He gives wisdom to wise men, and knowledge to men of understanding.'"
Daniel 2:20-21 (NASB)

I am Sovereign—do you believe this? My Word tells you that kings and presidents and rulers of all kinds obtain their power from me. Because I know the end from the beginning, I alone decide who will have positions of authority. When you do not understand what I allow to happen on earth, trust in me for I have perfect understanding of those I have created. My creation changes and responds to My Plan for I am all powerful. If you want wisdom and understanding, seek me more.

Week Two

SALVATION

S alvation came to me when I was eight years old. My family and I attended revivals every spring at our church where an evangelist would give a message and then call the congregation to repentance. One morning during revival week, I sat in our tiny kitchen with my mom and she led me to pray, asking Jesus to come into my heart and save me. I'll never forget the loud beating of my heart and the tears that fell as I made the most important decision of my life. Is there a distinct moment in time when you remember inviting Christ into your heart to forgive you for your sins and redeem you through his shed blood on the cross?

We live in a world where information bombards us from every direction, at times causing confusion and frustration. What are you to believe about God? Was Jesus really God's Son or just a wise prophet? Is salvation a reality because of Christ's death and resurrection, or just a belief system used by weak or ignorant people? Are there any absolutes?

1) <u>How can you obtain deliverance from the power of sin?</u>

God has given us the portal through which we can escape forever the power of sin. His name is Jesus. The Bible tells us that "the wages of sin is death, but the free gift of God is eternal life through Jesus Christ our Lord." Romans 6:23 (NLT). So, the power that would eventually lead to our death has been overcome by Jesus' death and resurrection. Everyone has access to Him – that includes you.

2) <u>How can you be liberated from ignorance or illusion?</u>

There are many who believe that Jesus is **not** the only way to heaven, and that it doesn't matter what you believe as long as you believe in <u>something</u>. That thinking **is** the illusion. If you want the Truth, look in God's Word for the answers to all of life's questions. Chief among those questions should be how you can be sure of your salvation. John 14:6 (NLT) quotes Jesus as saying, "I am the way, the truth, and the life. No one can come to the Father except through me." The Bible is God revealing Himself to man. It is both historical and relevant for all of life's issues.

3) <u>How can you be preserved from destruction?</u>

Psalm 92 (TLB) tells us in verse 7 "that although the wicked flourish like weeds, there is only eternal destruction ahead of them." Then, in verses 12–13, "But the godly shall flourish like palm trees and grow tall as the cedars of Lebanon. For they are transplanted into the Lord's own garden and are under his personal care."

I want to flourish in God's garden … how about you?

Reflections:

_____

_____

SALVATION

"Behold, I stand at the door and knock; if anyone hears my voice and opens the door, I will come in to him, and will dine with him, and he with Me." Revelation 3:20 (NASB)

I long to have a relationship with you. From the time I brought you into the world, I chose your earthly parents and gave you a path for discovering me. But I also gave you free will to accept or reject me. There is much I want to show you. I am always available to guide you and comfort you because I love you—just ask.

SOVEREIGNTY

"It is He who reveals the profound and hidden things; He knows what is in the darkness, and the light dwells with Him. To Thee, O God of my fathers, I give thanks and praise, for Thou has given me wisdom and power." Daniel 2:22–23a (NASB)

I see all and know all things hidden. Do not think that you hide even your innermost thoughts from me. Because the light dwells in me, I know what is in the darkness. There is much you do not understand; sometimes because you do not seek, but also because you are not yet ready for revelation. As you seek more of me, I will reveal profound truths to you. If you want wisdom and power, ask for it—and in all things, remember to have a thankful heart.

SOVEREIGNTY

"I, the LORD, search the heart, I test the mind, even to give to each man according to his ways, according to the results of his deeds."
Jeremiah 17:10 (NASB)

Know this about me: I search your heart and test your mind. I know you inside and out. I made you. Because you are uniquely made, I have special plans just for you. What I give to someone else may not be what I know you need. As you live your life, be aware that I follow not only what you do each day, but also the result of what you do which may not be evident for years. I want to bless you as your deeds produce good fruit. Enjoy the bounty of a righteous life.

MERCY

"But Thou, O God, the Lord, deal kindly with me for Thy name's sake; because Thy loving kindness is good, deliver me; for I am afflicted and needy, and my heart is wounded within me." Psalm 109:21–22 (NASB)

You can trust me to deliver you when you are in need. Sometimes your need is physical, but at other times it is a wounded heart that needs comfort. What is your need today? Remember that I love you more than anyone on earth, and my love is everlasting. You cannot do or say anything to separate yourself from my love. As you seek me in the quiet recesses of your heart, allow my peace to wash over you. Stay with me awhile and let your spirit rest.

MERCY

"Go home to your people and report to them what great things the Lord has done for you, and how He had mercy on you." Mark 5:19b (NASB)

Take time right now to think of five things I have done for you today. Is this hard for you, or do my blessings tumble off your tongue? If you want to be fulfilled, be thankful. Even on the darkest of days, if you acknowledge My Presence, My Light will fill you. Share the great things I have done for you with those you love, and more blessings will come your way. I love a thankful heart.

TRUST

"The LORD will also be a stronghold for the oppressed, a stronghold in times of trouble, and those who know Thy name will put their trust in Thee." Psalm 9:9–10a (NASB)

Do you know my name? I am the LORD. There is no one else like me. If you put your trust in me, I will be your stronghold in times of oppression and trouble. I will be your Hiding Place and your Comforter. Find rest in me. I will give you all you need to withstand the enemy. Trust me…trust me.

TRUST

"Ah, Sovereign LORD, you have made the heavens and the earth by your great power and outstretched arm. Nothing is too hard for you."
Jeremiah 32:17 (NIV)

I am Sovereign. This means that I alone made the heavens and the earth, and all who dwell within. I created all that you see, all that you know, as well as that which you do not know. Your knowledge is finite, but my knowledge is infinite. There is no power greater than my power and I rule over all I have created. You can choose to trust this truth or to reject it; though if you reject it, it remains true. There is absolutely nothing you can ask of me that I cannot do.

Week Three

SOVEREIGNTY

SOVEREIGNTY – God's absolute right to do all things according to His own good pleasure. *Easton's Bible Dictionary*

T he word "absolute" is powerful and exclusive. It describes His ultimate authority.

Several years ago when taking Beth Moore's *Daniel*[2] study at my church, I was intrigued by the many events in Daniel's life which pointed to God's sovereignty. The prophecies in his lifetime which have now been fulfilled and Daniel's faith in times of extreme circumstance gripped my attention. Near the end of the summer course, it was this precept that held me together for the unexpected events to come: our daughter's husband died suddenly at the age of 34. When events like this take you to the valley of despair, it is vital to know beyond a shadow of doubt in whom you can place your trust, believing that God is in control, even in the worst of times.

---

2   *Daniel*, A Woman's Bible Study, Beth Moore, 2006, LifeWay.com

Daniel's response to God in Daniel 2:20–23 (NIV) when He revealed Nebuchadnezzar's dream to him—the revelation that would save Daniel and all of the wise men—is a powerful reminder to us:

"Praise be to the name of God for ever and ever; wisdom and power are his. He changes times and seasons; he deposes kings and raises up others. He gives wisdom to the wise and knowledge to the discerning. He reveals deep and hidden things; he knows what lies in darkness, and light dwells with him. I thank and praise you, God of my ancestors; you have given me wisdom and power, you have made known to me what we asked of you, you have made known to us the dream of the king."

When life is hard and circumstances are beyond your control, what do you do? There is only one ultimate place to find both comfort and wisdom, and that is in the arms of our Lord. Psalm 34:18 (NASB) is a trustworthy promise: "The LORD is near to the broken hearted and saves those who are crushed in spirit." We may hate what has happened to us, we may be full of anger and frustration, but when we finally accept the reality of God's sovereignty over every event, we can then come to Him for comfort and direction. He alone can soothe our spirit and help us navigate through the deep waters of despair to the shores of hope and renewal.

Reflections:

_____

_____

SOVEREIGNTY

"The eyes of the Lord are in every place, watching the evil and the good."
Proverbs 15:3 (NASB)

There is no place on earth that is hidden from my eyes. I know the evil that is thought about in every dark corner of the mind, and I see the evil carried out all over the earth. I also see the good plans and actions taking place, and am pleased by the good intentions of each soul. I am watching—My eyes are everywhere. Love me, do what is good and enjoy peace.

SOVEREIGNTY

"O LORD, Thou hast searched me and known me. Thou dost know when I sit down and when I rise up; Thou dost understand my thought from afar. Thou dost scrutinize my path and my lying down, and art intimately acquainted with all my ways. Even before there is a word on my tongue, behold, O LORD, Thou dost know it all." Psalm 139:1–4 (NASB)

Be comforted that I know everything about you. I knew you before you were born and I know the number of your days. Nothing you do surprises me, and every thought you have is known to me. Your personality, your likes and dislikes, your strengths and your weaknesses, your greatest lifetime achievement, the degree of your faith moment by moment, your darkest thoughts and deepest needs—I know it all. Before you speak, I know what you will say. Be encouraged that you are understood and loved by the God of the Universe.

SIN

"For all have sinned and fall short of the glory of God."
Romans 3:23 (NASB)

Do you know that you are a sinner? As hard as you may try to be sinless, it is impossible. The darkness of the sin of man is juxtaposed against the resplendence of My Glory. Even the happiest, smartest, nicest, wisest person you know is flawed with a sinful nature. So how do you bridge the chasm between yourself and me? It is only through the blood sacrifice on the cross of Jesus Christ My Son. Ask me to cleanse you of your unrighteousness, and ascend from the hopelessness of sin and death to new life in Christ.

SIN

"If we say that we have no sin, we are deceiving ourselves, and the truth is not in us. If we confess our sins, He is faithful and righteous to forgive us our sins and to cleanse us from all unrighteousness. If we say that we have not sinned, we make Him a liar, and His word is not in us."
1 John 1:8–10 (NASB)

You may hear people say they don't "believe" in sin. They deceive themselves and do not speak the truth. So, when you say you haven't sinned, you make not only yourself a liar, but call me a liar at the same time. If My Word is in you, you know I want you to confess your sins … not for my sake (since I know your sin before you commit it), but for your sake. My desire is to cleanse you through confession, and forgive you when you ask to be forgiven. Believe and confess—this is My Way to your righteous living.

LOVE

"And He said to him, 'You shall love the LORD your God with all your heart, and with all your soul, and with all your mind.' This is the great and foremost commandment. The second is like it, 'You shall love your neighbor as yourself.'" Matthew 22:37–39 (NASB)

My Word commands that you first love me. How do you show your love to me? You acknowledge that I have given you this day; be thankful for your life and the abilities I have given you. Spend time with me each day—speak to me, but listen more. Learn of me and my desires for you. Then you will be able to joyfully participate in the second commandment, "love your neighbor as yourself." Work at showing others the same love and respect you receive from me. Your obedience will demonstrate your desire to please me.

OBEDIENCE

"Let the words of my mouth and the meditation of my heart be acceptable in Thy sight, O LORD, my rock and my Redeemer."
Psalm 19:14 (NASB)

How can you be confident that your words and thoughts are acceptable to me? If you are seeking my counsel, and obediently following my commands, if you are studying my Word to glean knowledge and wisdom, then you can be sure I am pleased with your efforts. When you come to me for reassurance, when you seek my face in times of trouble, when you praise me for My Presence, and when you confess that I have redeemed you through the sacrifice of My Son, then you will be confident of my pleasure.

OBEDIENCE

"He has told you, O man, what is good; and what does the LORD require of you but to do justice, to love kindness, and to walk humbly with your God?" Micah 6:8 (NASB)

I do not want animal or human sacrifice, or any of the treasures brought to the temple, as in the days before I sent My Son. I know that if you walk humbly by my side, your sacrifice will be that of obedience. You will be kind, loving and fair with your fellow man. You will treat them as you want to be treated. You will regard their life as important, because you will remember that I created them just as I created you. Remember that today, as you deal with those less educated, less beautiful, less confident, less moral or less lovable. I love you and I love them. Love them in remembrance of me.

CREATION

CREATION – "In the beginning," God created, i.e. called into being, all things out of nothing. *Easton's Bible Dictionary*

Genesis 2 (TLB) begins, "Now at last the heavens and earth were successfully completed, with all that they contained ... and God blessed the seventh day and declared it holy, because it was the day when he ceased this work of creation."

Each time I am confronted with a new creation, whether it is a flower opening, a butterfly leaving its cocoon, the first bright green leaves of spring, a new puppy or the soft cheeks of an infant, I am reminded of the vast limitless of God. To reflect on His ability to think of every detail in just these few examples is amazing enough, let alone all of creation.

Is it difficult for you to believe and accept that there is one Creator? Or, like me, do you find it even more difficult to believe that some forces came together in the universe over billions of years to evolve into our world today ... which still doesn't explain how the forces and the galaxies came into existence, if not for this one Creator whom we know as our God of the Universe.

God first showed His love for you before you knew Him. Psalm 139:13–16 (NASB): "For You formed my inward parts; You wove me in my mother's womb. I will give thanks to You, for I am fearfully and wonderfully made; wonderful are Your works, and my soul knows it very well. My frame was not hidden from You, when I was made in secret, and skillfully wrought in the depths of the earth; Your eyes have seen my unformed substance; and in Your book were all written the days that were ordained for me, when as yet there was not one of them."

How blessed we are to be part of this magnificent creation, and to have confidence that He who created us loves us with an unmatched love. He is there when the world goes away—when the friend forgets you, when the boss tells you your services are no longer needed, when the parent abandons you, when the spouse leaves, when the child dies, when life no longer seems to have purpose. Look to Him, and ask Him to reveal Himself all over again to you. He won't force Himself on you, so turn to Him—He will do the rest.

Reflections:

_____

_____

CREATION

"For Thou didst form my inward parts; Thou didst weave me in my mother's womb. I will give thanks to Thee, for I am fearfully and wonderfully made; wonderful are Thy works, and my soul knows it very well. My frame was not hidden from Thee, when I was made in secret, and skillfully wrought in the depths of the earth. Thine eyes have seen my unformed substance; and in Thy book they were all written, the days that were ordained for me, when as yet there was not one of them."
Psalm 139:13–16 (NASB)

Give thanks, for you **are** fearfully and wonderfully made. You were never hidden from me. Even though you were skillfully envisioned and created in secret from the world, I saw your unformed substance. I formed every part of you, inside and out, and wove you in your mother's womb. You were written in the Book of Life and all the days were ordained for you, even before you were born. Miracle of miracles, you were given life by the one and only Creator and God of the Universe. There is **no one else** just like you!

CREATION

"Do you not know that you are a temple of God, and that the Spirit of God dwells in you?" 1 Corinthians 3:16 (NASB)

What do you think of when you visualize a temple? Is it a beautiful structure of strong stone with precious metals and fine jewels inside? Even the most magnificent temple made with human hands is insignificant when compared to the treasure I have made in you. Every part of you—body, mind and soul—is a one-of-a-kind masterpiece made to be the dwelling place of My Spirit. What you allow into your mind and body will impact your soul. Guard it with the power of the Holy Spirit in you.

MERCY

"But God, being rich in mercy, because of His great love with which He loved us, even when we were dead in our transgressions, made us alive together with Christ (by grace you have been saved), and raised us up with Him, and seated us with Him in the heavenly places, in Christ Jesus." Ephesians 2:4–7 (NASB)

I am the LORD your God. You were without hope until I sent My Son Jesus Christ to save you from your sins and from the ultimate final death. Because of His sacrifice, you have been given GRACE: God's Riches At Christ's Expense. My mercy towards you is abundant because I have the greatest love for you—more than a parent, a spouse, a child. I want to raise you up to sit with me in the heavenly places I have prepared for those who accept the free Gift of Salvation.

PRAYER

"But if we hope for what we do not see, with perseverance we wait eagerly for it. And in the same way the Spirit also helps our weakness; for we do not know how to pray as we should, but the Spirit Himself intercedes for us with groanings too deep for words."
Romans 8:25–26 (NASB)

It takes great faith to continue hoping and waiting eagerly for something that you do not see happening. Yet, this is exactly what I want you to do—but not by yourself. I give you My Spirit to help you in your weakness. When you become discouraged, and can't even find the words to express in prayer, be confident that the Holy Spirit is interceding for you. You are not alone.

PRAYER

"In my distress I called upon the LORD, and cried to my God for help; He heard my voice out of His temple, and my cry for help before Him came into His ears." Psalm 18:6 (NASB)

Are you troubled today? Do you face something that seems insurmountable? I want you to turn to me for everything. Nothing you are concerned about is too small—nor is any problem too great. In your weakness, I am strong. Believe that I am All Powerful and Mighty to bring about the impossible. Confide in me and trust me. Then watch and see how I will honor your trust in ways you never dreamed possible.

DECEIT

"The heart is more deceitful than all else and is desperately sick; who can understand it?" Jeremiah 17:9 (NASB)

Your heart, your emotions, can deceive you far more than any other person. Because you desire things and relationships which you think will satisfy you and make you happy, you deceive yourself. They will all bring about disappointment, if they are not filtered through me. You were created with a deep soul need that cannot be satisfied by things on this earth. If you seek understanding, seek me. I will guide you and give you discernment for making good choices.

DISOBEDIENCE

"Therefore consider the members of your earthly body as dead to immorality, impurity, passion, evil desire, and greed, which amounts to idolatry. For it is on account of these things that the wrath of God will come." Colossians 3:5–6 (NASB)

Your body has become holy if you are my child. Do not defile it with immoral and impure thoughts of passion and evil desires. Those thoughts and desires are not my will for you, and will bring about my anger. Rather, consider your body dead to these kinds of impure desires so that you may remain obedient to me. Kindle afresh the passions with your husband or wife, and enjoy what I have given you in them, so that you may receive blessings rather than wrath.

Week Five

SACRIFICE

A cts of sacrifice command our attention. Today we see reports in the news as a fireman sacrifices his life to save victims from a raging fire; a soldier gives his life to save his platoon; a policeman takes a bullet to protect a citizen; a mother risks an unhealthy pregnancy to save her child; a father sacrifices everything to take care of his family. It seems that man can and does rise to the challenge of honor and sacrifice.

Conversely, we are repulsed by the human sacrifice associated with cultures of the past. The Phoenicians of Carthage were reputed to practice child sacrifice according to Plutarch (ca. 46–120 AD). Children were roasted to death on a heated bronze idol while still conscious.[3] In contrast, Leviticus contains many references to the Jewish blood sacrifices of animals, as well as bloodless sacrifices of grain and wine. God gave definite laws for them to follow concerning what and how to sacrifice. All of this was done in homage to their respective gods: the Phoenicians to an idol, the Jews to Jehovah God.

---

3   Stager, Lawrence; Samuel R. Wolff (1984). "Child Sacrifice in Carthage: Religious rite or population control?" *Journal of Biblical Archeological Review*. January:31–46

But where does the honorable sacrificial heart originate? As a Christian, my mind goes immediately to Christ's sacrifice on the cross. He gave up His life on earth at the age of 33 so that all who would believe that He is God's Son might have an eternal life with Him. He gave up His time with family and friends. He sacrificed His ministry to the multitudes. He withheld His power to prevent the physical agony and humiliation He experienced when soldiers nailed Him to a cross. Throughout history, there has been no other religion whose deity sacrificed his own life for his people. Jesus said, "Greater love hath no one than this: to lay down one's life for one's friends." John 15:13 (NIV). There exists no more noble and consequential sacrifice than Jesus Christ's act of perfect love.

If we conclude that there are both honorable and dishonorable sacrifices, and that Christ's death was the ultimate sacrifice for all mankind, what are we to do with this information? When we follow Christ's example in caring for the needs of others, and putting their interests ahead of our own, we honor His sacrifice for us. It is a way of acknowledging that we are His because of His great love for us; then translating that love to meet the needs of others. Why? To introduce them to the Savior.

Reflections:

_____

_____

SACRIFICE

"For even the Son of Man did not come to be served, but to serve, and to give His life a ransom for many." Mark 10:45 (NASB)

If I sent My Son to serve and teach mankind, and to offer up Himself as the blood sacrifice for all of your sins, does it not make sense that you should follow after Him in service to others? It delights me to see you put others before yourself, whether it is your family, a friend or a stranger. When you act selflessly, it gives you purpose and meaning beyond yourself. Find your calling serving others and show My Spirit until I return.

SACRIFICE

"For by one offering He has perfected for all time those who are sanctified." Hebrews 10:14 (NASB)

My Son Jesus is the only Sacrifice for your sins. He died on a cross to absorb all of your sin—once and for all. Do you understand that your disobedience will never be bad enough to keep you from my love ... and that all your good acts will never be good enough to give you eternal life? There is only one action you must take to give you eternal life, and that is to have a relationship with me by accepting the free Gift of Eternal Life through My Son Jesus Christ. Make today the day you invite me in, and let us build a relationship like no other.

PROTECTION

"But Thou, O LORD, art a shield about me, my glory, and the One who lifts my head." Psalm 3:3 (NASB)

My Glory, the brilliant essence of me, can form a shield around you. Ask me to go with you on your day, no matter what the day may bring. Whether you are taking the children to school, rehearsing an important presentation or having lunch with a friend, invite me to come alongside you. I can lift your head and give you confidence for what is coming. I can prepare you in ways you never imagined. Ask for my wisdom and my strength, and you will not be disappointed.

WORD OF GOD

"The words of the LORD are pure words; as silver tried in a furnace on the earth, refined seven times." Psalm 12:6 (NASB)

Purity ... what does this word bring to your mind? When something is pure, there can be no blemish found within. When something is pure, it is complete; there is no need to add or take away from it. Silver is refined seven times to become pure. My Word is pure simply because it is My Word; every letter inspired by me. My Word is blameless and trustworthy. It has the capability to stir the heart, convict the soul and cause incredible acts of faith and love to be demonstrated by those who believe it. What will you do with My Word today?

JUDGMENT

"And He said to His disciples, 'It is inevitable that stumbling blocks should come, but woe to him through whom they come! It would be better for him if a millstone were hung around his neck and he were thrown into the sea, than that he should cause one of these little ones to stumble.'" Luke 17:1–2 (NASB)

Ask me today for wisdom in what you say and what you do. It is bad enough to stumble with only yourself to blame. But, how much worse it is when you cause another to stumble? There is great consequence in leading others down the wrong path—you would be better off drowning. When you fail to remember your responsibility as a Light Giver, you stir the coals of my anger and judgment. Be wise and pay attention to this warning.

PRAISE

"But thanks be to God, who always leads us in His triumph in Christ, and manifests through us the sweet aroma of the knowledge of Him in every place. For we are a fragrance of Christ to God among those who are being saved and among those who are perishing." 2 Corinthians 2:14–15 (NASB)

Would you say your life is triumphant? Are you a natural-born winner? Does everything seem to go your way? If you answered "yes" to those questions, remember that I know your innermost thoughts. If you want to be triumphant, follow me to faith in the risen Savior, My Son Jesus Christ. His earthly birth and ministry were planned from the beginning. When you understand that you were part of my purpose in sending My Son to be the blood sacrifice for you, you will begin to find us everywhere, in everything. Yes, the sweet aroma of Christ in you is yours for the asking. When you determine to see us in every person, in every event, in every detail of nature, others will enjoy the sweet fragrance of your faith.

HOLY SPIRIT

"For God has not called us for the purpose of impurity, but in sanctification. Consequently, he who rejects this is not rejecting man but the God who gives His Holy Spirit to you."
1 Thessalonians 4:7–8 (NASB)

I have sanctified you for the purpose of consecrating all of you to all of me. If you make the choice to be impure in your body or in your thoughts, you are rejecting me and the Holy Spirit which I have given you. Be on guard against this temptation; rather be filled with My Spirit so that you can remain pure and ready for my purpose.

Week Six

HOLY SPIRIT

The Holy Spirit is the manifestation of Christ in us. The Holy Spirit is the third Person in the Trinity—God is our Creator, Jesus Christ is our Savior, and the Holy Spirit is God's gift of comfort and direction to us while Jesus is seated in heaven at the right hand of God until His Second Coming. When Jesus died for our sins, was buried, rose the third day, and then ascended to heaven to be with His Father, God gave us the Holy Spirit for instruction, revelation and power.

In the Old Testament book of Exodus, there is mention of God's Holy Spirit stirring the hearts of those giving gifts for the building of the Tabernacle. In Psalm 51, David pleads with God not to take the Holy Spirit from him. Isaiah 63 tells of the Israelite's rebellion and how this grieved God's Holy Spirit. Daniel was known to King Nebuchadnezzar as the man in his kingdom who had within him the "spirit of the holy gods."

The New Testament tells us that Mary's virgin pregnancy was a gift of the Holy Spirit in Matthew 1. Jesus was led by the Holy Spirit in Matthew 4 to be tempted by Satan. In Luke 3, when Jesus was baptized by John the Baptist in the Jordan River, the heavens opened and the Holy Spirit in the form of a dove settled upon Him. A voice from heaven said, "You are my much loved Son, yes, my delight." Luke 3:22 (TLB)

The Day of Pentecost is one of the most dramatic accounts of the power of the Holy Spirit, recorded in Acts 2. As the believers met together, there was the sound of a mighty rushing wind, and what appeared to be tongues of fire settled on their heads. These Christ-followers were filled with the Holy Spirit and began speaking in languages they didn't know. The Jews were amazed and perplexed that these men from Galilee were speaking to each of them in the native language of their birth.

Do you have Holy Spirit power? When you believe that Jesus has taken *your* sins to the cross, that His physical body has been resurrected and He has ascended to heaven to prepare a place for you, you have daily access to Holy Spirit power. God's gift of the Holy Spirit is your personal S-GPS—your Spiritual Guidance and Power System. Since you cannot know what day or season Christ will return for you, you have been given this power to help you navigate challenging circumstances, and embolden you to share what Jesus Christ has done for you.

Reflections:

_____

_____

HOLY SPIRIT

"Things which eye has not seen and ear has not heard, and which have not entered the heart of man, all that God has prepared for those who love Him. For to us God revealed them through the Spirit; for the Spirit searches all things, even the depths of God. For who among men knows the thoughts of a man except the spirit of the man, which is in him? Even so the thoughts of God no one knows except the Spirit of God." 1 Corinthians 2:9–11 (NASB)

I have given you the Holy Spirit that you may know me. If you seek me in the depths of your spirit, I will reveal things to you which you have neither seen nor heard. There is no other way to know me, except to know my Son and the Spirit which He left to guide you until He comes again. My Spirit knows you completely, and wants to be known by you. I have prepared an incredible life for those who seek to know me and love me. Believe this and live abundantly, always seeking me as your Advisor and Advocate.

HOLY SPIRIT

"But one and the same Spirit works all these things, distributing to each one individually just as He wills … For by one Spirit we were all baptized into one body, whether Jews or Greeks, whether slaves or free, and we were all made to drink of one Spirit."
1 Corinthians 12:11, 13 (NASB)

All spiritual gifts come from one Spirit, and each gift is given to individuals by me as I see fit. Whether I give you the gift of wisdom or knowledge or faith or prophesy or speaking in different tongues or healing—it is all from the Holy Spirit of My Son Christ in you. By one Spirit you are baptized, and from that same Spirit you drink. If you seek a spiritual gift, ask for it. If you know your spiritual gift, use it.

LOVE

"For now we see in a mirror dimly, but then face to face; now I know in part, but then I shall know fully just as I also have been fully known. But now abide faith, hope, love, these three; but the greatest of these is love." 1 Corinthians 13:12–13 (NASB)

How well do you think you know me? I give you glimpses of my nature as you seek me and become ready for each revelation. You see me only partially now, as if in a reflection; but one day we will be face to face. Then you will know and understand me fully, just as I have always known you. **Faith** is vital for you to believe what you do not see. **Hope** gives you the motivation to stay the course. But **Love** is the greatest of the three, as you experience my mercy and grace, until you see me face to face.

LOVE

"Greater love has no one than this, that one lay down his life for his friends. You are my friends, if you do what I command you. No longer do I call you slaves, for the slave does not know what his master is doing; but I have called you friends, for all things that I have heard from My father I have made known to you. You did not choose me, but I chose you, and appointed you, that you should go and bear fruit, and that your fruit should remain, that whatever you ask of the Father in My name, He may give to you." John 15:13–16 (NASB)

There is no greater love than losing one's own life to save others. Jesus did this for you because He loves you and wants you to be His friend. He wants to share with you all that I have revealed to Him. Remember that He chose you, and has appointed you to bear fruit in His name. Bearing fruit means simply to cause others to be drawn to Jesus as a result of your obvious obedience in all you say and do. When you do this, you will be able to ask anything of me in His name and I will give it to you.

TEMPTATION

"Therefore let him who thinks he stands take heed lest he fall. No temptation has overtaken you but such as is common to man; and God is faithful, who will not allow you to be tempted beyond what you are able, but with the temptation will provide the way of escape also, that you may be able to endure it." 1 Corinthians 10:12–13 (NASB)

Temptation is inevitable. What tempts one may not tempt another, but you will be tempted. You may think you have a distinctly different experience with temptation. But I know temptations are like the sands of the sea, too numerous to count, all having the same destructive tendencies. As the tide of temptation washes in, run from it using the escape I provide. When it washes back out to sea, take time to reflect on your obedience and how you used the blessing of My Power to escape the threat.

DIRECTION

"The steps of a man are established by the LORD; and He delights in his way. When he falls, he shall not be hurled headlong; because the LORD is the One who holds his hand." Psalm 37:23–24 (NASB)

Trust me to guide you on your path which I have established just for you. Walk with me and when you stumble, I will hold your hand and keep you from running headlong into disaster. I am delighted to show you more, as you trust me more.

DIRECTION

"The plans of the diligent lead surely to advantage, but everyone who is hasty comes surely to poverty." Proverbs 21:5 (NASB)

What are you planning for the future? Have you included me in your plan? Invite me to plan with you; tell me your ideas and then listen for my thoughts. Rushing to a conclusion may give you momentary satisfaction—whether it is your work, a hobby or a relationship. But diligently seeking me and waiting for a clear Word from me will give you confidence and peace as you move forward.

Week Seven

SPEECH

How good are your communication skills? Are you able to find the perfect words to articulate your question or statement? When you are angry or frustrated, do you fall back on language that is either inflammatory or perhaps profane? Conversely, what motivates you to speak in a manner that promotes peace and beckons understanding?

I love words. I am humored by the examples in the dictionary of word contradictions. For instance, there is the fact that "love" in the language of tennis means "nothing." In the world of texting and tweeting, word choice is critical. The reader has to "get" your meaning without the benefits of sight and sound. Proofread before you send!

I also love movies. I am fortunate that my husband does too, so most Friday nights you can find us munching popcorn and anticipating the thrill of a good story set in motion by a director and talented artists. You can probably guess where this is going … the inexplicable use of profanity that dots some movies and peppers others is becoming all too common. We came out of a movie tonight, enriched by the joy of the story and yet, disappointed and frustrated by the language. I can only surmise that the writer/director felt the story would have been mundane without the "colorful language" or that the rating required the profanity to attract the largest audience. They were regrettably mistaken. Great actors and great stories don't need profanity to weave their tale in a way that connects with the audience.

Our plight is described in James 3:8–10 (NLT). "But no one can tame the tongue. It is restless and evil, full of deadly poison. Sometimes it praises our Lord and Father, and sometimes it curses those who have been made in the image of God. And so blessing and cursing come pouring out of the same mouth. Surely, my brothers and sisters, this is not right!"

How, then, are we to control our tongue? We must replace our prideful desire to "have the last and loudest word" with God's desire to have us speak His Word. Ephesians 4:29 (NASB) says "Let no unwholesome word proceed from your mouth, but only such a word as is good for edification according to the need of the moment, that it may give grace to those who hear."

We must seek God's wisdom and His ways, as stated in James 3:13, 17–18 (NLT). "If you are wise and understand God's ways, prove it by living an honorable life, doing good works with the humility that comes from wisdom. But the wisdom from above is first of all pure. It is also peace loving, gentle at all times, and willing to yield to others. It is full of mercy and good deeds. It shows no favoritism and is always sincere. And those who are peacemakers will plant seeds of peace and reap a harvest of righteousness." Remember, your speech and sometimes your silence can be the very tools needed to reflect the wisdom of God.

Reflections:

_____

_____

SPEECH

"Let no unwholesome word proceed from your mouth, but only such a word as is good for edification according to the need of the moment, that it may give grace to those who hear." Ephesians 4:29 (NASB)

Does your language please me? I tell you to use words that edify others because I want you to give *grace*, just as it has been given to you. In moments of anger and passionate discourse, allow me to enter the conversation. Just as My Son displayed righteous anger in the temple, make sure it is My Honor you protect (and not your own), measuring your words with wisdom and self-control. Cursing has no place in your vocabulary. Ask for My Spirit to indwell you and take control, so that your speech honors me.

SPEECH

"This you know, my beloved brethren. But let everyone be quick to hear, slow to speak and slow to anger; for the anger of man does not achieve the righteousness of God." James 1:19–20 (NASB)

What is your first reaction to conflict? Do you speak immediately, as an impulsive child who cries when he doesn't get his way? Or do you take a moment to reflect and really hear what the person is saying? Does your temper immediately boil to anger? Or do you first breathe in My Spirit, and consider how you might show grace in the midst of conflict? You will show more of me in silence than in a harsh reply. Allow my righteousness to shine in you.

LOVE

"See how great a love the Father has bestowed upon us, that we should be called children of God; and such we are. For this reason the world does not know us, because it did not know Him. Beloved, now we are children of God, and it has not appeared as yet what we shall be. We know that, when He appears, we shall be like Him, because we shall see Him just as He is. And everyone who has this hope fixed on Him purifies himself, just as He is pure." 1 John 3:1–3 (NASB)

Do you see how great my love is for you, that I call you my children? There is no greater family to be part of than the Family of God! The world does not understand this, because the world does not know me. Though you do not fully comprehend what being my child means, you can look forward to the day when I will appear again, and know that you will see me just as I Am and that you will be like me. Be purified as you set your hope on me; because I am pure, you may be also.

THE LAW

FIRST COMMANDMENT
"You shall have no other gods before me." Exodus 20:3 (NASB)

I gave Moses the Ten Commandments written on two stone tablets to instruct my people of Israel, a holy nation set apart and devoted only to me. These commands are now for all Children of the Most High God, Jew and Gentile alike. If you are mine, you will put nothing above your worship of me. Things that take your allegiance away from me and the desire to do my will are gods. Do you unwittingly worship the god of money, your career, your body, fame, possessions? Maintain spiritual balance by keeping yourself centered on my purpose for you.

SPEECH

"But no one can tame the tongue; it is a restless evil and full of deadly poison. With it we bless our Lord and Father; and with it we curse men, who have been made in the likeness of God; from the same mouth come both blessing and cursing. My brethren, these things ought not to be this way." James 3:8–10 (NASB)

Do you have good intentions at the beginning of each day to speak kindly, only to spew forth derogatory or disrespectful language within a few hours? You must remember that your tongue is an instrument of your thoughts, so how you direct your thoughts will determine how you speak. Renew your mind in My Word, and ask for my wisdom to pervade your heart and mind. If you bless me, yet you curse the one who is made in my likeness, have you not cursed my workmanship? Ponder this and train yourself to place my image over the faces of all you meet, finding victory over what comes out of your mouth.

OBEDIENCE

"For it is Thou who dost bless the righteous man, O LORD. Thou dost surround him with favor as with a shield." Psalm 5:12 (NASB)

Who is righteous? You who believe you have been made righteous through the blood sacrifice of My Son Jesus. You who believe My Word is the ultimate Word, the final Authority, and seek to apply it to every aspect of your life. These acts of faith and obedience are so pleasing to me that I will surround you with favor and blessings as an invisible shield.

OBEDIENCE

"Yes, and all who desire to live godly in Christ Jesus will suffer persecution. But evil men and impostors will grow worse and worse, deceiving and being deceived. But you must continue in the things which you have learned and been assured of, knowing from whom you have learned them, and that from childhood you have known the Holy Scriptures, which are able to make you wise for salvation through faith which is in Christ Jesus." 2 Timothy 3:12–15 (NKJV)

Continue learning about me. Build on that which you have learned through scripture and from trusted teachers of My Word. You will gain wisdom for your salvation through faith in My Son Jesus Christ. But beware of evil men and imposters who will grow even worse as time goes by. There will be much deceit and you will be persecuted. Yes, all who desire to live godly in Christ will suffer persecution, so keep standing strong in your faith and rejoice in your salvation!

Week Eight

DECEIT

If Satan had a middle name, it would be Deception. Since the earth was formed and Adam and Eve were born, Satan has made it his goal to deceive mankind and draw them away from the Truth. He uses different tactics to match perfectly the weaknesses we each possess. For Adam and Eve, it was the desire for knowledge; for Abraham and Sarah, it was the desire for a child; for Jacob and Esau, it was the desire for the coveted birthright; for David, it was the forbidden fruit of another man's wife; for Judas, it was thirty pieces of silver.

1 Peter 5:8 (NASB) tells us to "Be of sober spirit, be on the alert. Your adversary, the devil, prowls around like a roaring lion, seeking someone to devour." What does this say to you? If the above-mentioned patriarchs and even one of the chosen twelve followers of Jesus Christ could be duped by the devil's deceitful ways, what chance do we have? Only One—that of daily throwing down the gauntlet of Jesus Christ. We are to be on the alert and guard our hearts and minds against the schemes of the devil. "Put on the full armor of God, so that you will be able to stand firm against the schemes of the devil." Ephesians 6:11 (NASB)

Now, let's get down to where you live. What does deceit look like in your world? Sometimes we do or say something that seems so innocent on the surface, and then are shocked when it unfolds into a terrible mess. Shakespeare is often mistakenly credited with this illuminating quote: "Oh what a tangled web we weave when first we practice to deceive" (It was actually penned by Sir Walter Scott (*Marmion*, 1808). No matter what the deception, does it not usually end in regret? As a child, my moments of terror over being found out were much worse than the actual punishment I received for breaking a rule. I have seen that same look of dread in my granddaughter's eyes, and I find it difficult to keep a straight face.

A less familiar quote from Johann Wolfgang von Goethe states: "It is better to be deceived by one's friends than to deceive them." It sounds like he may have known Jesus, or at least adhered to His teachings—"Do to others as you would have them do to you." Luke 6:31 (NIV). I was deceived by a group of women years ago, and I will never forget the terrible ache in my heart. As I readjusted my emotional compass—through lots of prayer and a dear friend who listened to my tale of woe—I was able to move forward without striking back. I came to realize that they were not Christians and would be watching my reaction. I've never been sorry that I remained faithful to God and the Golden Rule—deceit did not win that day.

Jeremiah 17:9 (NIV) states "The heart is deceitful above all things and beyond cure. Who can understand it?" This verse gets to the core of it—we are all born into sin and are able to deceive even ourselves. It is only through a daily relationship with Jesus Christ and the Holy Spirit's presence in us that we have the power to reject thoughts that lead to deception. Verse 10 goes on to say "I the LORD search the heart and examine the mind, to reward each person according to their conduct, according to what their deeds deserve." There is a reward for doing life God's way.

Reflections:

DECEIT

"Do not be deceived: 'bad company corrupts good morals.'"
1 Corinthians 15:33 (NASB)

Do you have a friend whom you enjoy, but who is not walking with me? Are your intentions to be "salt and light," but instead you succumb to their immoral influence over you? It may be their language, their situational ethics, their propensity to gossip, their general attitude of superiority. Or is it something less obvious, such as viewing life through the prism of negative thinking? I warn you to be on guard, because their attitude and lifestyle can corrupt the life you are trying to live for me.

DECEIT

"As a partridge that hatches eggs which it has not laid, so is he who makes a fortune, but unjustly; in the midst of his days it will forsake him, and in the end he will be a fool." Jeremiah 17:11 (NASB)

Don't be so overcome with the desire for riches that you are blinded to the way in which you seek them. Be careful to first desire those things which cannot be purchased with money—integrity, character, honesty, a clear conscience. All the money in the world won't be worth the price you have to pay when you place your needs and desires above those of your fellow man. In the end, your riches will mean nothing, so don't be a fool. Cast your sights on that which has eternal value, and I will take care of your earthly needs.

TEMPTATION

"Let no one say when he is tempted, "I am being tempted by God"; for God cannot be tempted by evil, and He Himself does not tempt anyone." James 1:13 (NASB)

Understand that temptation comes from the evil one in this world. I do not tempt you, but I have allowed the evil one to tempt for a time, until he is thrown into the lake of fire. Until the time I have ordained for his destruction, be aware of who is tempting you, and resist the temptation so that you may be strengthened in your faith until I come again.

SALVATION

"But as many as received Him, to them He gave the right to become children of God, even to those who believe in His name." John 1:12 (NASB)

Are you a child of God? I sent My Son Jesus to earth to show you who I am. He was born of a virgin into the Jewish lineage of King David. When Jesus began His ministry, not even His Jewish heritage could save Him from death on a cross. His fellow Jews, looking for another earthly king, rejected Him. But those that did receive His message of salvation and a Kingdom to come received the right to become my children because they believed in His Name. Then and now, I seek those who will believe by faith that Jesus is My Son, and that He prepares an eternal home for all those who believe in His name.

TRUST

"Know therefore that the LORD your God, He is God, the faithful God, who keeps His covenant and His loving kindness to a thousandth generation with those who love Him and keep His commandments."
Deuteronomy 7:9 (NASB)

I am the LORD your God. I am faithful to keep My Word, my covenant with you, to be with you until the end of the earth. If you love me and keep my commandments, I will surely show my love and kindness to all of your generations. I know you cannot be perfect in following after me, but trust me to know your motives in everything you attempt to do. Look forward to my love and kindness as you seek to be obedient.

TRUST

"For it is God who is at work in you, both to will and to work for His good pleasure." Philippians 2:13 (NASB)

Be glad that I am at work in you to will you towards my good pleasure. Think of the days before you knew me, and celebrate the newness of life that comes in following after me. The evil one wants to destroy you, but you are mine and nothing that I inhabit will be destroyed. Follow me and live forever!

HOLY SPIRIT

"The spirit of man is the lamp of the LORD, searching all the innermost parts of his being." Proverbs 20:27 (NASB)

Your spirit is precious to me. I have gifted you with intellect to do your job and manage your household. But it is your spirit that illumines your innermost thoughts and motives. When you are my child, you will be led by the Holy Spirit to think of others with the mind of Christ. You will possess compassion and understanding beyond your own ability, and will be given the strength and power to carry out my mission for you. Trust me—together we can accomplish more than you mind can conceive!

Week Nine

TEMPTATION

When you are drawn like a magnet to something that you know is not good for you—yet you lose all reason where this something or someone is concerned—that is temptation. Because Satan is allowed to "prowl around like a roaring lion, seeking someone to devour" (1 Peter 5:8 NASB), we must have a defense for evil enticements that come our way. We all have weak spots, vulnerabilities—and Satan has a laser pointed directly at these spots. What is your weakness? Is it emotional, physical, material, or intellectual? How do you say no when temptation comes?

First, understand that it is not a sin to be tempted, for even Jesus was tempted by Satan. The human part of Him was tempted, but the Spirit of God in Him kept Him from doing evil. He was literally God incarnate, God in human form. Yet, because He was tempted, we can have confidence that He understands our weakness when we fall to temptation.

Standing against temptation without spiritual armor is akin to going into battle without bodily protection or a weapon. There are several pieces of armor necessary to prevent your falling prey to the Enemy. As all good soldiers, you must train yourself to be fit for battle (Ephesians 6:10–17 NASB):

Helmet of Salvation: Are you saved? Have you been born again by trusting Jesus as your personal Savior? Are you certain if you died while reading this that you would be in the presence of the Lord for eternity?

Sword of the Spirit: Do you read the Word of God consistently? Do you trust it to be your guide through life? Do you hunger to know God better through scripture?

Belt of Truth: Are you confident of the Truth, and do you practice truth in everything? Does God's Truth change the way you think and react?

Breastplate of Righteousness: Are you confident of your righteousness through Christ? Are you willing to stand firm against the schemes of the devil using righteousness as your banner of courage and strength?

Feet Shod with Gospel of Peace: Have you prepared yourself with the message of the Gospel which brings peace to all mankind? Are you ready to share your faith? Can you speak of what God has done lately in your life?

Shield of Faith: Your faith will be like a shield to extinguish all the flaming missiles of the evil one. A strong exercised faith brings great confidence.

We must be ready, dressed in God's armor, and share our love of Jesus who died to save the world from temptation, sin and an eternity in hell. We must be ready to defend our faith at all costs, and let the whole world see what a great and mighty God we serve!

Reflections:

_____

_____

TEMPTATION

"For though we walk in the flesh, we do not war according to the flesh, for the weapons of our warfare are not of the flesh, but divinely powerful for the destruction of fortresses. We are destroying speculations and every lofty thing raised up against the knowledge of God, and we are taking every thought captive to the obedience of Christ." 2 Corinthians 10:3–5 (NASB)

Do you understand that the war you fight is not against the flesh, but against unseen forces? Therefore, you must seek my divine power to help you in the destruction of any theory or philosophy that contradicts your knowledge of me gained through My Word and the power of the Holy Spirit. Take every thought captive and, blending it with your spiritual knowledge, confirm your obedience and desire to magnify the Lord.

TEMPTATION

"Now flee from youthful lusts, and pursue righteousness, faith, love and peace, with those who call on the Lord from a pure heart." 2 Timothy 2:22 (NASB)

If you want to please me, you must set aside the lusts and pleasures of youth. When you were young, you selfishly pursued everything that pleased your mind and body. But now I want you to pursue righteousness, seeking to learn and grow in faith, love, and peace. Unite with others who call upon me with a pure heart, so that you have a common purpose, ready to encourage and inspire each other in love.

PRAYER

"Therefore I say to you, all things for which you pray and ask, believe that you have received them, and they shall be granted you."
Mark 11:24 (NASB)

How strong is your faith in me today? Do you know that I want to give you the desires of your heart? As you pray and ask me for what you want, you must believe with all your heart that you have received it. My Word promises if you do this in accordance with my will, your request will be granted.

PRAISE

"Shout joyfully to the LORD, all the earth. Serve the LORD with gladness; come before Him with joyful singing. Know that the LORD Himself is God; it is He who has made us, and not we ourselves; we are His people and the sheep of His pasture. Enter His gates with thanksgiving, and His courts with praise. Give thanks to Him; bless His name. For the LORD is good; His lovingkindness is everlasting, and His faithfulness to all generations." Psalm 100 (NASB)

Shout! Serve! Sing! I am the Lord your God and have made you to be my people. Be thankful unto me, let praise and thanksgiving be on your lips while blessings flow from your heart. I love you with an everlasting love; I will never fail you. My faithfulness is for you and to all generations. Sing with joy, serve with gladness!

PRAISE

"Then Hannah prayed and said, 'my heart exults in the LORD; my horn is exalted in the LORD, my mouth speaks boldly against my enemies, because I rejoice in Thy salvation. There is no one holy like the LORD, indeed, there is no one besides Thee, nor is there any rock like our God ... He keeps the feet of His godly ones, but the wicked ones are silenced in darkness; for not by might shall a man prevail.'" 1 Samuel 2:1, 2, 9 (NASB)

I am the LORD God and there is none Holy like me. I will keep you safe, you who are godly; but the wicked will be silenced when they least expect it. You will not prevail by your own might, but by trusting in me. Speak boldly against the enemies of My Name and rejoice in the salvation which I have provided for you. Let your hearts thrill in the power of My Holy Name!

SPEECH

"The heart of the righteous ponders how to answer …" Proverbs 15:28a (NASB)

Are there only two ways to answer: true or false, right or wrong? Or, are there shades of an answer to match the colors of the rainbow? What is the timing of an answer: immediate or delayed? There is much to consider when answering a question: is the question serious, urgent, meditative, philosophical, foolish, conditional, or incriminating? And who is asking the question: friend or foe? Prepare yourself in advance by pondering and seeking My Wisdom and Righteousness, so that you will have the appropriate answer, tone and countenance when the question is asked.

OBEDIENCE

"Do not be bound together with unbelievers; for what partnership have righteousness and lawlessness, or what fellowship has light with darkness?" 2 Corinthians 6:14 (NASB)

As a believer in Jesus Christ and follower of My Word, you ought not to partner with unbelievers. Righteousness and lawlessness have no relationship because you are in the light of my love, and darkness cannot abide in My Light. In marriage, business, friendships and family, live in the light of my love, in hopes of turning those you care about away from the darkness of sin and eventual death.

Week Ten

WITNESS

Have you ever been asked to give testimony in a court trial? If you witnessed a crime or a car accident, you may have been asked to give an accounting of the event from your perspective. Your testimony serves an important role in our legal system to provide truth about what was seen and heard.

In the world of Christianity, Creation itself is a powerful witness. Our faith has been built up through the testimony of Old Testament prophets as well as New Testament Disciples of Christ. It is through their experiences that we have come to know the Father, Son and the Holy Spirit. However, the Bible tells us in Romans 1:20 (NLT) that we have no excuse for denying who God is—even if we don't have access to His Word: "For ever since the world was created, people have seen the earth and sky. Through everything God made, they can clearly see his invisible qualities—his eternal power and divine nature. So they have no excuse for not knowing God."

Someone recently shared that she didn't like to hear people claim healing from God because it made all the others who had not been healed feel badly. That is a compassionate view, yet over and over the Bible tells us we are to shout aloud the good things God has done for us. According to Psalm 71:23 (NIV), "My lips will shout for joy when I sing praise to you—I whom you have delivered." When we experience God's mercy and grace, praise should be a natural response.

I am blessed to have a sister who has left an indelible mark on my life through her testimony. Before Bonnie left for college, she went on a mission trip to California, and was asked to give her testimony at church when she returned. Stepping up to the podium, she held her arms up like a ballerina and slowly turned a full circle. Facing the congregation again, she proclaimed that she might not look different on the outside, but that she had been changed on the inside. She went on to tell how the Lord had worked in her life on the trip; and she continues to witness concerning His grace and glory in her life. Her desire is for others to be drawn to Christ through her life ... and they are.

Who has made a spiritual impact upon your life? Are you giving testimony to God's grace in you? We are to be bold like Paul when he said, "For I am not ashamed of this Good News about Christ. It is the power of God at work, saving everyone who believes—the Jew first and also the Gentile. This Good News tells us how God makes us right in his sight. This is accomplished from start to finish by faith. As the Scripture says, 'It is through faith that a righteous person has life.'" Romans 1:16–17 (NLT)

Pray for opportunities to share your faith. God promises in Isaiah 55:11 (NIV), "So is my word that goes out of my mouth: it will not return to me empty, but will accomplish what I desire and achieve the purpose for which I sent it." God always honors our requests to share His Word and His Ways.

Reflections:

_____

_____

WITNESS

"You are the light of the world. A city set on a hill cannot be hidden ... Let your light shine before men in such a way that they may see your good works, and glorify your Father who is in heaven."
Matthew 5:14, 16 (NASB)

You who love me are the light of the world. When you feed the sick, comfort the bereaved, visit the lonely, teach a child, honor your parents, stand up for your friends, love your spouse, pray for others, share me with the lost, worship me in and out of church, I am glorified as your Father in heaven. As the world grows dim with sin and shame, just as a city set on a hill cannot be hidden, neither can your light of love and compassion. Let it shine!

WITNESS

"And Jesus came up and spoke to them, saying, 'All authority has been given to me in heaven and on earth. Go therefore and make disciples of all the nations, baptizing them in the name of the Father and the Son and the Holy Spirit, teaching them to observe all that I commanded you; and lo, I am with you always, even to the end of the age.'" Matthew 28:18-20 (NASB)

Do you care enough to share? When My Son Jesus had his earthly ministry, I gave Him authority over everyone and everything. He urged His followers to spread the good news of Christ and baptize all who believed. That is still the mission of all believers. He promised to be with you until the end of the world, so trust My Word and share your faith with others. People want to know about your hope in Christ—they are just waiting for someone to care enough to share.

WITNESS

"Therefore, since we have so great a cloud of witnesses surrounding us, let us also lay aside every encumbrance, and the sin which so easily entangles us, and let us run with endurance the race that is set before us, fixing our eyes on Jesus, the author and perfecter of faith, who for the joy set before Him endured the cross, despising the shame, and has sat down at the right hand of the throne of God." Hebrews 12:1–2 (NASB)

How are you doing today in running the race of faith for Christ? If you are laden with guilt and shame, remember that sin is subtle and seductive, and its author is always ready to entangle you. You must begin with me, laying your burdens down in admission and repentance. Are you filled with discouragement, delusion or confusion, even though you carry no responsibility or control over what is happening in your life? Remember that My Son Jesus, sinless and innocent, endured the cross, despising the shame He carried on our behalf, but looked towards the joy that was His for the redemption of our sins. Because of His sacrifice, He now sits at my right hand on the throne of God. The unsaved are watching you—give me your burdens daily so that you can run your race with endurance. Look forward to the prize which is eternal life with me where there will be no more tears or sadness.

SIN

"There is nothing outside the man which going into him can defile him; but the things which proceed out of the man are what defile the man ... For from within, out of the heart of men, proceed the evil thoughts, fornications, thefts, murders, adulteries, deeds of coveting and wickedness, as well as deceit, sensuality, envy, slander, pride and foolishness. All these evil things proceed from within and defile the man." Mark 7:15, 21–23 (NASB)

The food which goes into your body cannot make you impure. It is the evil which comes from your heart and mind that causes impurity. Ask me to fill you with My Spirit today and do this every day, so that evil thoughts and actions don't have a hiding place to germinate and grow. Fill your heart and mind with My Word so that you avoid corruption and displace evil.

SIN

"Therefore, to one who knows the right thing to do, and does not do it, to him it is sin." James 4:17 (NASB)

I have given you the Holy Spirit and My Word to guide you in discerning what is right. When you know what to do—when you hear my nudge to make the call, give the money, help the hurting, love the unlovely, work My Plan, let obedience rule—and fail to follow through, it is sin. You see, sin is not only what you do wrong, but what you *don't* do that you were inspired to do. Blessings abound for those who act upon their good impressions.

SPEECH

"Let your speech always be with grace, seasoned, as it were, with salt, so that you may know how you should respond to each person."
Colossians 4:6 (NASB)

There should be an underlying quality to your speech, whether you are speaking to a child, parent, spouse, good friend, co-worker, leader, or even one whom you do not respect. Just like salt is used to season food, enhancing the flavor, your words spoken with understanding and an attitude of grace will be received like the comfort of a warm blanket.

WITNESS

"Create in me a clean heart, O God, and renew a steadfast spirit within me. Do not cast me away from Thy presence and do not take Thy Holy Spirit from me. Restore to me the joy of Thy salvation, and sustain me with a willing spirit. Then I will teach transgressors Thy ways, and sinners will be converted to Thee." Psalm 51:10–13 (NASB)

Think about the important relationships in your life. Would they survive if you never called, wrote or spent time cultivating them? Sometimes when you feel I have moved away from you, when you can't feel My Presence, remember that our relationship depends upon your willingness and desire to spend time with me. Sin can make you feel separated from me, but know that I am here to cleanse your heart and renew your spirit. Your joy will be restored as you turn back to My Will and My Way. When that happens, others will notice and be directed to me because of your actions and attitudes.

Week Eleven

PRAISE

I was involved this morning in an unusual time of praise. Our church celebrated the 25th anniversary of the man God chose to lead our church away from loss and despair, and toward the liberating road to revival and renewal. We praised Pastor Jack Graham and reminisced through video and testimonials about the growth of the church under his leadership. We thanked him for not only staying the course, but pointing us toward God's plan for the future of our church.

Had this been the leader of a corporation or the commander of our armed forces, the focus would have been on the individual and all of his rightly-deserved accomplishments. Yet, in the instance of this celebration, the focus was not only directed at our pastor, but on our God who led him to us, gave him the vision for our future and inspires him still to move us onward and upward.

When praise is directed at the One who makes all things possible, it is true praise indeed. "For the LORD is great and greatly to be praised." Psalm 96:4a (KJV) "It is a good thing to give thanks unto the LORD, and to sing praises unto thy name, O Most High." Psalm 92:1 (KJV) "Oh that men would praise the

LORD for His goodness, and for His wonderful works to the children of men." Psalm 107:8 (KJV)

Our choir sings a song entitled "Total Praise," made famous by The Brooklyn Tabernacle Choir. The lyrics are taken from Psalm 121 beginning:

"Lord, I will lift mine eyes to the hills, knowing my help is coming from you.

Your peace you give me in time of the storm. You are the source of my strength.

You are the strength of my life. I lift my hands in total praise to you."

The song concludes with a series of Amens that crescendo and cascade over each other in a waterfall of praise. I have made a habit of starting each day by listening to this song, because it places me in a position of praise from which I can begin to worship the Most High God.

Praise comes from the Spirit of God in you. The more you reflect on God's power in your life, the more likely you are to thank Him and praise Him for His goodness, His direction, His mercy, His provision, His faithfulness, His love. God inhabits the praise of His people, so praise Him on the good days and even more on the days that deliver challenges. Praise Him and witness your own metamorphosis from ordinary to extraordinary; to a life of thanksgiving, hope, and expectancy!

Reflections:

_____

_____

PRAISE

"Thou hast turned for me my mourning into dancing; Thou hast loosed my sackcloth and girded me with gladness; that my soul may sing praise to Thee, and not be silent. O LORD my God, I will give thanks to Thee forever." Psalm 30:11–12 (NASB)

When you mourn the loss of a loved one, the loss of a job, the loss of a hope or dream—I understand your sorrow. I am here to comfort you, and I know exactly when to bring gladness back into your heart. Grief takes time, but as you experience renewed joy and hope, sing praises to me, just as David did. Don't be silent, for you are my witness that even during times of loss, I will return to you songs of praise.

PRAISE

"But as for me, I shall sing of Thy strength; yes, I shall joyfully sing of Thy lovingkindness in the morning, for Thou hast been my stronghold, and a refuge in the day of my distress. O my strength, I will sing praises to Thee; for God is my stronghold, the God who shows me lovingkindness." Psalm 59:16–17 (NASB)

Remember the last time you were distressed and you turned to me? That sense of My Presence with you in the middle of the storm is what I long to give you each time you face a crisis. If you will lean on My Strength, you will not only be able to survive, but thrive on My Love. Yes, even to the point of singing, because I am your stronghold. I will give you a new song to sing!

PRAISE

"How blessed are the people who know the joyful sound! O LORD, they walk in the light of Thy countenance. In Thy name they rejoice all the day, and by Thy righteousness they are exalted." Psalm 89:15–16 (NASB)

Walking in the light of My Countenance comes from being illuminated by My Counsel. Seek Me. Distractions are a tool of Satan. He will do whatever it takes to keep you busy doing anything other than developing your spirit. Determine to dedicate intentional time in My Word. You will find yourself rejoicing as you walk in My Light. You will be blessed and exalted—lifted up—by My Righteousness when you devote yourself to My Spirit.

THE LAW

SECOND COMMANDMENT

"You shall not make for yourself an idol, or any likeness of what is in heaven above or on the earth beneath or in the water under the earth. You shall not worship them or serve them; for I, the LORD your God, am a jealous God, visiting the iniquity of the fathers on the children, on the third and the fourth generations of those who hate Me, but showing lovingkindness to thousands, to those who love Me and keep My commandments." Exodus 20:4–6 (NASB)

The gods of today are not always made of stone, jewels and precious metals, but of money and things money can buy. Do you allow the desire for possessions to override your desire to love me? Do you want prestige and the praise of man? Those things are fleeting. I am a jealous God, and do not want you to serve any god alongside me or in opposition to me. This kind of iniquity can cause hardships for your children's children and beyond. My lovingkindness is for all who love me and keep my commandments. If you want to be blessed, serve me only.

STEWARDSHIP

"Give to him who asks of you, and do not turn away from him who wants to borrow from you." Matthew 5:42 (NASB)

When did you last give with pleasure to one of the least of my children? I am teaching much to those without the comforts of life, but I am also teaching you who are blessed beyond your needs. If you are to shine the Light of Christ in this world that forgets me more each day, then you must release back into the world the blessings I have given you. Be on guard against selfishness. Give of yourself to those I put in your path—it is never a coincidence!

STEWARDSHIP

"He who is faithful in a very little thing is faithful also in much; and he who is unrighteous in a very little thing is unrighteous also in much."
Luke 16:10 (NASB)

Have you ever found money that didn't belong to you, and put it in your pocket as if you earned it? Have you cheated on your taxes or stolen time from your employer? Have you taken someone's trust for granted? Remember I know all your tricks. I knew when you acted honorably toward your fellow man, and I knew when you brought shame to your name. Be honest in the small things of life, and I will trust you with more as you prove yourself trustworthy.

STEWARDSHIP

"And from everyone who has been given much shall much be required."
Luke 12:48b (NASB)

What have I given you? Is it financial wealth, a talent, a good business mind, the ability to teach, a heart of compassion? I know who will be faithful with much and who will squander their gifts. I allow financial success to those who will share. Others may not do well with extra money, so I may give them a special ability that others do not have. With whatever I give you, use it well. Be mindful that it is a temporary gift and a test for you to use it to benefit others as well as yourself. Take the responsibility seriously.

Week Twelve

PROTECTION

W hen I was a little girl, I was fortunate to have a mother and father who protected me from the harsh things of the world. They fed and clothed me, gave me a home, educated me and loved me consistently and well. I never really thought about their protection, but I certainly benefitted from it. In the same way, during most of my adult life, I seldom stopped to think about the outside forces at work to keep me from harm. The realization of God's protection over us may come when we land safely in another country, when the tornado strikes close enough to feel the vibration and experience the darkness, or when we pass a deadly crash, knowing it could have been us. For me, it has been a gradual awareness of the reality of God's presence in every area of my life.

Proverbs 30:5 (TLB) tells us that "every word of God proves true. He defends all who come to him for protection." We sing songs of praise and worship that speak of God as our Defender and Protector, so why is it that we forget to thank Him daily for defending us against unseen forces? When the driver next to us is texting while going 70 mph on the freeway, just making it home safely should be cause for praise!

So how do we find this deep assurance of God's protection? As always, look in His Word. Proverbs 19:23 (TLB) has a promise you can count on: "Reverence for God gives life, happiness and protection from harm." The word reverence has to do with a profound adoration and respect for another. If I say I revere God, but my lifestyle proves disrespectful to His Word, I fool only myself. God wants what is best for us, and we can obtain the best when we honor Him with obedience.

Psalm 91:1–2 (TLB) says "We live within the shadow of the Almighty, sheltered by the God who is above all gods. This I declare, that he alone is my refuge, my place of safety; he is my God, and I am trusting him." Visualize being in the shadow of Almighty God as you go about your day at work, at home with your children, or traveling to foreign lands. Just think, the same awesome God—who made heaven and earth and <u>you</u>—has your back. No matter where you go, He is there.

Reflection:

_____

_____

PROTECTION

"The LORD is good, a stronghold in the day of trouble, and He knows those who take refuge in Him." Nahum 1:7 (NASB)

When trouble comes your way, what is your first reaction? Do you panic, do you ask "why me," do you get angry—or do you come to me? I want you to learn to trust me—I am your stronghold. As you turn from running to trusting, you will find I know the shortest distance between trouble and triumph. I will comfort you and reveal My Wisdom to mend your spirit and build your character. Take refuge in me.

PROTECTION

"The angel of the Lord encamps around those who fear Him, and rescues them." Psalm 34:7 (NASB)

Did you know I have angels all around my children? When the enemy tries to harm you, my angels will fight for you and rescue you. Protection is promised to those who fear me, those who revere me and trust me to be their heavenly Father. Be comforted and strengthened by this knowledge—I protect those whom I love.

DISOBEDIENCE

Therefore God gave them over in the lusts of their hearts to impurity, that their bodies might be dishonored among them. For they exchanged the truth of God for a lie, and worshiped and served the creature rather than the Creator, who is blessed forever. Amen. For this reason God gave them over to degrading passions; for their women exchanged the natural function for that which is unnatural, and in the same way also the men abandoned the natural function of the woman and burned in their desire toward one another, men with men committing indecent acts and receiving in their own persons the due penalty of their error. Romans 1:24–27 (NASB)

I am the God of all truth. The instructions I have given you in My Word are to guide you toward the rewards of Godly living. But there are always going to be some who exchange My Truth for the lies of the world. They worship their bodies and temporary sensual pleasures; they abandon their natural functions between man and woman and crave their own sex. These acts have consequences, which may not be revealed until it is too late. The forfeiture of integrity, honor, family, health or life is at stake. If you are tempted with this, break free. Ask for my help to provide your way of escape from this life of heartache and destruction to one of Hope and Promise.

OBEDIENCE

SANCTIFIER—Jehovah-M'Kaddesh
And you shall keep my statutes, and practice them; I am the LORD who sanctifies you. Leviticus 20:8 (NASB)

Now that you have read my commands, remember to practice them so that keeping my commands becomes second nature. It is my desire that you learn to be obedient, and that you will be inspired to continue in obedience as you experience a sense of peace in doing my bidding. I am the only One who can sanctify you for my service. Seek me today to prepare you for what will come. Afterward, you will be wise to reflect on how My Presence made a difference.

SPEECH

"And put on the new self, which in the likeness of God has been created in righteousness and holiness of the truth. Therefore, laying aside falsehood, speak truth, each one of you, with his neighbor, for we are members of one another. Be angry, and yet do not sin; do not let the sun go down on your anger." Ephesians 4:24–26 (NASB)

When you put your trust in My Son Jesus Christ, you are a new creature. You now have my truth and righteousness in you, and have been given a holy calling. Therefore, let My Spirit work in you to speak only the truth with your family, friends, neighbors and co-workers. When there is disagreement, though anger may result, do not sin because of it. Use My Spirit in you to find understanding and compromise, so that your anger is diffused before night falls. Sleep peacefully knowing you have done my will.

PROTECTION

"Have I not commanded you? Be strong and courageous! Do not tremble or be dismayed, for the LORD your God is with you wherever you go."
Joshua 1:9 (NASB)

Be strong and courageous because I am with you all the time. Even when you can't feel My Presence, know that I am there. There is no need to be afraid or discouraged; these things are not of me. Trust me to give you everything you need as the need arises. When you experience this kind of trust and the accompanying deliverance, your faith will be made strong for what lies ahead.

PROTECTION

"As for God, His way is blameless; the word of the LORD is tried; He is a shield to all who take refuge in Him." Psalm 18:30 (NASB)

I am the LORD your God. I am Blameless, Flawless. My Word is tested and proven; no one successfully argues against it. The truth of My Word will shield you from danger when you take refuge in me. When you feel attacked and your burdens weigh heavy, open My Word and seek My Presence. Let me protect you and guide you to the Way of Perfect Peace.

Week Thirteen

HEALING

There are three kinds of healing—physical, emotional, and spiritual. We will look at each one since they are somewhat interdependent. Having witnessed this conundrum in the lives of friends and in myself, I find it both baffling and logical.

<u>Physical Healing</u>: Do you know someone who was healed from a terminal illness, where the doctors had no explanation? Or maybe you know one who should not have survived a accident, but walked away with no serious injuries? Yet, it seems there are more instances where permanent damage results from accidents; and terminal patients suffer and die after long and painful attempts to be healed. God's Word gives us hope as we see Jesus healing "every sickness and every disease among the people." Matthew 9:35 (KJV). The question remains, why are some people healed and some not? Isaiah 55:8–9 (NIV) reminds us, "For my thoughts are not your thoughts, neither are your ways my ways," declares the Lord. "As the heavens are higher than the earth, so are my ways higher than your ways and my thoughts than your thoughts." We must accept this truth and realize the boundless number of people changed for eternity when He chooses to

delay death in one and claim another early for His Kingdom. The ripple effect of God's power is beyond our comprehension.

Emotional Healing: I know two men who each lost their mother prematurely. It just so happens they are both highly intelligent, but because of this trauma, cannot "trust in a God who would take their mother from them." The paradox for them and so many others is that the very God they cannot trust is the only God who can give them all they truly need. No matter who or what event has caused us to suffer emotionally, we must be willing to lay all our burdens at Jesus' feet, and allow Him to give us the peace and love we so desperately seek. "Therefore humble yourselves under the mighty hand of God, that He may exalt you at the proper time, casting all your anxiety on Him, because He cares for you." 1 Peter 5:6–7 (NASB)

Spiritual Healing: To restore to original purity ... that is what Christ did when He died on the cross for our sins. The Christian life presents challenges for us as we struggle to keep our hearts, minds, and actions in line with God's Word. Even though the Bible tells us we have been made righteous through the blood of Christ Jesus, our sinful nature pulls us back into the maelstrom of temptation and subsequent sin and guilt. So, we must continually come back to the Throne of Grace for forgiveness and guidance. 1 Corinthians 6:19–20 (NLT) brings us full circle on the undeniable connection between healing of body, mind and soul (physical, emotional and spiritual): "Don't you realize that your body is the temple of the Holy Spirit, who lives in you and was given to you by God? You do not belong to yourself, for God bought you with a high price. So you must honor God with your body." Since our bodies are the sanctuary of the Holy Spirit, we must follow Peter's advice in1 Peter 2:2–3 (NIV): "Like newborn babies, crave pure spiritual milk, so that by it you may grow up in your salvation, now that you have tasted that the Lord is good."

The Lord *is* good ... come to the Source of love and mercy, and be healed.

Reflections:

_____

_____

HEALING

"Then your light will break forth like the dawn, and your healing will quickly appear; then your righteousness will go before you, and the glory of the LORD will be your rear guard. Then you will call, and the LORD will answer; you will cry for help, and He will say: 'Here am I'."
Isaiah 58:8–9 (NIV)

What causes me to respond with light and healing? Do you want My Righteousness and My Glory to surround you? Then begin with true worship. Let go of the bonds of wickedness and idolatry. Be done with selfishness and oppression. Seek and do my will. Have compassion on the poor and the hungry, the lost and forsaken. Pay attention not only to physical healing, but also emotional, mental and spiritual needs. Then My Light will break forth like dawn, and you will call on me and I will answer.

SUFFERING

"How long, O LORD? Wilt Thou forget me forever? How long wilt Thou hide Thy face from me? How long shall I take counsel in my soul, having sorrow in my heart all the day? How long will my enemy be exalted over me?" Psalm 13:1–2 (NASB)

Even King David, "a man after God's own heart," was separated from me for a time. It was not my choice, but his sin which drove him from me. Remember that nothing can separate you from my love—however, your own thoughts and actions can distance you from me. When you feel (as David did) that my face is hidden from you and there is loneliness and sorrow in your soul; when you feel that your enemies have been raised up and you are being trampled—seek me, search your heart, confess your sins and repent. Then our relationship will be healed and you will feel my love again, realizing that I have been there all along.

SUFFERING

Jehovah-Rophe, HEALER

"And He said, 'If you will give earnest heed to the voice of the LORD your God, and do what is right in His sight, and give ear to His commandments, and keep all His statutes, I will put none of the diseases on you which I have put on the Egyptians; for I, the LORD, am your healer.'" Exodus 15:26 (NASB)

Spiritual healing sometimes comes through physical illness. There are times when I may draw you back from your spiritual desert through the bitter springs of suffering. The questions you must ask yourself when you become ill or injured are these: 1) are you listening to God? 2) are you keeping His commandments and following His Way? Remember that others see your outward actions, but I alone know your heart. You are to love me first, your family second, your friends and neighbors after that. Sometimes, even good and noble deeds get in the way of time with me. Stay close and trust me to heal your mind, body and spirit.

FAITH

"Be on the alert, stand firm in the faith, act like men, be strong. Let all that you do be done in love." 1 Corinthians 16:13–14 (NASB)

You must stand firm in your faith and be on the alert for evil. Don't bow to the pressures of the world and become weak, taking the easy way out. Be strong in your commitment, filling your mind with My Word to protect you from evil thoughts. You must choose to think and act like My Son Jesus. Let everything be done in love for my sake.

FAITH

"As a result, we are no longer to be children, tossed here and there by waves, and carried about by every wind of doctrine, by the trickery of men, by craftiness in deceitful scheming; but speaking the truth in love, we are to grow up in all aspects into Him, who is the head, even Christ."
Ephesians 4:14–15 (NASB)

As a believer in My Son Christ Jesus, you cannot allow yourself to move back and forth between doctrines. There are always going to be deceitful men scheming to destroy your faith. Stand firm against any belief that does not meet the standard of the Living Word of God. Speak the truth in love, and continue to grow in all areas of your faith in Jesus Christ who demonstrated perfectly how to live a life that honors me.

FAITH

"It is a trustworthy statement: For if we died with Him, we shall also live with Him; if we endure, we shall also reign with Him; if we deny Him, He also will deny us; if we are faithless, He remains faithful; for He cannot deny Himself." 2 Timothy 2:11–13 (NASB)

Take comfort that I remain faithful even when your faith is weak. I know it is hard for you to understand when you are tested. You may struggle against the suffering, but do not deny me in the process. Remember that enduring the pain with faith is exactly what Jesus did when He took your sins to the cross. In essence, you died with Him when you accepted His sacrifice. And because of the evidence of your trust in Him by the way you live, your reward will be above all you imagine as you reign with Christ for all eternity. Live this promise!

SALVATION

"But when the fullness of the time came, God sent forth His Son, born of a woman, born under the Law, in order that He might redeem those who were under the Law, that we might receive the adoption as sons. And because you are sons, God has sent forth the Spirit of His Son into our hearts, crying, 'Abba! Father!' Therefore you are no longer a slave, but a son; and if a son, then an heir through God."
Galatians 4:4-7 (NASB)

When the time was exactly right, I sent My Son to be born of a woman who was under the Law, that Christ might redeem all those under the Law so they might receive adoption as sons. If you believe in me, My Spirit will cry out in your hearts to me, "Abba! Father!" Then you will no longer be a slave to the Law, but My Child; and if you are My Child, then you are My Heir. There is no greater aspiration than to be a Child of the King.

Week Fourteen

THE LAW

LAW—A rule of conduct or action prescribed or formally recognized as binding or enforced by a controlling authority. Law of Moses—The Pentateuch or Torah. *Merriam-Webster Dictionary*

You are probably familiar with the dramatic story in Exodus where Jehovah parted the Red Sea for the Israelites to escape Egyptian bondage and claim the Promised Land. Jehovah came down to Mount Sanai and called Moses to Him to give him instructions for the Israelites on how to live with their new found freedom. He wrote the Ten Commandments with His finger on two stone tablets and gave them to Moses so he could show the people what God had told him. Jehovah gave Moses a great deal of specific instructions, far beyond what was written on the tablets. Some believe this information was written down by Moses during the 40 days and nights he was on Mount Sanai with Jehovah. This seems logical since God's purpose was to teach the Israelites how to worship and live together as His people.

The above very condensed version of the origin of the Ten Commandments also known as The Law gives you historical perspective. Now, bring it forward, and consider how The Law applies to your life today. On the surface, it may appear that the Ten are easy to follow. After all, you are not planning to murder anyone and you certainly don't have any idols ... or do you?

I had the privilege of hearing a popular speaker last Sunday at church from Chorleywood, Hertfordshire, England, named Canon J. John. He has spoken at conferences and churches in 69 countries on six continents. His book entitled *just 10* is a contemporary application of the Ten Commandments. In an unusual move, our pastor requested that this guest speaker begin our series on The Law with the tenth commandment. How odd, I mused, until J. John refreshed my memory on the tenth: "Thou shalt not covet." He challenged that it was not really backwards at all to start with the last commandment, because coveting was the "gateway sin" to all other sins. Hmmm ... lying (check), stealing (check), idol worship (check), no other gods (check), murder (check)—you get the idea.

Our idols may not be calves carved in gold, but we are nonetheless tempted on all sides by things that would distract us from God's purpose for us. My husband and I are building a new home, the last for us as we ease towards retirement. We pray over our decisions for this house, and look forward to the time when we can enjoy the reality of our plan. But, in the process of planning, this good thing can become a distraction from God's best thing. In my case, it is the writing of *First Fruits*. Allowing God to lead me in the discipline of time management forces me to put away house plans, quit looking online for the perfect whatever, and begin praying as I wait for His words to form in my mind.

Which part of The Law is tugging at you?

Reflections:

_____

_____

THE LAW

"Now we know that whatever the Law says, it speaks to those who are under the Law, that every mouth may be closed, and all the world may become accountable to God; because by the works of the Law no flesh will be justified in His sight; for through the Law comes the knowledge of sin. Do we then nullify the Law through faith? May it never be! On the contrary, we establish the Law." Romans 3:19–20, 31 (NASB)

I gave you the Law to use as a guide, so that you are accountable for your actions. Your sin is made obvious by the Law, and no one is justified in my sight. But faith in the ultimate sacrifice of My Son Jesus' death, burial and resurrection makes your sins as white as snow. Does your faith then give you a "free pass" to continue in sin? No! The Law gives *direction* making you conscious of your sin. Your faith gives *salvation* pointing to forgiveness of your sin. My Plan has been for you all along, giving you direction leading to perfection.

THE LAW

"For Christ is the end of the law for righteousness to everyone who believes." Romans 10:4 (NASB)

I gave you the Law due to your sin nature. Because the Law points to your inability to be righteous, I also gave you My Son Jesus Christ. He provides you undeserved righteousness through His Grace. Therefore, you live under Grace, not the Law, once you embrace Christ's sacrifice and accept his free gift of Eternal Life.

DISCIPLINE

"You have wearied the LORD with your words. Yet you say, 'How have we wearied Him?' In that you say, 'everyone who does evil is good in the sight of the LORD, and He delights in them,' or, 'where is the God of justice?'" Malachi 2:17 (NASB)

Though I am the God of love, I do not love everything you do. I love you in spite of your sin. When I don't dispense justice immediately after your wrong doing, it does not imply that I approve of your actions. I choose when, where and how to chasten those I love, so don't consider your sinful actions as having slipped through my hands just because I did not administer swift discipline. Know that I love the sinner, not his sin—and that is exactly how I want you to respond to those with whom you find fault.

DISCIPLINE

"The LORD is slow to anger and great in power, and the LORD will by no means leave the guilty unpunished." Nahum 1:3a (NASB)

You may wonder why I do not punish the guilty immediately. Think of how you wish to be treated when you commit wrongdoing. Do you long for swift judgment? I am slow to anger on purpose. I have the power to chastise harshly and immediately, but I am slow to respond so that you may have time to come to repentance and find underserved grace.

TEMPTATION

"But I say, walk by the Spirit, and you will not carry out the desire of the flesh." Galatians 5:16 (NASB)

What fleshly desire keeps you imprisoned today? What thoughts creep into your mind during the day even when you are working on something else? What do you crave above all else? Is it knowledge, acceptance, respect, love, riches, protection, security, clothing, physical perfection, sensuality, beauty, power? The secret to a balanced life—and finding the strength to refuse the lure of self-centered desires—is to depend upon My Spirit in you to guard, guide and direct you.

WITNESS

"No one, after lighting a lamp, puts it away in a cellar, nor under a peck-measure, but on the lampstand, in order that those who enter may see the light. The lamp of your body is your eye; when your eye is clear, your whole body also is full of light; but when it is bad, your body also is full of darkness. Then watch out that the light in you may not be darkness. If therefore your whole body is full of light, with no dark part in it, it shall be wholly illumined, as when the lamp illumines you with its rays."
Luke 11:33–36 (NASB)

You are the lamp and the light is My Son Jesus in you. How bright is your lamp shining? I have told you that Jesus is love. Get to know Him, practice His priorities and recognize that the light of the knowledge of Him brightens your way. As you walk your enlightened path, others will notice the light of Jesus in your eyes and through your works, and be drawn to the light of Christ. Let your light shine!

WISDOM

"But if any of you lacks wisdom, let him ask of God, who gives to all men generously and without reproach, and it will be given to him." James 1:5 (NASB)

What is your challenge today? Do you feel you cannot overcome the obstacle by yourself? Come to me, ask me to give you the wisdom you need for this moment. I will give generously to you, and I am glad to do so. Oh, what I would give to you, if you would take the time to humble yourself and ask.

Week Fifteen

FAITH

Hebrews 11:1 (TLB) asks the question, "What is faith?" The answer ... "It is the confident assurance that something we want is going to happen. It is the certainty that what we hope for is waiting for us, even though we cannot see it up ahead." This chapter goes on to list the names of great faith-followers in the Bible such as Abel, Enoch, Noah, Abraham and Sarah, Isaac, Jacob, Joseph, Moses, Rahab, Gideon, David, and Samuel. In fact, the chapter is known as the Faith Hall of Fame, signifying the relationship between great faith and God's resultant blessings on those who believed.

One of the most dramatic depictions of faith occurred when Abraham followed God's command to offer Isaac as his sacrifice. As he trudged up that mountain, full of dread and fear and sadness, he was willing to follow God's command, but full of consternation as to why God would take the very gift of life He had given to Abraham and Sarah in their old age. Tying Isaac up and placing him on the altar, he could not see the ram coming up the other side of the mountain that would become God's provision of sacrifice. Because Abraham demonstrated his faith in the wisdom of God, he was rewarded with a solution he could not have imagined. How much we can learn from this event about trusting God's Way even when there seems to be no way.

Practicing your faith takes not only an understanding of what faith is, but hearing and reading the Word of God. "So faith comes from hearing, and hearing by the word of Christ"—Romans 10:17 (NASB). We must learn God's desires for us and His purpose for our lives. This takes intentional focus on God's presence. As you begin to see how God worked with people in the Bible, it will give you direction for developing a steadfast faith that God can use today.

Peter is another example of faith, as he stepped out of the boat and walked on the water towards Jesus. It was only when he looked away from Jesus that he began to sink. Are you willing to "step out of the boat" with a decision you are facing? God wants to know if you are serious about trusting Him with your challenge. When we are completely honest with Him (remember that He knows everything, whether we reveal it to Him or not), then we are able to trust Him.

Faith, then, is a spiritual exercise. If you want to become a strong man or woman of faith, you will need to exercise. Invite God to direct your steps on a specific matter—it may be a problem with your spouse, stress at work, or the right way to approach a friend on an important issue. Ask Him to give you direction and then trust that He will. That is faith in action.

Reflections:

_____

_____

FAITH

"By faith Abraham, when he was called, obeyed by going out to a place which he was to receive for an inheritance; and he went out, not knowing where he was going." Hebrews 11:8 (NASB)

Abraham is one of the great examples of faith. When I instructed him to go to a foreign place for his new home, he could have used the excuse of old age –he was 75 years old when he departed from Haran. He could have groaned with the dread of hard work ahead of him in loading all of his possessions. He could have lamented leaving the rest of his relatives in his father's home. He could have allowed the fear of not knowing where he was going to keep him at home. Yet he did none of these—he trusted me and obeyed me. When you follow my directions, your blessings will far outnumber the obstacles, just like Abraham and the number of his descendants.

FAITH

"I have fought the good fight, I have finished the course, I have kept the faith." 2 Timothy 4:7 (NASB)

My desire is for this proclamation of faith to be yours at the end of your life. Fighting the good fight is your resistance to the evil one, fighting for endurance against his schemes designed to lead you away from me. Stay strong in My Word and seek me in everything. Answer the call when you feel impressed to take action that will glorify me and unify my kingdom. Each act of obedience strengthens your resolve. When you have finished the course of your life, keeping your faith strong will bring satisfaction and peace because you have honored My Name.

FAITH

"I have been crucified with Christ; and it is no longer I who live, but Christ lives in me; and the life which I now live in the flesh I live by faith in the Son of God, who loved me, and delivered Himself up for me."
Galatians 2:20 (NASB)

Does Christ live in you today? Have you given yourself to Him, the one who sacrificed Himself for you? Walking in His love is not a burden as some think, but an absolute full measure of expectant joy. When you are certain that you were loved enough for Christ to die for you, how could you be anything but confident of your future with Him? Every day will bring renewed faith, revelation of His love, and a relationship bonded in trust.

DIRECTION

"I will bless the LORD who has counseled me; indeed, my mind instructs me in the night." Psalm 16:7 (NASB)

Seek my counsel daily and prove out my desire to be your Guide. I will instruct your mind even when you are sleeping, to keep you on the path I desire for you. Bless me with a thankful heart, and see what great things I will show you at just the right time for your edification.

DIRECTION

"The mind of man plans his way, but the LORD directs his steps."
Proverbs 16:9 (NASB)

What are you planning for today, next week, next summer? It is good to plan your calendar for work and for pleasure, but remember to include me. Ask for my guidance to enlighten your path and protect you from stumbling blocks. Because I know the future, trust me to guide you around and through the unknown. Seek me each day to go with you. Trust me to direct your path.

WORD OF GOD

"For whatever was written in earlier times was written for our instruction, that through perseverance and the encouragement of the Scriptures we might have hope." Romans 15:4 (NASB)

I want you to know that every part of the Bible is useful for your instruction. The Old Testament tells the history of creation and the origin of sin, the Covenant of the Law which I gave to Moses, Israel's rebellion, the reign of King David from whom Christ's lineage comes, the Psalms and Proverbs, and visions of things to come given to the Prophets. The New Testament tells of the birth and ministry of My Son, the New Covenant of Grace through Christ's death on the cross for the forgiveness of sin, the birth of the church after Christ's ascension, the letters of the apostles to give instruction and encouragement, and finally, the revelation of Christ's Second Coming. All of this is to give your life context in My Great Plan. Persevere in studying to know and do my will.

THE LAW

THIRD COMMANDMENT

"You shall not take the name of the LORD your God in vain, for the LORD will not leave him unpunished who takes His name in vain." Exodus 20:7 (NASB)

Have you taken my name in vain? How did it make you feel? Was it done in anger? Or did it flow from your mouth as easily as saying your own name? Do you understand that I am Holy, and that this action cannot go unpunished? You may not relate the adversity in your life to any one deed, but I *will* punish those who take my name in vain. Guard what comes from your mouth; desire to please me, and I will bless you.

Week Sixteen

SIN

Who is a sinner? The Bible tells us that everyone is a sinner. "For all have sinned and fall short of the glory of God." Romans 3:23 (NASB)

Why do we sin? *The Message* uses today's vernacular to give you a vivid picture of the apostle Paul as he laments his state of sinfulness, confronting the same frustration that today's Christian experiences. Settle in and be comforted by what Paul admits and concludes.

Romans 7:14-25 (MSG): "I can anticipate the response that is coming: 'I know that all God's commands are spiritual, but I'm not. Isn't this also your experience?' Yes, I'm full of myself—after all, I've spent a long time in sin's prison. What I don't understand about myself is that I decide one way, but then I act another, doing things I absolutely despise. So if I can't be trusted to figure out what is best for myself and then do it, it becomes obvious that God's command is necessary.

But I need something *more*! For if I know the law but still can't keep it, and if the power of sin within me keeps sabotaging my best intentions, I obviously need help! I realize that I don't have what it takes. I can will it, but I can't *do* it. I decide to do good, but I don't *really* do it; I decide not to do bad, but then I do it anyway. My decisions, such as they are, don't result in actions. Something has gone wrong deep within me and gets the better of me every time.

It happens so regularly that it's predictable. The moment I decide to do good, sin is there to trip me up. I truly delight in God's commands, but it's pretty obvious that not all of me joins in that delight. Parts of me covertly rebel, and just when I least expect it, they take charge.

I've tried everything and nothing helps. I'm at the end of my rope. Is there no one who can do anything for me? Isn't that the real question?

The answer, thank God, is that Jesus Christ can and does. He acted to set things right in this life of contradictions where I want to serve God with all my heart and mind, but am pulled by the influence of sin to do something totally different." [End of Romans 7:14–21 (MSG)]

And how did "Jesus act to set things right?" John 3:16–18 (MSG) says, "This is how much God loved the world: He gave his Son, his one and only Son. And this is why: so that no one need be destroyed; by believing in him, anyone can have a whole and lasting life. God didn't go to all the trouble of sending his Son merely to point an accusing finger, telling the world how bad it was. He came to help, to put the world right again. Anyone who trusts in him is acquitted; anyone who refuses to trust him has long since been under the death sentence without knowing it. And why? Because of that person's failure to believe in the one-of-a-kind Son of God when introduced to him."

He calls us to remove the shackles of sin's frustration and guilt by trusting in Him. To someone on trial, "acquitted" must be a beautiful sound coming from the judge. But even more so, from the King and Judge of the whole world. I have been acquitted—how about you?

Reflections:

_____

_____

SIN

"Flee immorality. Every other sin that a man commits is outside the body, but the immoral man sins against his own body. Or do you not know that your body is a temple of the Holy Spirit who is in you, whom you have from God, and that you are not your own? For you have been bought with a price: therefore glorify God in your body."
1 Corinthians 6:18–20 (NASB)

Your body is the temple of the Holy Spirit. Remember that you were bought with the high price of Christ's blood, and that the Holy Spirit has been given to you for power against the evil one. When you determine that your sensual needs are more important than obedience to my command, you sin against your own body, and against the Holy Spirit. Rather than feeling separated by your sin, wake up, throw off this destructive temptation, and glorify me in all you do.

SIN

"For they exchanged the truth of God for a lie …. And just as they did not see fit to acknowledge God any longer, God gave them over to a depraved mind, to do those things which are not proper, being filled with all unrighteousness, wickedness, greed, evil; full of envy, murder, strife, deceit, malice; they are gossips, slanderers, haters of God, insolent, arrogant, boastful, inventors of evil, disobedient to parents, without understanding, untrustworthy, unloving, unmerciful; and although they know the ordinance of God, that those who practice such things are worthy of death, they not only do the same, but also give hearty approval to those who practice them." Romans 1:25a, 28–32 (NASB)

Have you ever exchanged My Truth for the lies of Satan? Choosing to go the way of the world is denying me. Your heart is blinded by that which appears inviting, but issues only heartache and destruction in the end. Be on guard so that your heart is not hardened by acts of disobedience and depravity. I am a jealous God and when you prove your disdain for My Way by continuing to live in disobedience without my counsel, I may give you over to this mindset. There is always forgiveness when you come back to me, but the price of your rebellion may be higher than you can fathom. Therefore, do not be guilty of going your own way, but trust that My Way is always best.

FORGIVENESS

"He has not dealt with us according to our sins, nor rewarded us according to our iniquities. For as high as the heavens are above the earth, so great is His lovingkindness toward those who fear Him. As far as the east is from the west, so far has He removed our transgressions from us, just as a father has compassion on his children, so the LORD has compassion on those who fear Him." Psalm 103:10–13 (NASB)

When My Word speaks of fearing me, understand this type of fear includes love and respect for me. Though you are sinful, I do not punish you *because* of your iniquities, but rather to draw you back to me. I alone know what it will take for you to return to me. If you love me and fear me, I have removed your transgressions from you as far as the east is from the west. Because my lovingkindness is as high as the heavens are above the earth, you cannot lose my love, any more than a wayward child can lose the love of a compassionate father.

FORGIVENESS

"Never pay back evil for evil to anyone. Respect what is right in the sight of all men. If possible, so far as it depends on you, be at peace with all men. Never take your own revenge, beloved, but leave room for the wrath of God, for it is written, 'Vengeance is Mine, I will repay,' says the Lord. 'But if your enemy is hungry, feed him, and if he is thirsty, give him a drink; for in so doing you will heap burning coals upon his head.' Do not be overcome by evil, but overcome evil with good." Romans 12:17–21 (NASB)

There may come a time in your life when someone tries to hurt you or destroy your good name. The common man without faith will take revenge, but I tell you to be *uncommon* because of your faith. You have My Son's example and My Word to teach you that payback is never My Way. That means you are never to pay back evil for evil, because only I have the wisdom to use vengeance to achieve My Purpose. And I want you to go even further—not only do I want you to relinquish your revenge, but I want you to help your enemy if you are given opportunity. Overcome evil with good so that your enemy is silenced by your actions and you are blessed in the very act of obedience.

WISDOM

"But the wisdom from above is first pure, then peaceable, gentle, reasonable, full of mercy and good fruits, unwavering, without hypocrisy." James 3:17 (NASB)

Just as My Word is pure, so is the wisdom I give you. Ask this question to test wisdom in any situation: are the words or actions peaceable, gentle, reasonable, rich with mercy and good fruits, unwavering and without hypocrisy? If these words describe your desire when you seek wisdom from me, then trust me to give you solutions that will accomplish your desire. Seek wisdom each day and enjoy the harvest.

PRAYER

"Draw near to God and He will draw near to you." James 4:8 (NASB)

Do you feel close to me in this moment? If the answer is no, then come closer. Block out the world for a while, and still all distractions. Seek me in a quiet place, speak My Name—I am here. No matter how far away from me you feel, call on me and you will be in My Presence. Now, what would you like to say?

PRAYER

"Call to Me, and I will answer you, and I will tell you great and mighty things, which you do not know." Jeremiah 33:3 (NASB)

Have you ever been dumbfounded by learning something obscure that seemed obvious once you knew it? Or have you ever known the exhilaration that comes from seeking the truth and having no doubt that you have found it? You can trust that if you call on me for the answers to your questions, you will gain all this and so much more. There is much to learn from me, and I am eager to show you great and mighty things! Remember, I already know what you know. What you do not know, I can reveal. Seek me and learn.

Week Seventeen

FORGIVENESS

Forgiveness costs. The price involves relinquishing part of yourself, a part that may have comforted you for a very long time. When you are hurt by someone, it is human to feel justified in hanging on to the pain long after everyone else has forgotten about it. But, in the end, what have you accomplished? Pride interferes with your ability to clearly assess the damage being done to *you* as you hold on to anger and resentment.

God's Word is plain on this act of forgiveness in Matthew 6:14–15 (The Voice): "If you forgive people when they sin against you, then your Father will forgive you when you sin against Him and when you sin against your neighbor. But if you do not forgive your neighbor's sins, your Father will not forgive your sins."

Is it hard to forgive someone who has taken the love of your life from you? Absolutely! Is it hard to forgive someone who tells lies about you to make themselves feel good? You bet. Does it demand every God-filled part of you to forgive someone who hurt you as a child or teen? Yes! But do we have a God who is able to do "exceedingly, abundantly beyond all that we ask or think, according to the power that works within us?" Ephesians 3:20 (NASB). All praise to Him—the answer is yes!

The Message translates Psalm 130:3–4 like this: "If you, God, kept records on wrongdoings, who would stand a chance? As it turns out, forgiveness is your habit, and that's why you're worshiped." Forgiveness is God's habit—what a beautiful thought! So, as we become more like Christ with an intentional daily effort at living our life God's way, can we not form an intentional habit of forgiveness? If we ask to see others through the eyes of God, will it not allow us to have compassion on them just as He has compassion on us?

When you think of the ultimate reason to forgive those who have hurt you, you need only to look at the cross. Jesus hung there in agony, watching them spit upon him, listening to their mocking as they cast lots for his clothing. Enduring the worst pain and humiliation man had to offer, Jesus said, "Father, forgive them; for they know not what they do." Luke 23:34 (KJV)

Jesus, of course, was right. They had no idea they had crucified the Son of God. It is probable those who have hurt you have no idea of the deep and lasting pain they have caused. But God knows. Ask Him to take this burden from you and give you the courage to follow in His footsteps of forgiveness.

Reflections:

_____

_____

FORGIVENESS

"And be kind to one another, tender-hearted, forgiving each other, just as God in Christ also has forgiven you." Ephesians 4:32 (NASB)

When you think of the forgiveness you have received through My Son Christ's sacrifice, for past, present, and future sins, are you overwhelmed and in awe of this free gift, or do you take it for granted? You show your gratitude for this unspeakable gift by forgiving others. It costs you nothing to be tender-hearted, but your kindness may be the very thing that leads them to faith in Christ.

FORGIVENESS

"For if you forgive men for their transgressions, your heavenly Father will also forgive you. But if you do not forgive men, then your Father will not forgive your transgressions." Matthew 6:14–15 (NASB)

Search your heart and think of one whom you have not forgiven. When you remember the pain that you experienced from their words or actions, remember also My Son Jesus' pain and suffering on the cross. His pain was not limited to physical suffering. He bore the rejection and hatred of man. How does your pain compare to His? He was innocent. You may feel innocent, too, but you must acknowledge that I allowed this pain in your life so that you would learn from it. Though you may not want to accept it, even hurtful words can shed light on an area of your life that needs work. Seek the Truth and forgiveness will come. You will be forgiven as you forgive others – your act demonstrates your trust in the One who loves you.

OBEDIENCE

"And by this we know that we have come to know Him, if we keep His commandments." 1 John 2:3 (NASB)

It is not enough to know My Commandments. I have given you rules for living a life that will glorify me. When you are able to keep my commands because you want to please me, then you prove that you know who I am and my purpose for you. I know your heart, but the world knows only what they see you do. Let your actions point them to the Living Way.

OBEDIENCE

"But prove yourselves doers of the word, and not merely hearers who delude themselves. For if anyone is a hearer of the word and not a doer, he is like a man who looks at his natural face in a mirror; for once he has looked at himself and gone away, he has immediately forgotten what kind of person he was. But one who looks intently at the perfect law, the law of liberty, and abides by it, not having become a forgetful hearer but an effectual doer, this man shall be blessed in what he does." James 1:22–25 (NASB)

Do you desire to be blessed? I bless those who take My Word seriously. You make the decision every day to take time with me in the reading or hearing of My Word—or you go about your busy day without taking advantage of the wisdom that is available to you. Even still, it is not enough to hear and know scripture, or listen to a sermon. You must act on the knowledge you have been given by applying it to those you see and the decisions you make each day. As you read, ask me to remind you of the scripture, and for ways to help you demonstrate its truth.

OBEDIENCE

"Pay heed, you senseless among the people; and when will you understand, stupid ones? He who planted the ear, does He not hear? He who formed the eye, does He not see? He who chastens the nations, will He not rebuke, even He who teaches man knowledge? The LORD knows the thoughts of man, that they are a mere breath."
Psalm 94:8–11 (NASB)

Do you ever take for granted how and why you were created, and that I, God, made you? Do you forget that I, who made your eyes and ears, see and hear all that you have ever done or said? I have knowledge and wisdom available to all who seek, and therefore, I will rebuke those who do not choose to learn from me. Your thoughts are a mere breath, so use your opportunity to know My Word and please me while you still have the opportunity.

DIRECTION

"And the Lord will continually guide you, and satisfy your desire in scorched places, and give strength to your bones; and you will be like a watered garden, and like a spring of water whose waters do not fail."
Isaiah 58:11 (NASB)

My love for you is constant, like a spring whose waters bubble to the surface, continually adding fresh water, never slowing down, never bitter, never failing. I am all around you to guide you and comfort you, and to give you strength. You will be like a watered garden sprouting buds of love, joy, peace, kindness and gentleness as you reflect the dew drops of my love.

DIRECTION

"Teach me to do Thy will, for Thou art my God; let Thy good Spirit lead me on level ground." Psalm 143:10 (NASB)

Do you desire to know my will for your life? I am your God and I want to show you the way to keep from stumbling. You must have My Spirit in you, and the only way to have it is by faith in My Son Jesus. If you believe that He died for your sins, then declare it and ask for the Holy Spirit to fill you. My Word tells you how to live, but if you choose to experience life your way, your lessons will be hard. So spend time with me, and I will show you how to live abundantly.

Week Eighteen

SECURITY

The precept of security deals with the confidence we have in God through Christ Jesus. It is sometimes referred to as "the security of the believer." The believer bases his trust in God on the character of God which is understood through the study of His Word and the personal relationship formed through prayer.

When I was a child, I accepted Christ as my Savior through faith, God's gift to me. "For it is by grace you have been saved, through faith—and this is not from yourselves, it is the gift of God—not by works, so that no one can boast." Ephesians 2:8–9 (NIV) As I grew in knowledge of Him, I became more confident in His unchanging nature. "God is not a man, so he does not lie. He is not human, so he does not change his mind. Has he ever spoken and failed to act? Has he ever promised and not carried it through?" Numbers 23:19 (NLT)

We know when we have been called by God, and that also gives us a sense of security. Romans 8:28 (NIV) reminds us "And we know that God causes everything to work together for the good of those who love God and are called according to his purpose for them." This promise is often brought to mind when we go through a trial and are suffering. We must trust that He is in control of every situation we face, and relax in His grip.

I used to pray for different members of my family to have a closer walk with the Lord—lacking in confidence—but hoping God would answer my prayer. One day it dawned on me that when I ask Him for something that I know He desires, something for His Kingdom, I can be confident He will do it! Jesus said "You can ask for anything in my name, and I will do it, so that the Son can bring glory to the Father." John 14:13 (NLT). Asking for things in Jesus' name means asking for things that will bring glory to God.

Now some might think that continuing to ask for something that you haven't received shows a lack of faith. Jesus refutes that in His parable in Luke 11:5—13 (NLT). In essence, He tells of one going to a friend's house at midnight to borrow bread, and the friend tells him he can't help him. Jesus continues, "But I tell you this—though he won't do it for friendship's sake, if you keep knocking long enough, he will get up and give you whatever you need because of your shameless persistence. And so I tell you, keep on asking, and you will receive what you ask for. Keep on seeking, and you will find. Keep on knocking, and the door will be opened to you. For everyone who asks, receives. Everyone who seeks, finds. And to everyone who knocks, the door will be opened. You fathers—if your children ask for a fish, do you give them a snake instead? Or if they ask for an egg, do you give them a scorpion? Of course not! <u>So if you sinful people know how to give good gifts to your children, how much more will your heavenly Father give the Holy Spirit to those who ask Him?</u>"

Keep asking—keep seeking—keep knocking! James 4:8 (NASB) charges us to "Draw near to God and He will draw near to you." So, as you draw near to Him, remember "Let us hold tightly without wavering to the hope we affirm, for God can be trusted to keep his promise." Hebrews 10:23 (NLT).

Trust the authority of God to give you the ultimate in security.

Reflections:

_____

_____

SECURITY

"For you have not received a spirit of slavery leading to fear again, but you have received a spirit of adoption as sons by which we cry out, 'Abba! Father!'" Romans 8:15 (NASB)

When you were a child and afraid, you usually went to your parents or grandparents for comfort. But now that you are grown, to whom do you go for reassurance? Perhaps you still seek a parent or a good friend or spouse, but what if your fears are above the others' ability to comprehend or solve? You don't have to be a child to need comfort and security. The Spirit I offer you is love, not fear. I desire to comfort and encourage you as you walk with me today. Rejoice that I have adopted you, and you may call me Father!

SECURITY

"The LORD's loving kindnesses indeed never cease, for His compassions never fail. They are new every morning; great is Thy faithfulness. 'The Lord is my portion,'" says my soul, 'therefore I have hope in Him.'"
Lamentations 3:22–24 (NASB)

Count on me. Know that my compassion and love and kindness toward you are never failing. When you rise each day, I am there. When the challenges come your way, I am there. When you see the beauty of a sunset or the miracle of new birth, I am there. Put your faith and hope in me, for I will never leave you or forsake you.

SECURITY

"For Christ did not enter a holy place made with hands, a mere copy of the true one, but into heaven itself, now to appear in the presence of God for us." Hebrews 9:24 (NASB)

Be comforted in this. My Son does not reside in a man-made holy place, but because of His sacrifice on the cross, He is in My Presence as mediator for you. You have redemption through His blood if you have asked Him into your heart. And though it is beyond human explanation that His Holy Spirit could be in your heart and He Himself beside me in heaven, you know it to be true if you are a Child of the King.

JUDGMENT

"Then the LORD passed by in front of him (Moses) and proclaimed, "The LORD, the LORD God, compassionate and gracious, slow to anger, and abounding in lovingkindness and truth; who keeps lovingkindness for thousands, who forgives iniquity, transgression and sin; yet He will by no means leave the guilty unpunished, visiting the iniquity of fathers on the children and on the grandchildren to the third and fourth generations." Exodus 34:6–7 (NASB)

I love you. I give you mercy when you ignore my commands, because I choose to be slow to anger. If I immediately punish you when you do wrong, how will you learn to be patient with others and show them mercy? Learn from me—be steadfast in your love and in your forgiveness. Listen to me—though I may forgive you for every transgression, I must also teach you to learn from your mistakes. The sins that you commit will be forgiven if you seek my forgiveness, but your children and your children's children may reap the consequence of your disobedience. Think about this when you are tempted.

JUDGMENT

"For we must all appear before the judgment seat of Christ, that each one may be recompensed for his deeds in the body, according to what he has done, whether good or bad." 2 Corinthians 5:10 (NASB)

You will all, every one of you—whether you believe in the blood sacrifice of My Son, or whether you choose to ignore His virgin birth, life, crucifixion and resurrection—appear before the judgment seat of Christ. If you have received My Son as Savior, then your sins will be remembered no more as far as the east is from the west. You will be rewarded as to what you did to advance My Kingdom. But, if you have rejected Jesus Christ, you will then be judged according to all your deeds, both good and bad.

OBEDIENCE

"How blessed is the man who does not walk in the counsel of the wicked, nor stand in the path of sinners … he will be like a tree firmly planted by streams of water, which yields its fruit in its season, and its leaf does not wither; and in whatever he does, he prospers." Psalm 1:1, 3 (NASB)

I have planned a truly abundant life here on earth for those who will not yield themselves to the wicked, nor to the temptations of the world. Follow my path and prevent pain and destruction by those who would lead you away from My Presence. You will be like a tree, firmly planted by a stream and yielding good fruit – not like a seedling planted in the dust, blown by the destructive winds of deceit, decaying little by little until there is no life. If you want to prosper, give all of yourself to me. I alone know what you need.

OBEDIENCE

"But thanks be to God, who gives us the victory through our Lord Jesus Christ. Therefore, my beloved brethren, be steadfast, immovable, always abounding in the work of the Lord, knowing that your toil is not in vain in the Lord." 1 Corinthians 15:57–58 (NASB)

Rejoice and be thankful today. There is victory in Jesus – My Son overcame death to give you victory in this life and assurance of the life to come. Don't be swayed by false doctrines. Stand firm in your faith. Participate in Our Work to bring others to this great saving knowledge of Jesus Christ. Victory is yours.

Week Nineteen

DISOBEDIENCE

T hough we know defiance comes in many forms, let's first look at why children disobey. When mom tells Johnny to stay out of the street, he doesn't think about why—only that his ball has rolled across the street into the neighbor's yard and he needs to retrieve it. His mind is on that ball ... until he hears tires screeching to a halt just in time. Then he has an "ah-hah" moment.

Our adult "ah-hah" moments come in much the same way—after the fact. We know how to be responsible, how to teach our children the right way to do things, the right way to treat people, how to set a good example through our language, the books we read, the movies we watch, the things we say when others aren't around, the honor code we use in conducting business, the importance of punctuality, respect, loyalty, i.e., how to live a God-honoring life. So, why is it we fail in the very same rules of life we are trying to teach our children? There is a good reason for the phrase, "Hind sight is 20/20." We were born with a sin nature, but are we doomed to a life of defeat?

Romans 5:19–21 (NIV) explains "For just as through the disobedience of the one man the many were made sinners, so also through the obedience of the one man the many will be made righteous. The law was brought in so that the trespass might increase. But where sin increased, grace increased all the more, so that, just as sin reigned in death, so also grace might reign through righteousness to bring eternal life through Jesus Christ our Lord."

The Message says it like this: "Here it is in a nutshell: Just as one person did it wrong and got us in all this trouble with sin and death, another person did it right and got us out of it. But more than just getting us out of trouble, he got us into life! One man said no to God and put many people in the wrong; one man said yes to God and put many in the right. All that passing laws against sin did was produce more lawbreakers. But sin didn't and doesn't have a chance in competition with the aggressive forgiveness we call grace. When it's sin versus grace, grace wins hands down. All sin can do is threaten us with death, and that's the end of it. Grace, because God is putting everything together again through the Messiah, invites us into life – a life that goes on and on and on, world without end."

There you have it … "man said no to God and put many people in the wrong." How many times do we rebel against God's way by saying no to Him? As a result of our rebellion, how many people are influenced to do something similar? When we decide to ignore the narrow way, and go thoughtlessly down the wide way because it suits our needs of the moment, we not only displease our God, but we inadvertently take others with us. Thank God today for His grace through Jesus Christ.

Reflections:

_____

_____

DISOBEDIENCE

"There are six things which the Lord hates, yes, seven which are an abomination to Him: haughty eyes, a lying tongue, and hands that shed innocent blood, a heart that devises wicked plans, feet that run rapidly to evil, a false witness who utters lies, and one who spreads strife among brothers." Proverbs 6:16–19 (NASB)

Yes, there are things I hate—seven abominations: pride, the sin that leads to all other sin when your selfish nature takes control; lying by ignoring the truth, even to yourself; murdering the innocent, including the unborn child; planning to do any kind of wickedness toward others; running towards evil and forgetting its effect on those who love you; stretching the truth about yourself and others; and causing others to argue and disagree with each other. Rather, let your heart be moved to honor me. Become a peace maker and run rapidly to the Truth. Turn away from strife by loving others as yourself. Let them see the God you serve through your good acts.

DISOBEDIENCE

"But now that you have come to know God, or rather to be known by God, how is it that you turn back again to the weak and worthless elemental things, to which you desire to be enslaved all over again?"
Galatians 4:9 (NASB)

Do not think it surprises Me to see you fall back into old habits. I know your weaknesses better than you do. The reason I sent My Son to die for your sins was to save you from the punishment of these sins which is death. The habits which you find difficult to control are proof of your need of forgiveness. They are the catalyst for bringing you back to the Fountain of Forgiveness to receive hope and strength found only in me.

DISOBEDIENCE

"Because the sentence against an evil deed is not executed quickly, therefore the hearts of the sons of men among them are given fully to do evil." Ecclesiastes 8:11 (NASB)

I have given you free will to make the choice for good or evil. Do not expect that my punishment for the evil deeds you commit will come immediately after the offense, for I am patient and I have reasons for waiting. If you surmise that your sin is insignificant because I have not punished you, and you proceed to commit the same sin again and again, you have given yourself fully to doing evil. Your actions reveal the absence of repentance. My desire is that you learn from your mistakes, and it is only I who know whether you will learn on your own or whether I must intervene to show you through suffering. Believe that nothing you do escapes my notice, and repent immediately.

REPENTANCE

"But do not let this one fact escape your notice, beloved, that with the Lord one day is as a thousand years, and a thousand years as one day. The Lord is not slow about His promise, as some count slowness, but is patient toward you, not wishing for any to perish but for all to come to repentance." 2 Peter 3:8–9 (NASB)

Do you sin and dismiss the reality of consequences? Do you know anyone who thinks they have all the time in the world to get serious about their faith? Beloved, do not forget that time is different for me, the omnipotent One. I delay my judgment and consequences because I love you and wish for you to come to repentance on your own. After all, Love is patient.

REPENTANCE

"In the same way, I tell you, there is joy in the presence of the angels of God over one sinner who repents." Luke 15:10 (NASB)

Think back to the day you accepted My Son Jesus Christ as your personal Lord and Savior. The joy you felt that day paled in comparison to what my angels and I experienced at that exact moment of your repentance. And even now, whenever you repent before me, realize that this action of humble self-awareness is pleasing to me. We rejoice all over again as you seek to become more like Jesus.

Repentance

"I know your deeds, that you are neither cold nor hot; I would that you were cold or hot. So because you are lukewarm, and neither hot nor cold, I will spit you out of my mouth ... Those whom I love, I reprove and discipline; be zealous therefore, and repent." Revelation 3:15, 16, 19 (NASB)

Do you remember a time in your life when you were on fire for me? Was there a season when you thought of me first thing in the morning, talked with me throughout the day, and thanked me in the evening? Are you thirsty for My Word? Do you hunger for righteous living? When you are distracted by things of the world, you become lukewarm and don't even realize when you are moving away from me. I do not want just half a heart, and I will do what is necessary to turn your whole heart back to me, because I discipline those I love. Come back to me and taste the sweet fruits of My Spirit.

OBEDIENCE

"Put on the full armor of God, that you may be able to stand firm against the schemes of the devil. For our struggle is not against flesh and blood, but against the rulers, against the powers, against the world forces of this darkness, against the spiritual forces of wickedness in the heavenly places." Ephesians 6:11–12 (NASB)

I want you to be able to stand firm against the schemes of the devil. To do this, recognize the enemy. Your struggle is not against those you can see, but against rulers, powers, dark earthly forces and wicked spiritual forces in heavenly places. Satan will use every evil at his disposal to achieve his goal, including those who do not know the Savior. Be on the alert and equip yourself with my armor: Truth, Righteousness, Peace, Faith, Salvation, the Holy Spirit and My Word. I will not fail you.

Week Twenty
SUFFERING

I t has been 100 days since I last wrote. One hundred days since an ambulance carried me to the hospital to repair my shattered elbow after a fall; one hundred days of suffering, slow recovery, and physical therapy (aka pain & torture)! Traumatic injuries may be common, but they are not at all like planned surgeries, of which I have had a few. Unlike a scheduled surgery, there is no time before an accidental trauma to prepare your mind, body and soul. But one thing's for sure … there is plenty of time afterwards for reflection.

So I had many conversations with the Lord about what happened, the timing of it and the pearls of wisdom I might find in that oyster of suffering. I am quite sure Satan was having a hootenanny by tripping me up that day, but just like Joseph when his brothers betrayed him in Genesis 50:20 (NASB), "you meant evil against me, but God meant it for good." Satan doesn't want me, or any of you, to complete God's purpose in our lives, but God will use even our suffering for His good!

Suffering can be physical, mental or emotional. What kind of suffering have you experienced? Reflect on it, and ask yourself whether you used the power of God in your suffering to elevate the focus from your suffering to the Savior. Did you claim Him and thank Him for the ways in which He protected you during the trial? Your reaction to suffering has much to do with how you move through it. The apostle Paul had some advice for us in 1 Thessalonians 5:4–8 from *The Message*:

"But friends, you're not in the dark, so how could you be taken off guard by any of this? You're sons of Light, daughters of Day. We live under wide open skies and know where we stand. So let's not sleepwalk through life like those others. Let's keep our eyes open and be smart. People sleep at night and get drunk at night. But not us! Since we're creatures of Day, let's act like it. Walk out into the daylight sober, dressed up in faith, love, and the hope of salvation."

The accident changed my writing timeline in a flash, but what of God's? The path I was on, working furiously (indeed) on *First Fruits*, was a path where finishing had become the goal. I was so close! He showed me once again that He is interested in every detail of *First Fruits* (down to the last stroke on the computer), that learning is in the journey, and that His timing will be perfect. He brought me through a long surgery, muffled-but-never-silenced pain, dependence on others, and finally, a heart transformed to appreciate the details of His moment-by-moment provision, protection, and direction. My desire is to come to the close of *First Fruits*, not in a rush, but savoring the final pages of God-inspired writing to reflect Him. That's the bottom line. May He transform our faith from passive to passionate and our love from self-centered to God-centered as we live our lives of hope in the mighty name of Jesus!

Reflections:

_____

_____

SUFFERING

"Beloved, do not be surprised at the fiery ordeal among you, which comes upon you for your testing, as though some strange thing were happening to you; but to the degree that you share the sufferings of Christ, keep on rejoicing; so that also at the revelation of His glory, you may rejoice with exultation." 1 Peter 4:12–13 (NASB)

When suffering and trouble come your way, how do you react? Are you surprised by it, as though it is strange and unexpected? Don't be—in fact, look first to me so that you are reminded you are sharing in the suffering of My Son Jesus Christ. Suffering is never desired; it is an unwelcome result of sin in the world. When it comes, practice the habit of rejoicing because of and in spite of the suffering; I allow it to teach you things you can't learn any other way. Be comforted in knowing My Spirit will not only guide you through the suffering here on earth, but will lead you to exultant praise when His incredible Glory is revealed at the Second Coming.

THE LAW

FOURTH COMMANDMENT
"Remember the Sabbath day, to keep it holy." Exodus 20:8 (NASB)

Whether you observe the Sabbath on Saturday or Sunday, my command is to keep it holy. Do you use the day for your own pleasure? Can you keep the Sabbath holy if you are not in a church building? The answer is yes. But I have given you places of worship to come together as believers and worship me in unity. When you are able, I want you in a House of God on the Sabbath. I am pleased when you take the time to focus on My Word, praising me in song and lifting your spirits to me in prayer together. This type of worship will refresh and encourage you, and bring satisfaction to your soul as you prove your obedience to me.

SUFFERING

"We also exult in our tribulations, knowing that tribulation brings about perseverance; and perseverance, proven character; and proven character, hope; and hope does not disappoint, because the love of God has been poured out within our hearts through the Holy Spirit who was given to us … But God demonstrates His own love toward us, in that while we were yet sinners, Christ died for us." Romans 5:3–5, 8 (NASB)

I demonstrated my love toward you by sending My Son Jesus Christ to die for you, even though you were sinners. Therefore, when you experience tribulations, be comforted that trials and suffering bring about perseverance. Perseverance builds your character, and proven character brings hope. And you know that hope does not leave you disappointed, because I have poured out my love to you through the gift of the Holy Spirit. You have everything you need to stand firm in your faith.

SUFFERING

"For He has not despised nor abhorred the affliction of the afflicted; neither has He hidden His face from him; but when he cried to Him for help, He heard." Psalm 22:24 (NASB)

Do you cry out to me when suffering comes? Or do you suffer in silence, feeling that I am hidden from you? When disaster strikes, when your body and spirit are broken, when discouragement bears down so hard on you that you think not even I could possibly care—stop! This is the very time—sometimes the very reason—for you to take your eyes off the problem, lift up your voice and **cry out to me**. I will hear you and help you!

SALVATION

"Hence, also, He is able to save forever those who draw near to God through Him, since He always lives to make intercession for them. For it was fitting that we should have such a high priest, holy, innocent, undefiled, separated from sinners and exalted above the heavens; who does not need daily, like those high priests, to offer up sacrifices, first for His own sins, and then for the sins of the people, because this He did once for all when he offered up Himself." Hebrews 7:25–27 (NASB)

Rejoice in My Son Jesus Christ, for He is able to save you forever when you draw near to me through Him. Unlike the high priests before Him, who had to offer up sacrifices daily for themselves and their people, I have sent you the one permanent sacrifice: holy, innocent, undefiled, and yet offered up for the sins of man. Christ is now exalted in the heavens, making intercession for you. He did once for all what you could not do for yourself.

DIRECTION

"He brought me forth also into a broad place; He rescued me, because He delighted in me." Psalm 18:19 (NASB)

When suffering comes your way, call on me. Just as I delighted in King David and rescued him, I will rescue you because you are my creation and my delight. When your heart is overcrowded with fear, loneliness, and despair, cry out to me so that I can put you in a broad place of comfort, peace and hope. Though I do not always spare you the suffering, I will walk with you through the suffering. I know it well. Steady your eyes on me and seek for what I wish you to see through the suffering, that it may be shortened because of your desire to know me more.

DIRECTION

"Thou wilt make known to me the path of life; in Thy presence is fullness of joy. In Thy right hand there are pleasures forever." Psalm 16:11 (NASB)

As you seek me today, I will guide you on the path I have set just for you. Invite me in and I will guide your mind and guard your heart. Seek My Presence all day and find joy in walking with me as you go about your business. It can be a wonderful adventure as you set out to intentionally follow my lead. I have insights for you that you would never imagine on your own. Come along and enjoy your new Enlightened View.

Week Twenty-One
TRUST

How many people do you have in your life in whom you have complete trust? Equally important, how many have assured reliance upon you? It is daunting to think about the small number of people we each have in our lives in whom we can place utter and unfailing trust.

When I was young, my parents were my fail-safes. I never doubted their ability to meet all my needs and to love me unconditionally. And I was right, even during tough financial times and moments of marital discord, neither of which I was aware until many years passed. They made me feel safe and secure. It wasn't until I became a teen that I realized life was not perfect, and some things were just beyond their ability to fix for me.

My Heavenly Father then stepped in to see me through the challenges of being a little insecure and a lot naïve. As I went off to college, He became more and more important to me. It was then I asked Him to be Lord of my life. This was not an emotional decision at a BSU rally; rather, a compelling need to know He was with me in every facet of my life. That kind of trust can only be experienced with the One and Only Jesus who loved me enough to die for me.

Proverbs 3:5–6 (NIV) is the best known verse on trust: "Trust in the Lord with all your heart and lean not on your own understanding; in all your ways submit to him, and he will make your paths straight." This verse needs no explanation as it speaks the truth so plainly. But why then do we have such a difficult time following its command? Do we enjoy the pain we inflict upon ourselves when we go our own way?

There is no more beautiful promise and translation than the King James Version of Isaiah 26:3: "Thou wilt keep him in perfect peace, whose mind is stayed on thee; because he trusteth in thee." So, perfect peace comes when we trust in the Lord completely. This kind of ability to trust completely in the Lord comes from the Lord—making the Lord both the object of our trust as well as the power by which we trust.

Just as an athlete repeats the same exercises over and over, day after day, we too must practice this exercise of putting our complete trust in the Lord. Then, when the next trial comes and the evil one tries to steal our peace, we will be able with the Lord's help to keep our mind on Him, trusting Him with every detail … resting in His Peace.

Sing with me this old hymn: "Tis so sweet to trust in Jesus, just to take Him at His Word."

Reflections:

_____

_____

TRUST

"The LORD is gracious and merciful; slow to anger and great in loving kindness … The LORD is near to all who call upon Him, to all who call upon Him in truth." Psalm 145:8, 18 (NASB)

Draw near to me today—my desire is to have your complete and utter trust. You can share with me your deepest desires and your darkest secrets right now. Nothing you say to me will cause me to turn from you, because you are my great creation. I want the best for you! I am slow to anger, and have more grace and mercy to impart than you could ever comprehend or need. I love you and want to be the first one you come to in good times and bad. I am that Friend who loves at all times, unconditionally. Draw near.

TRUST

"Search me, O God, and know my heart; try me and know my anxious thoughts; and see if there be any hurtful way in me, and lead me in the everlasting way." Psalm 139:23–24 (NASB)

I know you. I know what you are thinking when you wake up. I know your anxieties as well as your aspirations. I know what motivates you, and what discourages you. I know the hurtful thoughts that diffuse your potential. There is a Way that is Everlasting, but it takes trust, time, courage and discipline. Spend time in My Word to learn the Way, then trust me to help you apply what you learn.

PROTECTION

"For He will give His angels charge concerning you, to guard you in all your ways." Psalm 91:11 (NASB)

How do you know that your steps are being guarded by my angels? First, you must believe that angels exist even though you cannot see them, and that they have the capacity to protect you from harm. Secondly, you must put all of your faith and trust in me. Be righteous in my sight by believing that My Son lived and died and rose again for you, as the Perfect Sacrifice for your sins. Then, be thankful that we value your life so much we have assigned you angels.

PROTECTION

"Do not fear, for I am with you; do not anxiously look about you, for I am your God. I will strengthen you, surely I will help you. Surely I will uphold you with my righteous right hand." Isaiah 41:10 (NASB)

In times when you feel alone—despairing, anxious, lost—do not fear, for I am with you. You do not have to look around with hopelessness and fear, because I am your God. I will help you, strengthen and comfort you. I know every feeling you are experiencing at this very moment, and I will uphold you with my righteous right hand.

PROTECTION

"Thou art my hiding place; Thou dost preserve me from trouble; Thou dost surround me with songs of deliverance." Psalm 32:7 (NASB)

Deliverance in Biblical times may have been from a storm, a famine, or the sword of an enemy. Deliverance today might be from the enemy of addiction, threat of financial destruction, fear, or persecution. Maybe you need deliverance from life-threatening disease, an abusive mate, an unfair bias at work, or an unhealthy relationship. Let me be your hiding place from today's troubles, where wisdom is waiting and songs of deliverance are sung.

TRUST

"For this reason I also suffer these things, but I am not ashamed; for I know whom I have believed and I am convinced that He is able to guard what I have entrusted to Him until that day." 2 Timothy 1:12 (NASB)

Have you entrusted your life to My Son Jesus Christ? Do you truly believe there is life after death? I sent My Son to live and die so that you would have physical evidence of His sinless life, death, burial and resurrection—to give you a picture of your own future. Do not be ashamed of this truth, for you have been given the gift of My Spirit and My Word. Be thankful that you can have conviction through faith that Jesus is your Savior who takes you from sin and judgment to abundant life and an eternal home.

TRUST

"Delight yourself in the LORD; and He will give you the desires of your heart. Commit your way to the LORD, trust also in Him, and He will do it." Psalm 37:4 (NASB)

Do you know what it means to delight yourself in me? When you trust me enough to let go of your life and commit it completely to me, you will begin to experience a lightness in your soul. You will have a spirit of expectancy as you seek out my will for you. As that happens, the desires of your heart begin to align with my desires for you. Delight yourself in me, and enjoy the blessings of a faithful servant.

Week Twenty-Two
WISDOM

WISDOM – A moral rather than an intellectual quality. Wisdom may be regarded not as a mere personification of the attribute of wisdom, but as a divine person. *Easton's Bible Dictionary*

Some use the words "wise" and "intelligent" interchangeably. Intelligence does not automatically beget wisdom and the converse is also true. I have known a few very wise individuals who would not be classified as intelligent in a scholarly sense. Which is to be more desired? If we accept the premise that ones' intelligence (IQ) and wisdom both come from God, which holds more value to God?

Using the online search engine for *Bible Gateway*, I found six verses concerning intelligence and 214 verses on wisdom. This suggests that the Author of the Bible is much more interested in the spiritual sense of our knowledge rather than mere intellect. A further comparison would be to classify the rank of these attributes in our children—would we rather our children be wise or just book smart? Of course, I want the best of both gifts for them, but if forced to choose, I choose wisdom.

Think of wisdom as a <u>divine person</u> as you read the following verses and enjoy the wisdom of Proverbs (NASB):

- "How blessed is the man who finds wisdom, and the man who gains understanding. For its profit is better than the profit of silver, and its gain than fine gold. She (wisdom) is more precious than jewels; and nothing you desire compares with her." Prov. 3:13–15
- "The beginning of wisdom is: Acquire wisdom; and with all your acquiring, get understanding. Prize her, and she will exalt you; she will honor you if you embrace her." Prov. 4:7–8
- "Do not reprove a scoffer, lest he hate you. Reprove a wise man, and he will love you." Prov. 9:8
- "The fear of the Lord is the beginning of wisdom, and the knowledge of the Holy One is understanding." Prov. 9:10
- "When there are many words, transgression is unavoidable, but he who restrains his lips is wise." Prov. 10:19
- "When pride comes, then comes dishonor, but with the humble is wisdom." Prov. 11:2
- "There is one who speaks rashly like the thrusts of a sword, but the tongue of the wise brings healing." Prov. 12:18
- "Through presumption comes nothing but strife, but with those who receive counsel is wisdom." Prov. 13:10
- "Do not speak in the hearing of a fool, for he will despise the wisdom of your words." Prov. 23:9
- "A fool always loses his temper, but a wise man holds it back." Prov. 29:11

Reflections:

_____

_____

WISDOM

"So teach us to number our days, that we may present to Thee a heart of wisdom." Psalm 90:12 (NASB)

What is your heart's desire today? Do you think about how many days you have on this earth? Do you want your life to count for something extraordinary? Then wake up each day with thanksgiving in your heart and seek wisdom. I have treasures of gold to give you, so don't settle for the insignificant scrap metal the world offers. Learn from My Word what is *true* and *right* and *just* for every circumstance. Keep My Words in your heart, and during times of testing they will enlighten you to guide you through. My Way is not always easy, but it is always right. For how can you love me if you do not know My Ways? Where else and from whom can you learn the deep mysteries of life? I have numbered your days, so search out my treasures while you still have time, and I will bless you.

WISDOM

"I love those who love me; and those who diligently seek me will find me." Proverbs 8:17 (NASB)

This proverb speaks of wisdom as a person. And who is wisdom? I am. Those who diligently seek wisdom will find me. For I am the basis for all truth; that which is noble and righteous comes from my lips. The wisdom I give to you is better than silver or gold—anything purchased with money cannot compare to the riches of wisdom. If you want true riches of wise counsel, understanding, justice and power, seek me.

WISDOM

"The fear of the LORD is the beginning of wisdom; a good understanding have all those who do His commandments; His praise endures forever."
Psalm 111:10 (NASB)

To fear me is to respect and honor me with your life. Every time you put my commands above your own desires, you are gaining wisdom. When you trust My Way to be better than yours, without having to test it against your own experience, you not only please me, but you save yourself from suffering and regret. Either way, my praise endures because My Way is best.

DECEIT

See to it that no one takes you captive through philosophy and empty deception, according to the tradition of men, according to the elementary principles of the world, rather than according to Christ. Colossians 2:8 (NASB)

If you know me, you understand that I alone have a purpose for you that will bless you here on earth and give you an eternal home. Be on the alert for philosophies and principles of this world that deceive and take your attention away from me. Sometimes these deceptions may seem harmless, but anything that moves your focus away from me has the potential to slowly move your allegiance from me, destroying the gains you have made in your faith. Stand firm and keep your eyes on me!

DECEIT

"Let no one deceive you with empty words, for because of these things the wrath of God comes upon the sons of disobedience. Therefore do not be partakers with them; for you were formerly darkness, but now you are light in the Lord; walk as children of light (for the fruit of the light consists in all goodness and righteousness and truth), trying to learn what is pleasing to the Lord." Ephesians 5:6–10 (NASB)

Walk in my Light as children of light—practice goodness, righteousness and truth, continually trying to learn what pleases me. Those who are disobedient are full of empty words and thoughtless actions. They lack sincerity, and consider their selfish desires before the needs of others. This does not please me! Do not be deceived, listening in the darkness, wasting time on ideas which do not produce the fruits of My Spirit. Hold the light of my truth next to anything you question, so that you may uncover any wicked way and run from it.

DECEIT

"For false Christs and false prophets will arise and will show great signs and wonders, so as to mislead, if possible, even the elect."
Matthew 24:24 (NASB)

If you have been born again through faith in My Son Jesus Christ, you are one of the elect. As such, stay on guard for false prophets and even false Messiahs who would use sorcery and evil powers to imitate the wonders and miracles performed by My Son. These counterfeits will use every trick to deceive you, so continually test their tactics against My Word.

SALVATION

"There is therefore now no condemnation for those who are in Christ Jesus. For the law of the Spirit of life in Christ Jesus has set you free from the law of sin and of death ... For whoever will call upon the name of the LORD will be saved." Romans 8:1–2 & 10:13 (NASB)

Have you been set free from the law of sin and death? My Son Jesus loved you enough to lay down His life for you. He conquered sin and death by dying on a cross and rising from the dead. He is preparing a place for you in heaven. There is no other way to be set free and heaven bound. Accept my free Gift of Salvation through Jesus Christ by repenting and turning from your sinful ways. Call upon His name and you will be saved.

Week Twenty-Three

UNBELIEF

T he year is 2014, July 12th to be exact. Tonight the moon will be just 222,611 miles away from Earth, the closest distance during its elliptical orbit around Earth, known as *perigee* (as opposed to *apogee* when it is its furthest distance away from Earth).[4] This startling visual enlargement has given way to the term "Supermoon."

During 2014 and 2015, there will be four "Blood Moons," total lunar eclipses, in an uninterrupted series known as a *"tetrad."* These blood moons are reddish in appearance due to refracted light from Earth's atmosphere when it aligns perfectly between the sun and Earth. The dates of April 15 and October 8 in 2014, and April 4 and September 28 in 2015[5] coincide both years with the High Holy Days of Passover and the Feast of Tabernacles on the Jewish calendar. Interestingly, there were blood moons in 1948 when Israel became the State of Israel, and in 1967 when Israel fought the Six Day War and recaptured Jerusalem.

---

4   *WND Faith* exclusive online report, "1st The Blood Moon, Now The Supermoon"
5   Bruce McClure; Deborah Byrd (March 30, 2014). "What is a Blood Moon?" *Earth & Sky*.

There has been a rash of skepticism associated with the blood moon events, demonstrating continued unbelief in the Master of the Universe. Critics of Christianity will many times point to science for their dissenting views; unless, as in the case of the blood moon, science points right back to the Jewish calendar and Old Testament prophecy. Ironically, skeptics are just like the Israelites of old in Jeremiah 6:16 (NIV) "This is what the Lord says: Stand at the crossroads and look; ask for the ancient paths, ask where the good way is, and walk in it, and you will find rest for your souls. But you said, 'We will not walk in it.'"

How hard these critics struggle to disprove the preponderance of evidence that is displayed in God's creation. Paul states in Romans 1:20 (NIV) "For since the creation of the world God's invisible qualities—his eternal power and divine nature—have been clearly seen, being understood from what has been made, so that people are without excuse."

David wrote in Psalm 19:1–4 (NIV) "The heavens declare the glory of God; the skies proclaim the work of his hands. Day after day they pour forth speech; night after night they reveal knowledge. They have no speech, they use no words; no sound is heard from them. Yet their voice goes out into all the earth, their words to the ends of the world."

Finally, Jesus said "There will be signs in the sun, moon, and stars. On the earth, nations will be in anguish and perplexity at the roaring and tossing of the sea. People will faint from terror, apprehensive of what is coming on the world, for the heavenly bodies will be shaken. At that time they will see the Son of Man coming in a cloud with power and great glory. When these things begin to take place, stand up and lift up your heads, because your redemption is drawing near." Luke 21:25-28 (NIV) Jesus said this—not to scare us—but to prepare us.

Reflections:

_____

_____

UNBELIEF

"The wicked, in the haughtiness of his countenance, does not seek Him. All his thoughts are, 'There is no God.'" Psalm 10:4 (NASB)

"The fool has said in his heart, 'There is no God.'" Psalm 14:1a (NASB)

Only the wicked and the foolish say "There is no God." They perceive their intellect to be far superior to other men and thus deceive themselves. They deny my existence and power because it points to their own weakness. Do not be foolish like one of them, but believe with all of your heart, soul, mind and spirit that I am the Living God who takes away the sin of the world through the death and resurrection of My Son, the Lord Jesus Christ.

UNBELIEF

"For since the creation of the world His invisible attributes, His eternal power and divine nature, have been clearly seen, being understood through what has been made, so that they are without excuse. For even though they knew God, they did not honor Him as God, or give thanks; but they became futile in their speculations, and their foolish heart was darkened. Professing to be wise, they became fools." Romans 1:20–22 (NASB)

No man will have an excuse on Judgment Day. I have enlightened every soul concerning my nature, my attributes and my power since the beginning of time. Even though everyone has had access to me and knowledge of me, they have not all honored me as God. They have not thanked me for my provision, and their hearts have been hardened. They tried to gain wisdom without me, and became fools.

UNBELIEF

"Take care, brethren, lest there should be in any one of you an evil, unbelieving heart, in falling away from the living God. But encourage one another day after day, as long as it is still called "Today," lest anyone of you be hardened by the deceitfulness of sin." Hebrews 3:12–13 (NASB)

Be careful not to fall away from me. Circumstances may come against you to cause doubt and discouragement which may lead to unbelief. Do not become hardened by the deceitfulness of sin and evil; you may not recognize the deception until sin is full blown. Be wise to look back and see the day you were first deceived. How might you have resisted the decision which caused your fall? You must stand firm in your faith, knowing I will be with you regardless of your strength or weakness. Encourage those you care about so they will see the profound difference that is made when you diligently seek me for strength and direction. Continue in your acts of faith while there is still time.

SALVATION

"I find then the principle that evil is present in me, the one who wishes to do good. For I joyfully concur with the law of God in the inner man, but I see a different law in the members of my body, waging war against the law of my mind, and making me a prisoner of the law of sin which is in my members. Wretched man that I am! Who will set me free from the body of this death? Thanks be to God through Jesus Christ our Lord!"
Romans 7:21–25a (NASB)

There is conflict between your spirit of hope and your body, which is destined to wear out and die. Though you wish to do well, and acknowledge My Presence in you, there is also evil lurking within. You feel like there is a war waging in your mind between the law of sin and the law of God. It is a conundrum, but not without hope. Rejoice with thanksgiving—the gift of My Son Jesus Christ can set you free from the bondage of sin.

SALVATION

"The LORD is my light and my salvation; whom shall I fear?"
Psalm 27:1a (NASB)

When you invite me—Giver of Salvation—to illumine your daily path, why should you be afraid? I have conquered sin and death through the sacrifice of My Son. There is nothing on this earth or the next that I do not control, so place your trust in me. I love you beyond measure!

SALVATION

"Now on the last day, the great day of the feast, Jesus stood and cried out, saying, 'If any man is thirsty, let him come to Me and drink. He who believes in me, as the scripture said, from his innermost being shall flow rivers of living water.'" John 7:37–38 (NASB)

Are you thirsty today for truth, comfort, hope, wisdom, love, peace? Have you been in the wilderness of the world, only to find disappointment and discouragement? Come to me and drink, and fill your innermost being with rivers of living water. Quench your thirst daily in My Presence and in My Word, and experience the bounty of blessings I have for you.

RIGHTEOUSNESS

"Therefore if any man is in Christ, he is a new creature; the old things passed away; behold, new things have come … He made Him who knew no sin to be sin on our behalf, that we might become the righteousness of God in Him." 2 Corinthians 5:17, 21(NASB)

Does the weight of your human condition cause you to forget that you are a new creature in Christ, or do you wake up each morning confident and strong in your righteousness? Because I made My Son Jesus Christ to become sin on your behalf, you are now the beneficiary of My Righteousness. Don't allow the evil one to destroy your image of who you really are. Let me transform your self-image into My God-image; then live victoriously in right standing with me.

Week Twenty-Four
POWER

P ower is attributed to people, words, actions, concepts, sounds, weather, cars, jets, machines, oceans, and much more. Its effects can enhance or destroy. Who doesn't love a beautiful blue-sky day in the 70's? It is so easy to feel God's comforting presence as the sun warms your skin. But when a tornado hurls its powerful funnel forward, blackening the skies with the sound of a locomotive, bringing with it winds strong enough to uproot giant oaks and pitch homes across a field of wheat, God's presence and power become daunting.

Jeremiah 32:17 (NIV) is my favorite verse on power: "Ah, Sovereign Lord, you have made the heavens and the earth by your great **power** and outstretched arm. Nothing is too hard for you." When you need God's power to effect a desired change in your life, remember that He is able to do <u>all</u> things—nothing is too hard for Him!

On a sparkling starry night just before sunrise in Zihuatanejo, Mexico, I was on the balcony of our condo, contemplating the majestic beauty of God's creation and His provision for us to be in this most enchanting place. Our son was getting married that next evening at sunset on the beach, surrounded by a host of family and friends. In the midst of counting my blessings, and speaking aloud this proclamation from Jeremiah, I felt God's powerful presence, as His joy flooded my soul. How amazing is this God who meets us anytime and anywhere we seek Him!

Isaiah had something to say about God's heavenly power as well in Isaiah 40:26 (NASB): "Lift up your eyes on high and see who has created these stars, the One who leads forth their host by number, He calls them all by name; because of the greatness of His might and the strength of His **power**, not one of them is missing." Isn't it great to know that not only does He know the stars by name, He knows your name?

My dad's favorite verse was 2 Timothy 1:7 (NASB): "For God has not given us a spirit of timidity, but of **power** and love and discipline." He was a strong man in my eyes, but I'm not sure I ever told him. He was extremely self-disciplined and he loved our mother and his four children long and well. When I think back on his childhood during the depression, losing his father too soon, his poor health and lack of higher education, he had many reasons to fail. But his faith and fortitude gave him the ability to trust in God's power. When he died in his sleep one Thanksgiving weekend at the age of 88, we grieved deeply; but we were also thankful to have had a dad who depended upon and acknowledged God's power in his life.

Reflections:

_____

_____

POWER

"I can do all things through Him who strengthens me." Philippians 4:13 (NASB)

What is your particular challenge today? Because My Son Jesus Christ has triumphed over sin and death, you can come to Him with confidence to accomplish anything through faith in Him. He will strengthen you and empower you to do what would be impossible without Him. My Word doesn't say *some* things—My Word says *all* things. Apply this promise to your challenge and watch Him work!

POWER

"But we have this treasure in earthen vessels, that the surpassing greatness of the power may be of God and not from ourselves; we are afflicted in every way, but not crushed; perplexed but not despairing; persecuted, but not forsaken; struck down, but not destroyed; always carrying about in the body the dying of Jesus, that the life of Jesus also may be manifested in our body." 2 Corinthians 4:7–9 (NASB)

Your body, your earthen vessel, is the embodiment of life and death, strength and weakness, building up and breaking down, survival and struggle. You will be afflicted, perplexed, persecuted and struck down, but never crushed, forsaken or destroyed because you have the treasure of Jesus. If you are mine, you carry within you both the suffering and dying of My Son Jesus, but also the life of Jesus through His resurrection. This dichotomy is to demonstrate the surpassing greatness of My Power manifested in you to overcome death through faith in My Son.

POWER

"For the word of the cross is to those who are perishing foolishness, but to us who are being saved it is the power of God." 1 Corinthians 1:18 (NASB)

I want you to know beyond doubt that your salvation is by My Power. I want you to know that even though the lost think you are foolish and weak, they will perish because of their unbelief. They will know one day that the cross of Christ was for the purpose of redemption of all sinners who would humble themselves and believe that He shed His blood for their sins. It is by My Power that He sits at my right hand today, waiting for all who will accept our Gift.

POWER

"But you shall remember the LORD your God, for it is He who is giving you the power to make wealth, that He may confirm His covenant which He swore to your fathers, as it is this day." Deuteronomy 8:18 (NASB)

You may not perceive yourself as wealthy, but be assured there is someone who would love to walk in your shoes. Remember that whatever you have—the next meal, clothing, a meager income, or billions in the bank—it is I who have given you the power to make wealth. Whatever you have is what I know you need to fulfill my purpose. Manage it well and be generous to others. Trust me to guide you as you give freely to those in need. You will be rewarded greatly in blessings money cannot buy.

THE LAW

FIFTH COMMANDMENT

"Honor your father and mother, that your days may be prolonged in the land which the LORD your God gives you." Exodus 20:12 (NASB)

How do you honor your parents? Whether they are alive or with me in heaven, are you quick to remember their admonitions and teachings? Did you submit to their direction and correction? If you have children, are you letting them know that you delight in them? Are you giving them appropriate discipline that will lead them to become conscientious adults? Do you tell them you love them? Do you understand the most important gift you give both your parents and your children is your time? When you honor your parents, you delight me. My affirmation to you will be more time with them as you seek to honor them in word and deed.

END TIMES

"For the time will come when they will not endure sound doctrine; but wanting to have their ears tickled, they will accumulate for themselves teachers in accordance to their own desires; and will turn away their ears from the truth, and will turn aside to myths." 2 Timothy 4:3–4 (NASB)

My Word is prophetic, and you can look forward to promises of heavenly perfection. You must also be on guard for teachers and preachers who profess false doctrines and myths. Many who are weak in their faith, and who do not understand the power of arming themselves with My Word, will fall victim to enticing words that promise what will not be delivered. They search to find a teacher who will profess their beliefs to justify their own actions. If what you read and what you hear does not pass the test when the light of My Word shines on it, be confident it is false doctrine and not from Me.

END TIMES

"But the present heavens and earth by His word are being reserved for fire, kept for the day of judgment and destruction of ungodly men … But the day of the Lord will come like a thief, in which the heavens will pass away with a roar and the elements will be destroyed with intense heat, and the earth and its works will be burned up." 2 Peter 3:7, 10 (NASB)

There is much debate about heaven and hell, and whether hell is a real place of fire, or just separation from me. Do not be deceived by the ideas of mere men, but believe My Word that what you know as heaven and earth are being reserved for fire on the Day of Judgment. The Lord will come like a thief (when you don't expect Him), and there will be intense heat as the heavens pass away with a roar, and everything on earth will be burned up. Those who are ungodly will be judged and destroyed, so be sure you are ready to meet Jesus and reign with us in the new heaven we are preparing for all who trust in us.

Week Twenty-Five
PRIORITIES

In today's world, it's all about prioritizing. As technology and machinery thrust us forward, enabling us to create and produce faster than ever before, we must constantly prioritize our time, making sure we allocate enough time to our job, our family, our friends and, oh yes, our faith! If we are not careful, our spiritual growth can come to a screeching halt while meeting all of the demands and commitments that bombard us each day. Sound familiar?

So how do we make time for God? Intentionally. This book, *First Fruits*, was born out of my desire to write, and God's directive to me to write for Him first. As you use this perpetual devotional tool, I hope you understand that I didn't always "feel like" writing. And other days, I wanted to write, but I had commitments to my family and friends. So, just as with you and your responsibilities, we all have to make time each day for the Lord.

I look back to a time in my adult life when I was at a crossroads, and tempted to take a different path than the one I had distinctly been told to take—the path of marriage to my husband, C.J. We had been married about sixteen years, and though we had two great kids and lots going for us, I lost my focus on all the "right stuff." Satan was trying his best to reel me in, but on one of the worst mornings of that time, God spoke to me: "Choose you this day whom you will serve." I was just walking through my bedroom—not studying the Bible—how grateful I am for the scriptures I memorized as a child. I knew exactly what He was saying.

"Choose you this day whom ye will serve ... but as for me and my house, we will serve the Lord." Joshua 24:15 (KJV). That famous speech given by Joshua to the people of Israel about their priorities and their commitment to God as opposed to the gods their fathers served when they wandered in the desert and during their captivity in Egypt is worth re-reading (Joshua 24). Hearing that command was a turning point for me, and I have never regretted staying the course. We have been celebrating anniversaries since 1968—not always easy, but always right, because it was the path God ordained for us. When we turn everything over to Him, we can live expectantly in the light of His love and direction.

We must choose. What does your priority list look like? If you haven't made one lately, take time to think about who and what is most important in your life. If God is anything other than first in your life, think about this fact: He created and controls everything—the sun, moon and stars, the oceans, the planets, and galaxies—and all that dwell within. When we are able to come before Him in humility, and confess that we know we are not in charge; and then ask Him to cover us with His wisdom to fulfill His purpose for our lives, He can help us prioritize in a way that makes heavenly sense.

Reflections:

_____

_____

PRIORITIES

"Do not lay up for yourselves treasures upon earth, where moth and rust destroy, and where thieves break in and steal. But lay up for yourselves treasures in heaven, where neither moth nor rust destroys, and where thieves do not break in and steal; for where your treasure is, there will your heart be also." Matthew 6:19–21 (NASB)

In this generation, as in every generation, there are false treasures that distract you from your true calling. They may be earthly possessions, obsessive activities, or they may be less obvious desires of the mind that you share with no one. How do you spend your time? What thoughts pervade your mind as you go through each day? Remember that you have a set amount of time on the earth, and how you spend that time directly relates to your definition of treasure. I have blessed you with much. Do you desire to share with others or keep it all for yourself? Concentrate on giving of yourself each day, and find the true treasures of life lived as I meant it to be lived.

PRIORITIES

"He who loves father or mother more than Me is not worthy of Me, and he who loves son or daughter more than Me is not worthy of Me. And he who does not take his cross and follow after Me is not worthy of Me ... He who receives you receives Me, and he who receives Me receives Him who sent Me." Matthew 10:37, 38, 40 (NASB)

I desire your love for My Son Jesus Christ to be above every other relationship in your life. Though I have given you family to love, do not put them above Him. If He is first in your life, then My Word and My Spirit in you will guide you to love them as He does. Follow after Him, search His Ways, make knowing Him your priority. Then, you will be worthy to call Him Master.

LOVE

"If, however, you are fulfilling the royal law, according to the Scripture, "You shall love your neighbor as yourself," you are doing well." James 2:8 (NASB)

The Royal Law: "Love your neighbor as yourself." It is a simple phrase, but a challenging action. It means considering the feelings of others, practicing kindness, gentleness, patience, forbearance, forgiveness, selflessness, humility, generosity, encouragement and grace. Prove out your love for me by obeying this Royal Law and refresh those you meet today with my kind of love.

LOVE

"There is no fear in love; but perfect love casts out fear, because fear involves punishment, and the one who fears is not perfected in love. We love, because He first loved us. If someone says, "I love God", and hates his brother, he is a liar; for the one who does not love his brother whom he has seen, cannot love God whom he has not seen." 1 John 4:18–20 (NASB)

I have loved you perfectly. If you then have My Spirit in you, fear cannot exist within you. Therefore, enjoy the peace that My Spirit brings, rather than the fear of punishment that those who have chosen to ignore me will experience. A liar will say He loves me, yet hates his brother. He deludes himself because He cannot hate one he has seen, and love me whom he has not seen. When you feel hatred boiling up against someone, remember to ask me to help you love them with My Perfect Love.

WORD OF GOD

"For the word of God is living and active and sharper than any two-edged sword, and piercing as far as the division of soul and spirit, of both joints and marrow, and able to judge the thoughts and intentions of the heart. And there is no creature hidden from His sight, but all things are open and laid bare to the eyes of Him with whom we have to do." Hebrews 4:12–13 (NASB)

Think of this: My Word is living and active. My Word sharply pierces the soul and spirit—actually divides it when there is discord between the two. Your intentions are not hidden from me, but laid bare before me. Let My Word show you the difference between your natural thoughts and my thoughts. Confess your intentions to me and allow me to reveal Truth to you. As you walk in My Light, your path will become clear.

WORD OF GOD

"Seek the LORD while He may be found; call upon Him while He is near ... so shall My word be which goes forth from My mouth; it shall not return to Me empty, without accomplishing what I desire, and without succeeding in the matter for which I sent it." Isaiah 55:6, 11 (NASB)

You have many opportunities to learn from me through My Word and through the Holy Spirit as you pray and seek my face. Do not delay in finding me and trusting me with your life. There will come a time when I will not be easy to seek or find, so seek me now. When you read, speak, and obey My Word, My purpose is fulfilled in you. I have sent My Word to you, not only to give you eternal life, but to guide you this very day. Come, let us see what My Word can accomplish in you today.

SALVATION

"Do you not know that when you present yourselves to someone as slaves for obedience, you are slaves of the one whom you obey, either of sin resulting in death, or of obedience resulting in righteousness? For the wages of sin is death, but the free gift of God is eternal life in Christ Jesus our Lord." Romans 6:16, 23 (NASB)

To whom is your obedience directed? Do you want to obey me, trusting that My Way has proven through the ages to be the right way, the way of righteousness? Or would you rather take the way that seems easy, the way of the world and of sin? For the wages of sin is death, but the free gift I give is eternal life in Christ Jesus the Lord.

Week Twenty-Six
SOWING AND REAPING

"Whoever sows sparingly will also reap sparingly, and whoever sows generously will also reap generously." 2 Corinthians 9:6 (NIV)

I attended a memorial service recently which put me on my knees before God. It was not for a family member or a child. It was for a friend, a minister who, like David, was "a man after God's own heart." For many years, we sat by each other in choir practice, so I got to know his audacious sense of humor and his extreme love for the Lord. Mike Fechner was a successful businessman and faithful Bible teacher who was called to full-time ministry at our church.

In 1995, Mike was led to begin H.I.S. BridgeBuilders in South Dallas. Their goal: "to bring about city transformation by building bridges of hope between the rich and the poor, the corporate CEO and the unemployed father, the private school student and the high school dropout, the doctor and the single mother—but most importantly between Jesus Christ and the unbeliever."[6]

6   H.I.S. BridgeBuilders, mikefechner.com; www.hisbridgebuilders.org

During his memorial service, numerous leaders spoke of Mike's unwavering goal to reach "the least and the lost." His desire ran deep and was infectious. Sowing seeds of kindness and inspiring people to reach for greater heights through following and serving the Lord—that was his spiritual gift. It was as if he stepped out of the confining jumpsuit of self-absorption and slipped on the soaring wings of freedom found in Christ. Mike sowed his seeds of love deep and wide, never considering the cost, and certainly not stopping to tally his reward. That reward came too soon for the thousands that loved him, but how we celebrate his Godly example.

You are probably familiar with Galatians 6:7–10 (NASB): "Do not be deceived, God is not mocked; for whatever a man sows, this he will also reap…" *The Message* says it this way: "Don't be misled: No one makes a fool of God. What a person plants, he will harvest. The person who plants selfishness, ignoring the needs of others—ignoring God!—harvests a crop of weeds. All he'll have to show for his life is weeds! But the one who plants in response to God, letting God's Spirit do the growth work in him, harvests a crop of real life, eternal life. So let's not allow ourselves to get fatigued doing good. At the right time we will harvest a good crop if we don't give up, or quit. Right now, therefore, every time we get the chance, let us work for the benefit of all, starting with the people closest to us in the community of faith."

God is ready to do amazing work through all of us. It begins with prayer. Ask Him to give you an assignment for sowing eternal seeds. Get excited, because His purpose is beyond your wildest dreams.

Reflections:

_____

_____

SOWING AND REAPING

"Do not be deceived, God is not mocked; for whatever a man sows, this he will also reap. For the one who sows to his own flesh shall from the flesh reap corruption, but the one who sows to the Spirit shall from the Spirit reap eternal life." Galatians 6:7–8 (NASB)

What are you going to reap? The answer is in your soul this very minute, so pay attention. Has your life been all about you—or have you spent your time doing things that will have spiritual impact on those around you? I cannot be fooled and I do not want you to be fooled either. If you want the rewards of eternal life, spend time pondering and praying in the Spirit about what I want you to do in love and obedience. Because I first loved you, seek ways to show my love to others.

SOWING AND REAPING

"Now this I say, he who sows sparingly shall also reap sparingly; and he who sows bountifully shall also reap bountifully. Let each one do just as he has purposed in his heart; not grudgingly or under compulsion, for God loves a cheerful giver. And God is able to make all grace abound to you, that always having all sufficiency in everything, you may have an abundance for every good deed." 2 Corinthians 9:6–8 (NASB)

My Word commands you to love each other. How you go about sowing love is an individual process, so do not compare yourself to the way another shows love. Love comes in different forms: nurturing, giving wise counsel, sharing wealth, providing physical labor, listening, understanding, encouraging, comforting. But as you give of yourself, act upon my impressions because you want to, not because you have to. I love a cheerful giver. My grace will abound in you, supplying more than enough for every good deed.

SOWING AND REAPING

"And let us not lose heart in doing good; for in due time we shall reap if we do not grow weary. So then, while we have opportunity, let us do good to all men, and especially to those who are of the household of the faith." Galatians 6:9–10 (NASB)

Do you ever find yourself tired and resentful of serving others? Are you tempted to give up? I have given you the ability, time, energy and opportunity, so while you have these resources, continue on and don't lose heart. Pay attention to those who believe in my promises, and build them up in their faith by caring for them. Remember that in my timing, you will reap blessings from these seeds of unselfish love you have sown.

SOWING AND REAPING

"Do not neglect to show hospitality to strangers, for by this some have entertained angels without knowing it." Hebrews 13:2 (NASB)

How do you react when a stranger speaks to you or asks for help? Is your expression, your body language, your speech closed or open? Are you so busy with your own problems that you don't have time for them? This stranger may be a waitress, store clerk, policeman, child, beggar or banker. Stop, and in My Name, treat them heavenly ... they just might be.

Sowing and Reaping

"Give, and it will be given to you; good measure, pressed down, shaken together, running over, they will pour into your lap. For by your standard of measure it will be measured to you in return." Luke 6:38 (NASB)

This is the Law of the Harvest. When the currency of the time was grain, a good measure was grain pressed down and shaken together in the container. An image of grain rising up over the top and pouring into your lap is the picture I want you to see, demonstrating the overflowing blessing of giving. Being a generous steward of that which I have entrusted to you involves giving for the physical, mental and spiritual benefit of others. When you give, you not only prove out your obedience to me, but you will also be blessed in ways that cannot be measured: pressed down, shaken together, running over … an illogical mathematical mystery producing a heavenly harvest.

WISDOM

"When pride comes, then comes dishonor, but with the humble is wisdom." Proverbs 11:2 (NASB)

Pride is obvious in others, yet subtle in oneself. It lurks behind every acquisition and accomplishment, and even disguises itself as self-confidence. When it is full blown, and your desire is the applause of man rather than my approval, then dishonor will be your reward. But the wise man knows to be humble in all things, for he understands that nothing is possible unless I allow it. It is good to be happy and thankful for what you accomplish and have—just remember each blessing is from me.

SALVATION

"I pray that the eyes of your heart may be enlightened, so that you may know what is the hope of His calling, what are the riches of the glory of His inheritance in the saints, and what is the surpassing greatness of His power toward us who believe. These are in accordance with the working of the strength of His might which He brought about in Christ, when He raised Him from the dead, and seated Him at His right hand in the heavenly places, far above all rule and authority and power and dominion, and every name that is named, not only in this age, but also in the one to come." Ephesians 1:18–21 (NASB)

I am glorified by the words of this prayer because I have such great plans for you. My desire is for you to experience my strength and power by believing in My Son Jesus Christ whom I raised from the dead. He sits with me now in heaven and His Name is above every name. His authority is greater than all rulers, kings, presidents and prime ministers combined. Your hope is Christ. I want you to comprehend the riches of my glory which is your inheritance as a believer in Him. What are these riches? Wisdom, knowledge, peace, joy, hope and love … for all eternity.

Week Twenty-Seven
STEWARDSHIP

The precept of stewardship is the basis for this devotional book, *First Fruits*—giving God our first and best. We have been entrusted with time, talents, and resources which we are to carefully and responsibly manage. The Bible has much to say on this subject, I believe, because our motivation for the way we give of ourselves is as important as the act itself.

2 Corinthians 9:7–8 (NIV): "Each of you should give what you have decided in your heart to give, not reluctantly or under compulsion, for God loves a cheerful giver. And God is able to bless you abundantly, so that in all things at all times, having all you that you need, you will abound in every good work."

After we got married, we gave our offering on Sundays and felt pretty good about it, both having grown up in Christian homes, understanding the concept of giving to help the church continue its ministry to "the least and the lost." We were living on the meager salaries of a high school teacher/coach and a secretary. One Sunday morning, a very successful member of our church gave a testimony on tithing. I was surprised to learn that he had not invested on Wall Street, but what he said next struck a chord within me. He said he had found that investing in the Lord's work was all he and his wife would ever need; that other investments were up and down, but the consistency of giving to God paid dividends that could not be measured by earthly standards.

He used Luke 6:38 as his reference. The NIV states "Give and it will be given to you. A good measure, pressed down, shaken together and running over, will be poured into your lap. For with the measure you use, it will be measured to you." My husband and I began to tithe ten percent of our income to the work of the Lord, and soon found that we truly could not out-give God. It has been a source of encouragement to us that even though we may not have the gift of teaching or preaching, we can share in the work of God's church to reach people in need of a Savior.

Of course, giving our money is only part of the equation. If we truly want to please God, we have to think about the other needs believers and non-believers share. Remember the parable Jesus told His disciples in Matthew 25:31–43 (NLT), paraphrased—Jesus returns with all His angels and sits on His throne, all the nations gather and He separates them, putting the sheep on the right and goats on the left. He tells the sheep on His right to take their inheritance because "I was hungry, and you fed me. I was thirsty, and you gave me a drink. I was a stranger, and you invited me into your home. I was naked, and you gave me clothing. I was sick, and you cared for me. I was in prison, and you visited me." Then his sheep, the righteous, ask him when they had done these things. His reply: "I tell you the truth, when you did it to one of the least of these my brothers and sisters, you were doing it to me!"

God expects us to use the gifts He has given us, whether it is our money, cooking, sewing, repairing, singing, writing, encouraging, teaching, listening, inspiring—whatever we can give to others to make their life better will be remembered and rewarded when Jesus returns. What a glorious inheritance awaits us!

Reflections:

_____

_____

STEWARDSHIP

"He who is gracious to a poor man lends to the LORD, and He will repay him for his good deed." Proverbs 19:17 (NASB)

When you perform an act of kindness to someone poor, you are, in effect, lending this help to me. If you are compassionate to those less fortunate than you, whether by your wealth or abilities—and when you take the time to consider their needs and help them, you show grace in action. I do not forget the good deeds done in My Name, and I will repay you. May my grace abound in you!

STEWARDSHIP

"Unless the LORD builds the house, they labor in vain who build it ... Behold, children are a gift of the LORD; the fruit of the womb is a reward. Like arrows in the hand of a warrior, so are the children of one's youth." Psalm 127:1a, 3–4 (NASB)

If I have blessed you with children, it is both a gift and a reward. With the blessing comes immense responsibility. So take seriously your role as mother and father, grandmother and grandfather. Teach your children My Ways so that your struggles and efforts won't be in vain. Build your home with My Word as the foundation. As your children grow into adults, they will provide love, protection and direction for you in old age, just as you provided for them when they were like arrows in your warrior hand, protecting, guiding and loving them to adulthood.

STEWARDSHIP

"The generous man will be prosperous, and he who waters will himself be watered. He who trusts in his riches will fall, but the righteous will flourish like the green leaf." Proverbs 11:25, 28 (NASB)

Generosity is a two-fold gift I give you. First, I have given you something of value to give others—time, talents, money, compassion, love. Second, I have given you the desire to give—sharing your time unselfishly, using your talents to serve others, spending whatever wealth you have to help those in need, and leading a compassionate life with humility and understanding. Do not trust in the gift itself, but trust me, the Giver, to lead you in using your gifts. You will flourish and be refreshed as you experience the mystery of a full heart each time you give part of it away.

SALVATION

"And Peter said to them, 'Repent, and let each of you be baptized in the name of Jesus Christ for the forgiveness of your sins; and you shall receive the gift of the Holy Spirit.'" Acts 2:38 (NASB)

My Word tells you exactly what to do to have the gift of the Holy Spirit. If you repent of your sins and ask My Son Jesus Christ to forgive you of your sins, you will be forgiven. Because Jesus Himself was baptized by John the Baptist in the River Jordan, you are to be baptized in front of fellow believers to signify your faith in Jesus Christ to save you. The gift of the Holy Spirit is given to every believer to guide you towards fulfilling my purpose for you until Jesus comes again.

OBEDIENCE

"Brethren, I do not regard myself as having laid hold of it yet; but one thing I do: forgetting what lies behind, and reaching forward to what lies ahead, I press on toward the goal for the prize of the upward call of God in Christ Jesus." Philippians 3:13–14 (NASB)

Paul was letting his fellow apostles and friends know that he knew he had not yet arrived to claim his eternal prize. He wanted them to know that even though his past was full of ungodly acts, he was able to put the past behind him because of the grace of My Son Christ Jesus on his behalf. His goal was to move forward in faith, buoyed by his high calling, looking toward the prize of eternity with Christ. Do not let your past failures keep you from this hope you can have in Christ. Come to me, believe My Son died for you and repent of your sins. If you have a relationship with Christ, but have fallen away, begin again! With a heart of thanksgiving, assurance of forgiveness, and joy for your salvation, place your confidence in the Holy Spirit's help to guide you inexorably to eternity with your Lord and Savior.

WITNESS

"Every branch in Me that does not bear fruit, He takes away; and every branch that bears fruit, He prunes it so that it may bear more fruit. I am the vine, you are the branches; he who abides in me, and I in him, he bears much fruit, for apart from me you can do nothing. My Father is glorified by this, that you bear much fruit, and so prove to be My disciples. If you abide in me, and my words abide in you, ask whatever you wish, and it shall be done for you." John 15:2, 5, 8, 7 (NASB)

My Son is the True Vine. When you trust in Him, then you are the branches. I want you to share your faith in Christ to lead others to Him—that is how you bear fruit as a branch of the True Vine. When you do this, you will be pruned (cut back) so that you can bear more fruit. Pruning can be painful, as I begin to cut away that which impairs your witness. You glorify me and prove your love when you are willing to let go of everything that stands in the way of others seeing Christ in the way you live. Abide in me and ask whatever you wish, and it will be done.

OBEDIENCE

"And whoever in the name of a disciple gives to one of these little ones even a cup of cold water to drink, truly I say to you he shall not lose his reward." Matthew 10:42 (NASB)

When you follow Christ's example, know that even the smallest effort of giving a cup of cold water to a child will not go unnoticed. His ministry displayed His priority in meeting the needs of the least of His followers. Do not get so caught up in doing the big things that you miss the opportunity to do the small thing which may lead to an even greater outcome for My Kingdom.

Week Twenty-Eight
FRUIT OF THE SPIRIT

FRUIT OF THE SPIRIT - The fruits of the Spirit are those gracious dispositions and habits which the Spirit produces in those in whom he dwells and works. *Easton's Bible Dictionary*

What are the fruits of the Spirit? Galatians 5:22–23 (NIV) gives the answer: "But the fruit of the Spirit is love, joy, peace, forbearance, kindness, goodness, faithfulness, gentleness, and self-control. Against such things there is no law." This tells us that these qualities are from the Spirit of God and there is no law against any of them. Since Christians should desire to possess them, let's consider each one, allowing God's Spirit to illumine and expand our thoughts.

LOVE is the action of putting someone else's desires above your own. In marriage, parenting and grand-parenting, the opportunities are legion!

JOY is the unseen exuberance inside derived from the fulfillment of a desire. Answered prayer is the best example of Spirit-filled joy as we receive concrete evidence of God at work in us.

PEACE is the result of the trust we place in the Lord to accomplish what we cannot; we have a calm spirit as we let Him take over while we rest in the confidence we have in Him.

FORBEARANCE is the diligent patience we give to someone during a difficult situation, wrapped in a spirit of love and generosity.

KINDNESS is the Golden Rule—treat others as you would have them treat you—even when you are being treated unfairly. Ask yourself, "What would Jesus do?"

GOODNESS is that virtue of sincere trustworthiness and honesty that draws others to us.

FAITHFULNESS is trusting the Lord to not only save us for eternity, but to give Him every part of us so that we live life in a way that points others to Jesus.

GENTLENESS is the softness in our attitude, countenance and speech, borne out of the gift of understanding.

SELF-CONTROL is the ability we have through the Spirit to hold our tongue, refrain from "rolling our eyes" and resisting temptations of all kinds, thereby disallowing outside forces to define our reactions.

It is impossible to possess these qualities without the help of the Holy Spirit. There are times I go through an entire day, and then in retrospect, wonder why I lost my temper or felt such profound discouragement. Without exception, I didn't start my day with the most important conversation of the day—asking my Lord and Savior to fill me with the Holy Spirit. When we are filled with Him, we are better equipped to handle the veiled fiery darts of the evil one.

Reflections:

_____

_____

FRUIT OF THE SPIRIT

"But the fruit of the Spirit is love, joy, peace, patience, kindness, goodness, faithfulness, gentleness, self-control; against such things there is no law." Galatians 5:22–23 (NASB)

Do you hope for love—joy—peace—patience—kindness—goodness—faithfulness—gentleness—self-control? These are the qualities of temperament available to you as you become one with My Spirit. Just think, if you believe in me, and ask to be filled with My Spirit daily, these attributes will become a part of you, as you seek to know me through My Word. You will find no opposition or law against behaving in this manner, because these fruits promote good will as My Spirit is manifested.

HOLY SPIRIT

"Truly I say to you, all sins shall be forgiven the sons of men, and whatever blasphemies they utter; but whoever blasphemes against the Holy Spirit never has forgiveness, but is guilty of an eternal sin."
Mark 3:28–29 (NASB)

You know that I sent the Holy Spirit to live in you after My Son Jesus' death, burial, and resurrection. As my child, all of your sins have been forgiven and paid for by Jesus' blood shed on the cross. There are many degrees of vile utterances, but only one that brings eternal guilt. Do not be irreverent concerning the gift of the Holy Spirit, and do not deny the Holy Spirit's presence and power. This is blasphemy against the Holy Spirit, the one sin for which there is no forgiveness. Rather, ponder this supernatural Gift with reverence and awe.

HOLY SPIRIT

"But when He, the Spirit of truth, comes, He will guide you into all the truth; for He will not speak on His own initiative, but whatever He hears, He will speak; and He will disclose to you what is to come."
John 16:13 (NASB)

My Son's death and resurrection was not the final chapter. He explained to His disciples that the Holy Spirit would come and guide them after He departed. Though they did not understand completely, and you do not fully understand now, it was always in my plan to infuse the Truth into you through My Spirit. Wherein Jesus spoke to thousands, My Spirit speaks to *all* who seek, with no barriers of space, time, language or knowledge. You can trust what the Spirit reveals to you because He reveals nothing except what He hears from me. Draw near to hear.

LOVE

"In this is love, not that we loved God, but that He loved us and sent His Son to be the propitiation for our sins." 1 John 4:10 (NASB)

I love you. Three simple words, and yet they hold the power to change your heart. You are loved with a love so deep the oceans could not contain it, and so high the night skies could not cover it. I chose to sacrifice My Son on a cruel cross to atone for your sins—not because you loved me, but because I loved you. As you consider the depth of this love, let it flow unrestrained through you so that others might see the power of authentic, sacrificial love.

HOPE

"For I know the plans that I have for you, declares the Lord, plans for welfare and not for calamity to give you a future and a hope." Jeremiah 29:11 (NASB)

I know you. I know your life from beginning to end. I know your hopes and dreams, and all the visions you have for happiness and contentment. My plans for you, however, are beyond your wildest imagination. When you make mistakes, I want to show you a better way—because my way is for your best future. Look ahead with hope—that is my desire for you. Seek My Way and your path will be illuminated.

POWER

"Greater is He (Jesus) who is in you than he (Satan) who is in the world."
1 John 4:4b (NASB)

I am all powerful. You do not have to fear Satan and his ploys as long as you have My Spirit in you. Nothing can happen to you, except I allow it. Sometimes the only way I can teach you and mature you is through suffering. Be certain that it is temporary as you seek to learn from me. Trust the type and timing of the suffering to be exactly what I allow in teaching you a specific lesson. Be bold and trust this promise. Together we can show My Power and Love to the world through your faith, proving that Christ is greater than he who is in the world.

THE LAW

SIXTH COMMANDMENT
"You shall not murder." Exodus 20:13 (NASB)

This command I give you is about respecting life. How do you suppose someone goes about planning to take the life of another? Emotions such as anger, bitterness, selfishness, jealousy, hatred and deceit might be the starting point for the process which could end in death. When any of these emotions rise up in you, do not allow it to fester by dwelling on yourself and how you have been wronged. Rather, realize that none of these characteristics are Godly. As much as you feel justified in your feelings, seek me to move you away from human emotion to Godly understanding. The prison of regret has no escape. Resolve negative emotions through forgiveness and understanding so that Mercy and Grace triumph.

Week Twenty-Nine

JUDGMENT

What emotion wells up inside you at the mention of the word judgment? Are you soothed by it or agitated? In a court of law, life changes in an instant when the court's judgment is read. A victim might receive some consolation when their offender is convicted. Because our judicial system is not perfect, however, the innocent may go to prison. They are sometimes sentenced to death by execution. Then, due to new DNA evidence, their convictions must be posthumously overturned. Judgment can be tragic.

Or how about the way you feel when others judge you for the way you talk, the way you look, the friends you have, the color of your skin, your size, your religion or your education? Bullying has become rampant in our schools where children have not been taught the Golden Rule: "Do to others as you would have them do to you." Luke 6:31 (NIV) Regardless, if you are a student or an adult, remember that even playful kidding around can cause harm. Beyond the well-known mantra, "Judge not, that ye be not judged," Matthew 7:1 (KJV), God's Word has more to say on this topic:

- On good judgment: "Teach me knowledge and good judgment; for I trust your commands. Psalm 119:66 (NIV)
- On anger: "But I tell you that anyone who is angry with a brother or sister will be subject to judgment." Matthew 5:22 (NIV)
- On speech: "But I tell you that everyone will have to give account on the Day of Judgment for every empty word they have spoken." Matthew 11:24 (NIV)
- On God's judgment: "You, therefore, have no excuse, you who pass judgment on someone else, for at whatever point you judge another, you are condemning yourself, because you who pass judgment do the same things. Now we know that God's judgment against those who do such things is based on truth. So when you, a mere human being, pass judgment on them and yet do the same things, do you think you will escape God's judgment?" Romans 2:1–3 (NIV)
- On mercy: "Speak and act as those who are going to be judged by the law that gives freedom, because judgment without mercy will be shown to anyone who has not been merciful. Mercy triumphs over judgment." James 2:12–13 (NIV)
- On our own judgment: "For we must all appear before the judgment seat of Christ, so that each of us may receive what is due us for the things done while in the body, whether good or bad." 2 Corinthians 5:10 (NIV)

God's Word bids us to think before we speak, and beyond that, to seek His wisdom for our thoughts as well as our actions. In our endeavor to become more like Christ, we need to leave judgment to God and show others the same mercy and grace we have been given.

Reflections:

_____

_____

JUDGMENT

"But whoever causes one of these little ones who believe in me to stumble, it is better for him that a heavy millstone be hung around his neck, and that he be drowned in the depth of the sea. Woe to the world because of its stumbling blocks! For it is inevitable that stumbling blocks come; but woe to that man through whom the stumbling block comes!" Matthew 18:6–7 (NASB)

You have a grave responsibility to nurture the children in your life. Little children have a purity in their faith that becomes clouded as they grow. The cloud of confusion comes from what they see and hear from adults. Bad attitudes, selfishness, quick tempers, gossip, bad language, laziness, lack of self-control and disrespect for authority—these are stumbling blocks. Though stumbling blocks are inevitable, it would be better to drown in the sea than to cause a child to stumble. Work at being a good example!

JUDGMENT

"Therefore let us not judge one another anymore, but rather determine this—not to put an obstacle or a stumbling block in a brother's way."
Romans 14:13 (NASB)

I am the Lord your God and only I have authority to judge. Because you lack my wisdom and mercy, I have warned you not to judge, lest you be judged by others. And do not cause others to stumble because of your actions. The burden is twice as heavy because of your guilt and their sin. Rather, strive to set a good example in your attitudes and behavior, always allowing my love to shine through you.

JUDGMENT

"Do not judge lest you be judged. For in the way you judge, you will be judged; and by your standard of measure, it will be measured to you."
Matthew 7:1-2 (NASB)

My Word refers many times to the consequence of judging others. This warning is repeated because a judgmental attitude requires constant awareness. It takes diligence to refrain from slipping into this mode of seeing your neighbors' weaknesses, while being blind to your own. You must understand and accept that your imperfections are just as obvious to others as their imperfections are to you. Therefore, remember that you will be judged by the same measure you use to judge others.

SPEECH

"When there are many words, transgression is unavoidable, but he who restrains his lips is wise." Proverbs 10:19 (NASB)

When you find yourself in a situation where the more you try to explain yourself, the worse the situation gets, close your mouth. Restraint takes a disciplined, intentional effort. Think before you speak, and lean on me to give you discernment and wisdom, so that your words edify others and honor me.

SPEECH

"Keep your tongue from evil, and your lips from speaking deceit. Depart from evil, and do good; seek peace, and pursue it." Psalm 34:13–14 (NASB)

Keeping your tongue from evil and deceit is perhaps the most difficult challenge of all. If you think you are exempt from this statement, you lie to yourself. The mind conceives ungodly thoughts, but sin comes when the thought is born on the cradle of your tongue. Ask for the indwelling of the Holy Spirit to remove the desire to speak evil, no matter how small. Then seek the Holy Spirit to replace this ungodly behavior with positive speech and good actions. Seek peace in all you say, and pursue peace with those you meet today.

ENCOURAGEMENT

"And let us consider how to stimulate one another to love and good deeds, not forsaking our own assembling together, as is the habit of some, but encouraging one another; and all the more, as you see the day drawing near." Hebrews 10:24–25 (NASB)

My desire is for you to assemble with other believers at My House and in your homes. You each have been given certain gifts which serve to stimulate and encourage each other. Sometimes, it is not what is said, but what is left unspoken that inspires others to right living and obedience. Give of yourself, your time and effort, because no one knows when the Day is coming. Have no regrets. Be My Standard Bearer today.

ENCOURAGEMENT

"How beautiful are the feet of those who bring glad tidings of good things!" Romans 10:15 (NASB)

How does it affect you when you receive good news? Do you enjoy giving good news to others? There is something exciting about sharing good news and bringing a smile to someone's face. Do you remember how you felt when you first heard the Best News ... that you could call upon the name of the LORD and be saved? When you share your faith in Christ with others, My Light is reflected in your face, and I call you beautiful.

Week Thirty
MERCY

W hen was the last time you cried out for mercy? Was it for something you did or said—or possibly an attitude that had infected your disposition? Inherent in the plea for mercy is the need for forgiveness, and compassion the characteristic through which mercy is given. This concept is relatively easy for a parent to understand due to the limitless number of times mercy has to be administered during the rearing of a child. It is our best view of what God does when we miss the mark.

King David is a vivid example of God's mercy in the Old Testament. He allowed pride, coveting, lust and murder to invade his mind, and then came the actions that left him pleading for mercy. David did what we all do to greater or lesser extents—he allowed his strengths to become his weaknesses. He had the ultimate power of his kingdom and all the respect, riches and pleasures that came with the title. Yet those entitlements became the very tools Satan used to bring David down. God had raised him up to be king, knowing all the time that David would fall short ... because we all do.

Personalize this familiar passage from Psalm 51:1–17 in the *New Living Translation*:

"Have mercy on me, O God, because of your unfailing love. Because of Your great compassion, blot out the stain of my sins. Wash me clean from my guilt. Purify me from my sin. For I recognize my rebellion; it haunts me day and night. Against you, and you alone, have I sinned; I have done what is evil in your sight. You will be proved right in what you say, and your judgment against me is just. For I was born a sinner—yes, from the moment my mother conceived me. But you desire honesty from the womb, teaching me wisdom even there.

Purify me from my sins, and I will be clean; wash me, and I will be whiter than snow. Oh, give me back my joy again; you have broken me—now let me rejoice. Don't keep looking at my sins. Remove the stain of my guilt. Create in me a clean heart, O God. Renew a loyal spirit within me. Do not banish me from your presence, and don't take your Holy Spirit from me.

Restore to me the joy of your salvation, and make me willing to obey you. Then I will teach your ways to rebels, and they will return to you. Forgive me for shedding blood, O God who saves; then I will joyfully sing of your forgiveness. Unseal my lips, O Lord, that my mouth may praise you. You do not desire a sacrifice, or I would offer one. You do not want a burnt offering. The sacrifice you desire is a broken spirit. You will not reject a broken and repentant heart, O God."

David received God's mercy, but God's ultimate act of mercy came when He allowed His only Son to take the punishment for our sin and shame. Jesus' blood became the mercy sacrifice that was necessary for our forgiveness and eternal salvation. Let us remember this sacrifice each time we need forgiveness and mercy.

"Therefore, since we have a great high priest who has ascended into heaven, Jesus the Son of God, let us hold firmly to the faith we profess. For we do not have a high priest who is unable to empathize with our weaknesses, but we have one who has been tempted in every way, just as we are—yet he did not sin. Let us then approach God's throne of grace with confidence, so that we may receive mercy and find grace to help us in our time of need." Hebrews 4:14–16 (NIV)

Reflections:

_____

_____

MERCY

"Blessed be the God and Father of our Lord Jesus Christ, who according to his great mercy has caused us to be born again to a living hope through the resurrection of Jesus Christ from the dead, to obtain an inheritance which is imperishable and undefiled and will not fade away, reserved in heaven for you, who are protected by the power of God through faith for a salvation ready to be revealed in the last time." 1 Peter 1:3–5 (NASB)

I, God and Father of the Lord Jesus Christ, have rained down mercy upon you so that if you believe in the resurrection of Jesus Christ, you will be born again. You can have a living hope for an inheritance reserved in heaven, to be revealed when Christ returns for you at His Second Coming. You are protected by My Power through faith for this imperishable gift of salvation that will not fade away.

MERCY

"Thus has the LORD of hosts said, 'Dispense true justice, and practice kindness and compassion each to his brother; and do not oppress the widow or the orphan, the stranger or the poor; and do not devise evil in your hearts against one another.'" Zechariah 7:9–10 (NASB)

My Word has Godly advice running like rivers through it. I am pleased when you are kind and compassionate to those around you. Be aware of the needs of others at all times; smile and be friendly to those you pass during each day. Widows and orphans, strangers and the poor have special needs that must not be ignored. They do not have the same financial, emotional and spiritual support that you may have, so pray for them and help them in areas where you can. And if you are in a position to dispense justice, whether to your family or groups or in a hall of justice, dispense it using truth and fairness. Finally, keep your heart from evil and love one another.

MERCY

"For judgment will be merciless to one who has shown no mercy; mercy triumphs over judgment." James 2:13 (NASB)

Be honest with yourself, and try to understand why you find it appealing to judge others. Does it make you feel better about yourself when you can point to the weakness of someone else? Though the temptation is great, I want you to remember that I alone am Judge. Remind yourself that you have been shown great mercy by the One who has known no sin. Let the Spirit of Christ in you reflect that same mercy to others. There is no better witness for My Kingdom than laying aside your natural tendency to judge, and replacing it with the uncommon response of mercy—let mercy triumph!

OBEDIENCE

"Who may ascend into the hill of the LORD? And who may stand in His holy place? He who has clean hands and a pure heart, who has not lifted up his soul to falsehood, and has not sworn deceitfully. He shall receive a blessing from the LORD and righteousness from the God of his salvation." Psalm 24:3–5 (NASB)

Do you want to receive a blessing from me? Do you want righteousness? Those who want to stand in my holy place must have clean hands and a pure heart. How clean are your hands—what sin have you committed with your hands lately? A rude gesture, an object thrown in anger, an act of violence, hurtful words typed in a phone text —what act does your mind reveal? How pure is your heart? Do not lie or swear deceitfully, but speak the truth in all things. Test your motives and keep them pure by examining them under the light of My Word. Then you will receive my blessings, and righteousness will flow from you.

OBEDIENCE

"Finally, brethren, whatever is true, whatever is honorable, whatever is right, whatever is pure, whatever is lovely, whatever is of good repute, if there is any excellence and if anything worthy of praise, let your mind dwell on these things. Philippians 4:8 (NASB)

Rise above the mind of man and seek the mind of Christ. The one who dwells on My Word will sift through the dissonant notes of human defiance, doubt and despair, and find the resounding timbre of truth, honor, hope, purity, and love. Thoughts of excellence will transform your speech into ideas worthy of praise.

UNBELIEF

"If anyone advocates a different doctrine, and does not agree with sound words, those of our Lord Jesus Christ, and with the doctrine conforming to godliness, he is conceited and understands nothing; but he has a morbid interest in controversial questions and disputes about words, out of which arise envy, strife, abusive language, evil suspicions, and constant friction between men of depraved mind and deprived of the truth, who suppose that godliness is a means of gain. But godliness actually is a means of great gain, when accompanied by contentment."
1 Timothy 6:3–6 (NASB)

There are many who enjoy the controversy of debate and disputes over doctrines. They think highly of their intellect and their vast knowledge and vocabulary, when they actually understand nothing. For whoever disassociates themselves from the doctrine of Christ and advocates any other doctrine, is literally deprived of the truth. Their conceit in stirring up controversy causes envy, strife, abusive language, evil suspicions, and constant friction. They mistakenly believe that godliness is used only as a means of selfish gain. In reality, it is a means of far greater gain than they can imagine; for unlike their view of gain, peace and contentment can only come from me when genuinely sought by seekers of the Truth.

LOVE

"But I say to you, love your enemies, and pray for those who persecute you in order that you may be sons of your Father who is in heaven; for He causes His sun to rise on the evil and the good, and sends rain on the righteous and the unrighteous." Matthew 5:44–45 (NASB)

I know it is hard for you to love your enemies and pray for those who mistreat you. You may wonder why I allow good things to happen to bad people, and bad things to happen to good people. The truth is that both good and bad happen to all people. Due to sin, there is purpose in everything that happens to you, beyond what you can see. Because I know each individual heart and what each needs, I am dispensing mercy and grace as well as judgment and consequences at different times, to different people. The purpose in every situation, for each one who suffers and for each one who experiences triumph, is that all men should come to know me as Lord. Therefore, pray for those who hurt you and treat you unfairly, so you can be known as believers who respond to crisis with an uncommon love taught to them by their Heavenly Father.

DISCIPLINE

DISCIPLINE—Training that <u>corrects</u>, <u>molds</u> or <u>perfects</u> the mental faculties or moral character. *Merriam-Webster Dictionary*

<u>iscipline that corrects</u> is like that between a parent and a child. Proverbs 13:24 (NIV) states, "whoever spares the rod hates their children, but the one who loves their children is careful to discipline them." Rebellion is learned at an early age, so the parent has to convince the child through discipline that they must obey the parent. Proverbs 22:15 (NIV) says "folly is bound up in the heart of a child, but the rod of discipline will drive it far away." Parents who desire to be wise in discipline, then, must pay attention to Proverbs 9:20 (NIV) and "listen to advice and accept discipline, and at the end you will be counted among the wise." Likewise, adults must accept Godly discipline regarding their own personal failures to achieve Godly wisdom.

<u>Discipline that molds</u> reminds me of the extraordinary feats of seasoned Olympians who first have to discipline their minds to endure the long physical training necessary to compete at the highest level. Hebrews 12:11 (NLT) states

"No discipline is enjoyable while it is happening—it's painful! But afterward there will be a peaceful harvest of right living for those who are trained in this way." These athletes do not allow their momentary impulsive desires to overtake their desire to become the best at their sport. Their training supersedes all else, molding them day by day into a world class athlete who looks not to the left or right, but straight ahead at the goal.

Discipline that perfects is described when Paul uses the runner metaphorically in Hebrews 12:1–2 (NIV): "Therefore, since we are surrounded by such a great cloud of witnesses, let us throw off everything that hinders and the sin that so easily entangles. And let us run with perseverance the race marked out for us, fixing our eyes on Jesus, the pioneer and perfecter of faith. For the joy set before him he endured the cross, scorning its shame, and sat down at the right hand of the throne of God."

A former pastor once preached a sermon on God's discipline being in one of two categories—correction or perfection. That has stayed with me because it is both simple and true. Each of us has a race to run that is tailored to our gifts and strengths. When we get off the path, God **corrects** us through discipline. When we are ready to learn new strategies for Godly living, He **perfects** us through discipline.

Revelation 3:19 (NIV) provides us comfort as we struggle to find meaning when we are disciplined. "Those whom I love I rebuke and discipline. So be earnest and repent." Though we don't enjoy discipline, we are assured that through it, God is consistently placing His arms around us, reminding us that we are loved even when we disappoint the very One who created us.

Reflections:

DISCIPLINE

"My son, do not reject the discipline of the LORD, or loathe His reproof, for whom the LORD loves He reproves, even as a father, the son in whom he delights." Proverbs 3:11–12 (NASB)

I know it is hard for you to accept my discipline, but you must see my love as the basis for all reproof, just as a father reproves the son whom he loves. Discipline and correction are at times the only means through which repentance and turning away from disobedience can happen. My love for you is constant, and though I am patient, I know what it will take for you to turn back to My Way. Seek My Will and receive the blessings that come with obedience.

DISCIPLINE

"As you therefore have received Christ Jesus the Lord, so walk in Him, having been firmly rooted and now being built up in Him and established in your faith, just as you were instructed, and overflowing with gratitude." Colossians 2:6–7 (NASB)

For you who have received My Son Christ Jesus as your Lord and Savior, make sure you are firmly grounded in Him. Establishing and building your faith as instructed in My Word takes intentional time and effort. You must choose to fellowship with me daily in prayer, and hunger for Holy Scripture which will answer the deepest longings of your heart. My Word is instructional, inspirational, motivating, convicting—the only true guide to leading a life that honors me. Gratitude and thanksgiving will flow from you as you learn the Truth.

DISCIPLINE

"He who is slow to anger is better than the mighty, and he who rules his spirit, than he who captures a city." Proverbs 16:32 (NASB)

How do you deal with anger? When you allow anger to become master, you become victim to its power over you. This anger can not only hurt others, but overshadow the spirit of My Son Christ in you. When you master anger, however, My Word says you are better than the mightiest warrior or ruler in the world. Why? Because it takes great discipline and strength to overcome anger. It means looking at the full scope of a situation, rather than just your own view. Ask for self-control and understanding, so that in moments of great provocation, Christ shines in you.

TEMPTATION

"There is a way which seems right to a man, but its end is the way of death." Proverbs 14:12 (NASB)

How many times have you gone your own way, only to discover too late that you have made a mistake? You may feel certain you are doing the right thing, but the result is still disappointment or failure. Satan is always working to mask his evil intentions with acts that may seem good at first glance, but result in destruction. He knows your weaknesses and just how to disguise his plan. Be on guard, then, and seek wisdom from me—wait for spiritual clarity before you act, and your plan will have a perfectly timed and successful conclusion.

TEMPTATION

"Be of sober spirit, be on the alert. Your adversary, the devil, prowls about like a roaring lion, seeking someone to devour. But resist him, firm in your faith, knowing that the same experiences of suffering are being accomplished by your brethren who are in the world. And after you have suffered for a little while, the God of all grace, who called you to His eternal glory in Christ, will Himself perfect, confirm, strengthen and establish you." 1 Peter 5:8–10 (NASB)

You must be on the alert at all times for the vicious schemes of the devil who prowls about like a roaring lion, seeking someone to devour. Do not take this description from My Word lightly, because his depravity can lead the weak-willed into dangerous and deadly circumstances. You must resist him by being strong in your faith, knowing that your brothers and sisters in Christ deal with the same temptations. When you suffer through these times, know that I am perfecting, confirming, strengthening and establishing you for eternity with Christ.

TEMPTATION

"The thief comes only to steal, and kill, and destroy; I came that they might have life, and might have it abundantly." John 10:10 (NASB)

Satan is a counterfeit. He presents temptation in a way that makes it seem good and right and justified. You may get what you want in the beginning, but soon enough you will realize that he has tricked you and shattered your integrity. It may be your honor, your reputation, your health, your wealth, your allegiance to your family, your respect among your peers, your word. If you have fallen to his schemes, come to the One who has laid down his life for the very sins you have committed. Choose abundant life through My Son Jesus Christ who loves you, forgives you and can make your life whole again.

DIRECTION

"Iron sharpens iron, so one man sharpens another." Proverbs 27:17 (NASB)

Think about how iron sharpens iron—there is friction and heat causing sparks to fly. When you come up against a fellow believer that irritates you, ask yourself why. If it is merely a personality difference, then maybe a measure of patience will suffice. However, if there is something they are doing or saying that fits with My Word but does not fit with your view of me, stop to ask me if they have been put in your path to sharpen your view—or vice versa. Iron also depicts strength. As strong Godly personalities collide, the result can be jealousy, resentment, and other negative emotions. But when these personalities determine to use their gifts in spiritual concert, their efforts produce strong chords of harmony in the Savior's Symphony of Love and Redemption.

Week Thirty-Two
HOPE

HOPE—To cherish a desire with anticipation; to desire with expectation of obtainment. *Merriam-Webster Dictionary*

The word "hope" elicits a certain anticipation and excitement in me. When I was young, I hoped for a new puppy or for a friend to sleep over. I hoped to win a giant stuffed animal at the state fair. I hoped I would make an "A" on my spelling test. When I became a teen, I hoped for a certain boy to ask me to homecoming … I hoped for a new outfit to wear if he did.

As I grew older, hope took on new meaning. I hoped my first pregnancy would give me a healthy baby girl. That hope was crushed when I went for my weekly checkup two days before my due-date. In 1972, there were no advanced sonograms to help doctors detect abnormalities. During the examination, my doctor realized something was wrong and sent me for x-rays. What I found out later that day changed my life. This tiny little baby girl, while kicking inside me the next morning as I went into surgery, could only live inside my womb. She died during delivery.

I could tell you my hope died along with her that day—but it didn't. You see, though I was only 23 and had plenty of misconceptions about God, I was already His child. At the kitchen table when I was only eight years old, I sat with my mother and asked Him to forgive me of my sins and to save me. I grew in my faith through church attendance, Bible study and prayer, thanks to parents who understood the importance of all three. So, when this huge crisis came, my faith in God was intact. There was suffering and grief, but God gave me renewed hope in Him.

That is why I can say with certainty that God provides for every need, even renewed hope when life goes wrong. 1 Peter 3:15 (TLB) says, "Quietly trust yourself to Christ your Lord, and if anybody asks why you believe as you do, be ready to tell him, and do it in a gentle and respectful way."

The greatest hope for mankind is the hope we find in Jesus Christ. 1 Peter 1:3–5 (MSG) "What a God we have! And how fortunate we are to have him, this Father of our Master Jesus! Because Jesus was raised from the dead, we've been given a brand-new life and have everything to live for, including a future in heaven—and the future starts now! God is keeping careful watch over us and the future. The Day is coming when you'll have it all—life healed and whole." Now, *that* is hope. And so, I hope—no, I expect—to see my vibrant little girl, perfect and whole, when I get to heaven … "and hope does not disappoint, because the love of God has been poured out within our hearts through the Holy Spirit who was given to us." Romans 5:5 (NAS)

Reflections:

_____

_____

HOPE

"I will climb my watch tower now and wait to see what answer God will give to my complaint. And the LORD said to me, 'Write my answer on a billboard, large and clear, so that anyone can read it at a glance, and rush to tell the others. But these things I plan won't happen right away. Slowly, steadily, surely the time approaches when the vision will be fulfilled. If it seems slow, do not despair, for these things will surely come to pass. Just be patient! They will not be overdue a single day!'"
Habakkuk 2:1–3 (TLB)

Just because I know the past, present and future, do not be confused about prayer. I want you to make your pleadings and desires known to me—speak it, write it down for all to see, that they may pray with you concerning it. I hear you when you ask me to grant your prayer. I may not choose to answer you overnight, but be confident that I am planning my answer. Do not become impatient or disillusioned, because my answer will surely come at exactly the right time—**it will not be overdue a single day**!

HOPE

"And we know that God causes all things to work together for good to those who love God, to those who are called according to His purpose."
Romans 8:28 (NASB)

When you are my child, and you know that I have called you for my purpose, then be confident of My Grand Plan for you—that all things will work together for good in the end. If you love me, stay strong during times of suffering and sadness, and claim my promise. I am your salvation even when it seems impossible. I am by your side in moments of desperation. I am there when your hope seems lost. Call on me and I will hold you close.

HOPE

"He who loves his life loses it; and he who hates his life in this world shall keep it to life eternal." John 12:25 (NASB)

I have given life to you, and I want you to live it in anticipation of your eternal life in heaven. If you love life so much here on earth that I am a mere shadow of thought in the way you live your life, then you will lose out on eternity. But if you hate the sin in this world enough to keep your eyes on My Purpose for you, then you can have confidence of life eternal. Your relationship with me right now is but a glimpse of things to come when we live together for all eternity.

HEAVEN

"For behold, I create new heavens and a new earth; and the former things shall not be remembered or come to mind ... And I saw a new heaven and a new earth; for the first heaven and the first earth passed away, and there is no longer any sea." Isaiah 65:17, Rev. 21:1 (NASB)

I gave Isaiah a prophetic vision about the future of mankind after Jesus returns. I will create new heavens and a new earth with no sea. In this new world, those who have put their faith in me will not remember what the old world was like. Everything will be brand new and life will be sustained with the perfection of my plan. I know it is impossible to imagine; just trust that My Word is true, and it will come to pass.

HEAVEN

"Let not your heart be troubled; believe in God, believe also in Me. In My Father's house are many dwelling places; if it were not so, I would have told you; for I go to prepare a place for you. And if I go and prepare a place for you, I will come again, and receive you to myself; that where I am, there you may be also." John 14:1–3 (NASB)

My Son wants to comfort you and give you hope for the future. Because you believe in me, believe also in My Son Jesus who died, rose and ascended to heaven to prepare a place for you. Your heavenly home will be magnificent and far beyond what you can imagine. The most opulent mansion on earth is a shack when compared to the glory and splendor that await all those who believe in me. Jesus Christ is coming again to take all who know Him as Lord and Savior to a celestial home of unparalleled beauty, unimagined music and worship with unending joy. Look forward to this eternal feast of the senses with the One who has loved you with an everlasting love.

HEAVEN

"And the city has no need of the sun or of the moon to shine upon it, for the glory of God has illumined it and its lamp is the Lamb … and nothing unclean and no one who practices abomination and lying, shall ever come into it, but only those whose names are written in the Lamb's book of life." Revelation 21:23, 27 (NASB)

My Word says that there will be a new heaven and a new earth when My Son Jesus returns. In this new heaven, there will be no need of the sun or the moon because My Glory will illumine it all. And Jesus, the perfect sacrificial Lamb of God, will be its lamp. No one will be admitted who has not been washed by the blood of the Lamb. His truth will shine in them and liars will be forbidden. Only those who have been perfected in Christ Jesus and whose names are written in the Lamb's Book of Life will enter. Aren't you eager to see the Lamb who took away your sins and wrote *your* name in the Book of Life?

HEAVEN

"And He is the radiance of His glory and the exact representation of His nature, and upholds all things by the word of His power. When He had made purification of sins, He sat down at the right hand of the Majesty on high; having become as much better than the angels, as He has inherited a more excellent name than they." Hebrews 1:3–4 (NASB)

I gave you Jesus to provide an exact flesh and blood representation of my nature. He upheld my every thought, my character, my power and my love for all mankind. He became God in human form. After His sacrifice on the cross, He rose from the grave and ascended into the heavens to sit at the right hand of the throne of Majesty. His radiance is a reflection of My Glory, and His name is above all the angels. Mere words cannot describe the glorious and eternal spectacle of heaven! We invite you to come see for yourself.

Week Thirty-Three

COMFORTER

I n Job's distress, after losing his family and his entire land and livestock, he lamented that his friends were "miserable" comforters, Job 16:1 (NIV). A tragic indictment, indeed; and one we hope not to be said of us. But comforting someone who is hurting is not always comfortable.

I can remember a time twenty-five years ago when a friend at church lost her teen son to suicide. I said something remarkably naive and insensitive to his mother as we stared at his body lying in the casket; something like, "well, at least he is happy now". I know now from having some premature losses of my own that she was not ready to hear that. She needed me to put my arms around her and let her know of my sorrow for her loss. She needed a listening ear and a compassionate heart. Though I felt compassion for her, my inexperience with such devastating circumstances was glaring and inept.

In an even more devastating circumstance, God allowed Satan to take everything from Job to test his faith, and in the end, Job remained faithful. Our Father allows suffering and tragedy in our lives as well, always drawing us to His purpose for our lives. We are to use these painful lessons to give us knowledge and understanding so that our lives reflect God's love when we minister to those we love.

This concept of learning to comfort is expressed in 2 Corinthians 1:3–4 (NASB): "Blessed be the God and Father of our Lord Jesus Christ, the Father of mercies and God of all comfort, who comforts us in all our affliction so that we will be able to comfort those who are in any affliction with the comfort with which we ourselves are comforted by God."

I understood the full weight of this verse when my unmarried daughter adopted out her baby boy. The ministers of our church showed such compassion to us as a family. Our children's minister, Sondra Saunders, gave us words of wisdom that I have never forgotten: "No one can know your pain." That was comfort at its finest – she validated our pain as the memory of my daughter passing that precious baby to his new parents flooded my soul.

Paul demonstrated further where our comfort lies in 2 Thessalonians 2:16 (NASB): "Now may our Lord Jesus Christ Himself and God our Father, who has loved us and given us eternal comfort and good hope by grace, comfort and strengthen your hearts in every good work and word."

Let us begin again to use God's comfort to strengthen us so that every one of our "good works and words" will bring comfort to a hurting world of people just like you and me.

Reflections:

_____

_____

COMFORTER

"For I satisfy the weary ones and refresh everyone who languishes."
Jeremiah 31:25 (NASB)

When you are tired and weary, even small problems seem to take on added significance. Whether physical, mental or spiritual weariness, the response should be the same. Come lay down beside me and give me your burdens. No one cares for you or understands you the way I do, because I made you and know you infinitely well. I knew you would be weary before you were, so let me refresh you and give you a new perspective, washed in wisdom.

COMFORTER

"The LORD is near to the brokenhearted, and saves those who are crushed in spirit." Psalm 34:18 (NASB)

Are you brokenhearted today? Do you know someone who is? Lift up this brokenness to me—not because I don't know about it, but because it proves both your trust in me and your compassion for others. There are many reasons for crushed spirits, yet I understand them all. Be confident that I am near to you, because I am the Great Comforter. Trust me. Let me heal the brokenness and give you a new song to sing.

THE LAW

SEVENTH COMMANDMENT
"You shall not commit adultery." Exodus 20:14 (NASB)

Remember that I made you. My desire is for you to love only the one to whom you have vowed your love. I know when you are tempted by the looks and verbal advances that come your way. I tell you to withstand the temptation and desire to think about someone besides your mate, because it leads to devastation. The one luring you is being led by Satan who wants only one thing—to destroy your marriage. The sin of adultery has a high price to pay. Are you willing to sacrifice your integrity, your mate and your family on the altar of lustful desire? Seek me, trust me to lead you away from those evil desires that would consume you and destroy your life. My plan for you is full of rewards and hope for the future.

SUFFERING

"For this finds favor, if for the sake of conscience toward God a man bears up under sorrows when suffering unjustly. For what credit is there if, when you sin and are harshly treated, you endure it with patience? But if when you do what is right and suffer for it you patiently endure it, this finds favor with God. For you have been called for this purpose, since Christ also suffered for you, leaving you an example for you to follow in His steps." 1 Peter 2:19–21 (NASB)

Suffering unjustly may be the one experience that brings you to the greatest understanding of your Savior's sacrifice. He knew no sin, and yet was accused of breaking laws which ultimately led to His death on the cross. It is one thing to suffer when you do wrong, for this is just punishment; but to suffer when you have done nothing is a true test of endurance in the race of faith. This kind of patient suffering pleases me as you follow My Son Christ's example.

SUFFERING

"Blessed is a man who perseveres under trial; for once he has been approved, he will receive the crown of life, which the Lord has promised to those who love Him." James 1:12 (NASB)

What trials have you experienced? Pain, job loss, divorce, rebellion, disapproval, hatred, hunger, loneliness, death of a loved one? I know you intimately, and I have seen your struggles. I know when you have wanted to give up, and I have witnessed your determination to persevere. You are blessed when you persevere, for it is in that struggle that you will hear from me and understand my purpose for allowing the trial in your life. Once you have stood the test, you will receive the crown of life, your eternal reward, because you have loved me and depended on my strength in the midst of suffering.

COMFORTER

"Blessed be the God and Father of our Lord Jesus Christ, the Father of mercies and God of all comfort; who comforts us in all our affliction so that we may be able to comfort those who are in any affliction with the comfort with which we ourselves are comforted by God. For just as the sufferings of Christ are ours in abundance, so also our comfort is abundant through Christ." 2 Corinthians 1:3–5 (NASB)

Have you experienced My Comfort? When you were distressed, did you cry out to me? Or have you never known the comfort I can give? I want to comfort you in all of your suffering, so that when you suffer as My Son Christ did, you can have the abundant comfort I give through Christ. And when you have been comforted, you will be able to comfort others with the same comfort you have received. You glorify me when you display mercy and comfort to others.

COMFORTER

"It is better to take refuge in the LORD than to trust in man." Psalm 118:8 (NASB)

When you are burdened, when you have failed miserably, when you have been harmed, when your spirit has been crushed, come to me. Who else knows your innermost thoughts? I alone can comfort you, dispel the pain, and make you whole. I want the fewest trials, the least suffering, and the straightest path for you—that will lead you to become the person I have purposed you to be. Trust me, for I Am the Great Comforter, Counselor, and Mighty God.

Week Thirty-Four
PEACE

"Each one has to find his peace from within. And peace to be real must be unaffected by outside circumstances."—Mahatma Gandhi

"We don't realize that, somewhere within us all, there does exist a supreme self who is eternally at peace."—Elizabeth Gilbert, *Eat, Pray, Love*

"There is no such thing as inner peace. There is only nervousness and death."—Frances Ann Lebowitz

The world has some strikingly different views about peace, but what does God say? The answers to the following questions are found in His Word:

Is peace given to us? "Peace I leave with you, <u>my peace I give unto you</u>; not as the world giveth, give I unto you. Let not your heart be troubled, neither let it be afraid." John 14:27 KJV.

Jesus' promise confirms that it is He who gives us peace. So, if peace is a gift that we know we have been given through faith in Jesus Christ, why are we unable to have a sense of peace in all circumstances? What action is required to elicit this peace we long for, especially in desperate times? You will find the answer in the next question.

Is peace conditional?

"Thou wilt keep him in perfect peace, whose mind is stayed on thee; because he trusteth in thee." Isaiah 26:3 KJV

Yes, we will have perfect peace when our mind continually trusts in Him. But how do we cope with the distractions of this world which rob us of our peace? It is a matter of practice—an exercise of the mind. A good example is the writing of this book, *First Fruits*. It is especially easy to have peace when I focus on God's Word and listen to inspirational music through my headset. The world is blocked out and I feel God's presence wash over me as I write my impressions from Him. Pondering the many facets of God's character builds strength and confidence to help fight off the negative thoughts that would steal my joy and peace when the headset comes off and the Bible is closed. I do not always win the battle against negative thoughts, but my percentage is better because I know the key to peace is keeping the mind of Christ … knowing His Word and allowing my communication with Him to be fluid throughout the day.

"And the peace of God, which passeth all understanding, shall keep your hearts and minds through Christ Jesus." Philippians 4:7 KJV. We cannot understand it completely … so we just trust.

Reflections:

_____

_____

PEACE

"Be anxious for nothing, but in everything by prayer and supplication with thanksgiving let your requests be made known to God. And the peace of God, which surpasses all comprehension, shall guard your hearts and your minds in Christ Jesus." Philippians 4:6–7 (NASB)

I am Peace. What are you worried about? What stands in the way of your confidence in me to provide every need? Are you so focused on what you do not have that you cannot be thankful for what you have? Talk to me and ask for what you want, but do it with a spirit of thanksgiving for that which I have already given you. Give your burdens to me and I will cover you with My Peace which surpasses everything you understand, to guard your hearts and your minds in the name of Jesus.

PEACE

"When a man's ways are pleasing to the LORD, he makes even his enemies to be at peace with him." Proverbs 16:7 (NASB)

Do you know a person who is respected by the masses, though they may not be especially beautiful or wealthy or powerful? Perhaps they are not even successful in the world's view. Is there a quiet contentment in them that may contradict their circumstances? When your ways are pleasing to me, others take notice and respect you even if they disagree with you. Strive then to please me, and be at peace.

PEACE

"These things I have spoken to you, that in me you may have peace. In the world you have tribulation, but take courage; I have overcome the world." John 16:33 (NASB)

My Son Jesus comforted His disciples by telling them that though He was leaving them and they would grieve, they could have peace in Him. His words, "in this world you will have trouble," are still true today, but take heart because He has overcome the world. My Plan will triumph over all the trouble in the world when the heavens open and the King of Kings and Lord of Lords returns to earth for His millennium reign!

SECURITY

"What then shall we say to these things? If God is for us, who is against us?" Romans 8:31 (NASB)

Because I created you and love you and support you, it really doesn't matter if others are against you. My Power and My Plan for you trump what others might say or do. I hold the keys to the Kingdom, and when you choose me as your God, there is nothing to fear. I will protect you and guide you; no enemy shall conquer you because you are mine.

SECURITY

"For I am confident of this very thing, that He who began a good work in you will perfect it until the day of Christ Jesus." Philippians 1:6 (NASB)

Be confident that I planned and created you for my work. What I began in you before you were even born, I will perfect until the day Christ returns. This perfection takes a lifetime, so do not be discouraged in times of doubt and defeat. Just get up and try again, clinging to my promise that you are a work in progress on the path to perfection.

OBEDIENCE

"Do not love the world, nor the things in the world. If anyone loves the world, the love of the Father is not in him. For all that is in the world, the lust of the flesh and the lust of the eyes and the boastful pride of life, is not from the Father, but is from the world. And the world is passing away, and also its lusts; but the one who does the will of God abides forever." 1 John 2:15–17 (NASB)

What in this world has captured your thoughts and desires today? Is it some new possession, the applause of mankind, attainment of wealth or rank among friends? I tell you that all of these things encompass the pride of life, and are from the world—not from me. You know that the world and those in the world who do not love me will pass away, and all of their lusts will die with them. But if you do My Will, you will abide forever. Keep this in mind as you set your goals for today. Live for me and live forever!

OBEDIENCE

"I urge you therefore, brethren, by the mercies of God, to present your bodies a living and holy sacrifice, acceptable to God, which is your spiritual service of worship. And do not be conformed to this world, but be transformed by the renewing of your mind, that you may prove what the will of God is, that which is good and acceptable and perfect."
Romans 12:1–2 (NASB)

Do you realize that your bodies are a living and holy sacrifice, and an important part of how you worship me? Be sure to present yourself as acceptable to me by renewing your mind in My Word. Do not conform yourself to this world where the moral compass deteriorates more each day, but be transformed by applying what you learn from scripture to your life. Ask me to reveal my perfect will for you in every circumstance.

Week Thirty-Five

WORSHIP

WORSHIP – Homage rendered to God which is sinful to render to any created being (idolatry). *Easton's Bible Dictionary*

Worship is a privilege. Worship is a gift. Worship is public. Worship is private. Worship is silent. Worship is song. Worship is facing upwards toward God. Worship is bowing low before Him. Worship is personal—no matter how or where you worship—it is between you and God. "Since we are receiving a Kingdom that is unshakable, let us be thankful and please God by worshiping him with holy fear and awe." Hebrews 12:28 (NLT)

Known as Elohim—Yahweh—Adonai—El Shaddai—I Am—Alpha & Omega—God: do you ever stop to think about the incredible privilege we have through Jesus Christ to worship and pray directly to our Master and Creator? And that the great I AM cares for us in a way we can't begin to comprehend? If you are feeling insignificant, think on that! A privileged few get to have conversations with great international leaders, CEO's of mega corporations, the most acclaimed movie stars and super athletes, etc. But *we* have a direct line to commune with the One True God, through whom anything is possible. Now *that* is significance.

I am privileged and blessed to belong to one of the great churches of the 21st century, Prestonwood Baptist Church in Plano, Texas. Though this church has over 35,000 members, I say I "belong" to it because my husband and I have invested our lives here. Our closest friends are those we have known through Bible Fellowship for over 30 years. We have a ministry staff who has held our hand in dark days and inspired us to grow in greater knowledge of The Lord. The church goal is simple—to reach souls for Christ until He comes again.

Corporate worship happens not only when thousands gather together to make a "joyful noise," but when even two or three gather together in Jesus' name, joining their hearts in praise to the King of Kings and Lord of Lords. For some, worship occurs during a prelude before the service begins. For others, it happens in the midst of praise music. Still others worship deeply during the sermon as they apply what God is saying to them through the minister. It is amazing to me that God gets us together in one big room and, in the span of an hour, uses the same conduits of music and sermons to connect with each of us individually, effecting different outcomes as each person applies His message to their life! How great is that?

In John 4:23–24 (NLT), Jesus explained to a Samaritan woman the essence of worship: "But the time is coming—indeed it's here now—when true worshipers will worship the Father in spirit and in truth. The Father is looking for those who will worship him that way. For God is Spirit, so those who worship him must worship in spirit and in truth."

No matter where or when we worship, God is honored when we not only set aside the time to commune with Him, but when we prepare for that time of worship by inviting the Holy Spirit to indwell our beings before we begin. Let's not miss what God has to say to us.

Reflections:

_____

_____

WORSHIP

"Therefore also God highly exalted Him, and bestowed on Him the name which is above every name, that at the name of Jesus every knee should bow, of those who are in heaven, and on earth, and under the earth, and that every tongue should confess that Jesus Christ is Lord, to the glory of God the Father ... for it is God who is at work in you, both to will and to work for His good pleasure." Philippians 2:9–11, 13 (NASB)

Is My Son Jesus Christ your Lord today? Do you realize that you have the *privilege* of bowing to Him? For I have highly exalted Him, that at the mention of His name, angels, humans and even demons should bow and confess that Jesus Christ is Lord! This is my plan, and it pleases me to work in you through the power of the Holy Spirit, so that you honor and glorify Him. When you glorify Him, you glorify me.

WORSHIP

"But an hour is coming, and now is, when the true worshipers shall worship the Father in spirit and truth; for such people the Father seeks to be His worshipers. God is spirit, and those who worship Him must worship in spirit and truth." John 4:23–24 (NASB)

I seek those whose human spirit invites My Holy Spirit to fill them with the truth of My Word. I desire for you to worship me when you are alone, as well as when you worship with fellow believers. It pleases me when you are focused not on a sanctuary or a soloist, but on the message of hope in Christ, and how you can strengthen your faith by hearing and reading My Word. Wherever you are, worship me in Spirit and in Truth—that is true worship.

WISDOM

"Cease striving and know that I am God; I will be exalted among the nations, I will be exalted in the earth." Psalm 46:10 (NASB)

You desire peace, and yet you become defiant when another nation tests you. Do you think aggression is the only answer when diplomacy fails? I am the Most High God who raises leaders and deposes them at my discretion. Understand that I will be exalted among the nations and in all the earth. My power is greater than all the missiles and nuclear energy man can produce. Cease striving against other nations, and come back to me. Prove you trust me by seeking my wisdom with a humble spirit, and encourage others to follow after me. My Way is the Perfect Path to Peace and Life Everlasting.

SPEECH

"Let him who means to love life and see good days refrain his tongue from evil and his lips from speaking guile. And let him turn away from evil and do good; let him seek peace and pursue it. For the eyes of the LORD are upon the righteous, and His ears attend to their prayer, but the face of the LORD is against those who do evil." 1 Peter 3:10–12 (NASB)

Life is a gift from me. I watch my righteous ones and I hear their prayers. You must choose to live a life that glorifies me. First of all, control your tongue! It is important to think before you speak, and let your words bring edification and comfort to those who hear. Inspire others by your own behavior to speak with respect and do acts of kindness; let these very actions point others to me. Seek peace with others, no matter what comes from their mouth. When your actions display the principles you learn from me, your days will be enriched and your life will honor My Name.

WORD OF GOD

"But know this first of all, that no prophecy of Scripture is a matter of one's own interpretation, for no prophecy was ever made by an act of human will, but men moved by the Holy Spirit spoke from God."
2 Peter 1:20–21 (NASB)

My Word was written by men of my choosing, directed and inspired by the Holy Spirit of God. The prophecies foretold were never and could never be written by mere human thought, but by My Spirit alone. For it was I who instructed the Spirit, who in turn impressed the prophets to write. The proof of prophecy is in its revelation. History proves out the accuracy of all true prophetic utterances, marking the fulfillment of each one in the passage of time.

OBEDIENCE

"For the mind set on the flesh is death, but the mind set on the Spirit is life and peace, because the mind set on the flesh is hostile toward God; for it does not subject itself to the law of God, for it is not even able to do so … if anyone does not have the Spirit of Christ, he does not belong to Him … for all who are being led by the Spirit of God, these are sons of God … and if children, heirs also, heirs of God and fellow heirs with Christ, if indeed we suffer with Him in order that we may also be glorified with Him." Romans 8:6, 7, 9b, 14, 17 (NASB)

Are you choosing to be led by My Spirit today? Do you realize what opportunity you have in this choice as a child of mine, and fellow heir with My Son Jesus Christ? The laws I have given to all mankind are unimportant to the man of flesh, and he doesn't understand what he is giving up. You will have life and peace, but the mind set on the flesh will end in death. Those who are hostile to me think they have all the answers and are not even able to follow me. But you who accept the suffering of Christ and walk in His Spirit have wisdom and will be glorified with Him for all eternity.

PRAISE

"Rejoice always; pray without ceasing; in everything give thanks; for this is God's will for you in Christ Jesus." 1 Thessalonians 5:16–18 (NASB)

Thanksgiving should be every day. Look around you and rejoice in all that you have been given. I want you to think about your physical capabilities, your talents and skills, your family and friends, and the grace that abounds in your relationship with me. Make each day a conversation with me that begins and ends with thanksgiving for the forgiveness of sin and the hope you have found in My Son Jesus Christ. Learn to be thankful in all things, confident that I will provide exactly what you need as you keep your eyes on me.

Week Thirty-Six
GRACE

Before we can begin to understand the depth of God's grace, He gives us glimpses of grace through others. Upon first glance, you may not relate these "lucky days" to God's grace, but look again. Remember the day you got caught speeding—and then for some unknown reason, the officer looked at you and smiled as he tore up the ticket and told you to slow down? What about the understanding friend who forgave your stressed-out reaction to something they had no control over? And then there's Charlie, the adorable Bassett hound who just picked the wrong day to get under your feet. You yell, and he cowers with those hang-dog eyes. The next thing you know, Charlie is sidled up right next to you, with those same big eyes full of love and admiration. Unmerited grace indeed!

Now God, on the other hand, already knows before we are born how many times and in which ways we are going to break the rules and need His pardon, His amazing grace. In addition to the ways in which He graces us with mercy and understanding from others, He covers every last sin committed until the day we die. His Word tells us that we are saved, not because we deserve it, but because it is His gift to us. Ephesians 2:8 (NASB) "For by grace you have been saved through faith; and that not of yourselves, it is the gift of God." He goes on to say in verse 9 that we can't earn it—"not as a result of works, so that no one may boast." Finally, He tells us why in verse 10—"For we are His workmanship, created in Christ Jesus for good works, which God prepared beforehand so that we would walk in them."

Grace seems illogical. The apostle Paul certainly wrestled with the concept, as he asked the Lord three times to take away his "thorn in the flesh." Each time the Lord told him, "My grace is all you need. My power works best in weakness." 2 Corinthians 12:9 (NLT). And so it is in our lives—that which keeps us somewhat humble allows God to grace us with His power, not ours. Even when we can't see it or explain it, God is using us to show Himself to others.

In sheet music, there is a small note called a "grace note." The grace note is always attached to a larger note, and is typically played less than a second before the larger note. And yet, it is this small accent which adds color and character and purpose to the main note. I like to think that just as the Lord has added color and character and purpose to our lives through His grace, we can do the same in other's lives as we find moments to play our grace notes for them and for Him.

"Then the name of our Lord Jesus will be honored because of the way you live, and you will be honored along with him. This is all made possible because of the grace of our God and Lord, Jesus Christ." 2 Thessalonians 1:12 (NLT)

Reflections:

_____

_____

GRACE

"Gracious is the LORD, and righteous; yes, our God is compassionate. The LORD preserves the simple; I was brought low, and He saved me." Psalm 116:5–6 (NASB)

When do you feel my grace and compassion? Is it on the mountaintops of life when you have success at every turn? Or is it when you have been brought low by your circumstances? Think about My compassion: it does not begin at the point of your need, but before you even have the need. For how would you experience compassion unless you had a need? And how would you have a need unless I allowed it? There is purpose in the low times of life, so that you might realize my righteousness and power to heal every hurt. Depend on me for all things.

GRACE

"But He gives a greater grace. Therefore it says, 'God is opposed to the proud, but gives grace to the humble.'" James 4:6 (NASB)

I am the Lord your God. To know that I am opposed to the proud should give you pause. Understand that when you act proud of your accomplishments or possessions, you deny my power. You must stay constantly aware that you have nothing except by my grace. That is why I give greater grace to the humble, for they recognize the contrast between their humanness and my attributes as God. This comprehension is necessary so that you receive the Holy Spirit as my *gift* to guide you into all knowledge and understanding. Recognize that the indwelling of the Holy Spirit is not something you have earned or deserve, but is a blessing of My Grace.

SPEECH

"And I say to you, that every careless word that men shall speak, they shall render account for it in the Day of Judgment. For by your words you shall be justified, and by your words you shall be condemned."
Matthew 12:36–37 (NASB)

Words matter. Be careful when you speak. I warn you now that you are responsible for every careless word—whether it be hurtful, crude, obscene, angry, arrogant, antagonistic or blasphemous. Judgment Day will demand an accounting of your speech. By your words you will be justified, and by your words you will be condemned. Let words of wisdom, encouragement, respect and love flow from you so that I am glorified. Words matter.

SPEECH

"There is one who speaks rashly like the thrusts of a sword, but the tongue of the wise brings healing." Proverbs 12:18 (NASB)

Have you ever been pierced by someone's words as though a sword had been thrust into you? The pain can actually feel physical as you struggle to find your balance. Conversely, when have you caused pain in another by hurtful words of your own? Your speech is critical in being known as a Christ-follower; you must think before you speak. Therefore, be wise and let your words bring healing. Encourage one another, and above all, love others as I love you. The result will always be pleasing to me.

SALVATION

"And there is salvation in no one else; for there is no other name under heaven that has been given among men, by which we must be saved." Acts 4:12 (NASB)

There are many places in My Word that tell you My Son Jesus is the only name under heaven by which you must be saved. That means that there are no other religions and no other gods—none—that will save your soul and give you eternal life. No other religion or faith provides a Savior who gave the ultimate blood sacrifice of death so that your sins could be forgiven. He rose again, defying death and hell, to claim you for all eternity. If it was worth His dying, isn't it worth your living?

OBEDIENCE

"Train up a child in the way he should go; even when he is old he will not depart from it." Proverbs 22:6 (NASB)

Train your children in My Ways. When they learn my commands and to love as My Son Jesus loved, then they will be able to apply this profound knowledge to any walk of life they choose. They will consider the feelings of others in what they do and say, and they will respect others' reputations, property, and life. They will speak the truth in love with everyone. They will honor their commitments and honor their parents all of their days. These character traits, when learned as a young child, will stay with them into old age.

ASSURANCE

"Truly, truly, I say to you, if anyone keeps My word he shall never see death." John 8:51 (NASB)

You may ask, "How do I keep all of your Word?" And I will tell you to begin with love. If you first love me and show it by your obedience and desire to please me, you will then love those I have created in my image. All sin comes in some form of rebellion to the principle of loving me first, and loving others as yourself. If you want assurance of life everlasting, then know and follow My Word. I will join you on this journey to joy—let us begin today.

Week Thirty-Seven
LOVE

hat exactly is love? Is it a feeling—a thought—or an action? In John Bisagno's book, *Love is Something You Do,*[7] the focus is on relationships; the message being not only to *say* you love someone, but to show them love through your actions. Whether the object of your affection is your spouse, parent, child, friend, pet, teacher, boss or pastor, they interpret your love by how you treat them.

Are there different kinds of love? The Bible speaks of four distinct forms of love from the Greek:

- **Agape**: Unconditional love; that love which our heavenly Father shows us in the person of Jesus Christ who first loved us. He did not wait for us to love Him, but proved His love for us through His suffering and death on the cross for the redemption of sins.
- **Storge**: Natural affection between a parent and a child. I think of my Dad when the word "love" comes up. He died Thanksgiving, 2012,

7   Bisagno, John R., *Love is Something You Do,* www.amazon.com

at 88. Though he was a very reserved man and found it difficult to express his love verbally, during his last decade he developed the habit of saying just the word "love" at the end of phone conversations. That one word said it all, and is now my fondest memory of him.

- **Phileo**: Brotherly love, where there is give and take, loyalty and understanding.
- **Eros**: Physical, emotional love which can exist with or without logic.

There is an entire chapter in the Bible dedicated to the subject of love. In fact, 1 Corinthians 13 is known as the Love Chapter. Many couples use it as the scripture reading for their wedding. It begins so beautifully, "If I speak with the tongues of men and of angels, but do not have love, I have become a noisy gong or a clanging cymbal" (NASB).

In today's vernacular, *The Living Bible* translates the verse like this: "If I had the gift of being able to speak in other languages without learning them and could speak in every language there is in all of heaven and earth, but didn't love others, I would only be making noise."

So then, what is the most accurate definition of love for the Christian?
<u>God is Love</u>
- 1 John 4:10 (NASB)—In this is love, not that we loved God, but that He loved us and sent His Son to be the propitiation for our sins.

And how do we respond to this authentic, extreme example of love?
<u>Love One Another</u>
- 1 John 4:12 (NASB)—No one has seen God at any time; if we love one another, God abides in us, and His love is perfected in us.

Reflections:

_____

_____

LOVE

"But love your enemies, and do good, and lend, expecting nothing in return; and your reward will be great, and you will be sons of the Most High; for He Himself is kind to ungrateful and evil men. Be merciful, just as your Father is merciful. And do not judge and you will not be judged; and do not condemn, and you will not be condemned; pardon, and you will be pardoned." Luke 6:35–37 (NASB)

Look for opportunities today and search your heart for ways to love the unloving; love those with whom you do not agree. Follow my example and be kind even to those who are ungrateful. When you give of your time or money, expect nothing in return. Your reward will be great because you follow My Way. Just as I am merciful to those who do not deserve mercy, practice mercy with others, remembering my mercy to you. Do not judge and condemn others in your own mind, but pardon them just as you want to be pardoned. Let me take care of the sins of others; your opportunity is to love!

LOVE

"Then make my joy complete by being like-minded, having the same love, being one in spirit and of one mind. Do nothing out of selfish ambition or vain conceit. Rather, in humility value others above yourselves, not looking to your own interests, but each of you to the interests of the others." Philippians 2:2–4 (NIV)

As believers, you are to be like-minded in Christ, having *His* Love, *His* Spirit and *His* Mind. Following Christ's example, be humble in your opinion of yourself and put others first. Think of them and their interests rather than preferring to talk about yourself and what is important to you. Think of what they would like to do, what they would like to discuss, how they feel. Selfish ambition and vain conceit are like tarnished metal attempting to reflect the light of Christ. Shine brightly like silver as His Spirit works in you.

LOVE

"Charm is deceitful and beauty is vain, but a woman who fears the LORD, she shall be praised." Proverbs 31:30 (NASB)

Beauty and charm are gifts from me, though they can be both a blessing and a curse. Through no fault of your own, beauty can cause jealousy, and charm can be taken as insincere. Women, what is the answer then? Fear Me—not as one who is afraid to approach me—but let your love and respect for My Way point others to me and you will be praised. There is nothing so beautiful as a spirit of love and grace.

SALVATION

"Jesus said to him, 'I am the way, and the truth, and the life; no one comes to the Father, but through me.'" John 14:6 (NASB)

I have loved my creation since the beginning of time, and have used people, angels and miracles to communicate this love. I gave Israel the Ten Commandments (Covenant of The Law) to guide them and provide a blueprint for living a God-honoring life. Because of sin, I chose to send My Son Jesus to live a righteous life, then suffer and die for the sins of all mankind. This is My New Covenant so that you can be saved by Grace rather than experience the futility of trying to live up to the Law. No one can earn salvation by right living or good works. My Son **Jesus provides** the way to walk with me—**Jesus personifies** the truth of Who I Am—**Jesus perfects** eternal life through His death and resurrection. Trust Jesus.

DIRECTION

"And let the favor of the Lord our God be upon us; and do confirm for us the work of our hands; yes, confirm the work of our hands." Psalm 90:17 (NASB)

Do you go about your business without thinking of asking me to join you? Then do not wonder when things go wrong. I want you to look to me for assurance and undergirding in whatever you set out to do. When you begin your day—with a project, an important conversation, a crucial meeting—ask me to go before you and guide you. Then look forward with anticipation to the confirmations I will provide along the way.

THE LAW

EIGHTH COMMANDMENT
"You shall not steal." Exodus 20:15 (NASB)

What have you stolen? Was it an object, an idea, a reputation, a relationship? Taking from others eventually brings pain and remorse. Have I not given you that which I know is right for you? I know the right time, the right season for giving you the desires of your heart. And when you have been denied that which you desire, accept that it is either not the right time or the desire will harm you. Be patient, because when you do receive your desires honestly, without hurting anyone, you will know that I have given them to you. Receiving what I give you will bring the added blessing of joy.

LOVE

"Little children, let us not love with word or with tongue, but in deed and truth." 1 John 3:18 (NASB)

You are my child and I want you to show love in what you do, rather than in what you say. Just as children show their love to their parents by the way they act, I want to see your acts of love, not mere words. Good intentions are just the beginning, for they are the inspiration you receive from me. When you act on that inspiration by ministering to others, you prove out your love to them and you glorify me.

PRAYER

PRAYER—Prayer presupposes a belief in the personality of God, his ability and willingness to hold intercourse with us, his personal control of all things and of all his creatures and all their actions; the intercourse of the soul with God. *Easton's Bible Dictionary*

As Christians, we believe prayer is our opportunity to commune with the Most High God. Prayer should be personal, but not necessarily private. It is our privilege to "come boldly unto the throne of grace, that we may obtain mercy, and find grace to help in time of need." Hebrews 4:16 (KJV)

HOW DO WE PRAY—Jesus instructed the early Christians to pray as follows: "After this manner therefore pray ye: Our Father which art in heaven, Hallowed be thy name. Thy Kingdom come, Thy will be done in earth, as it is in heaven. Give us this day our daily bread. And forgive us our debts, as we forgive our debtors. And lead us not into temptation, but deliver us from evil: For thine is the kingdom, and the power, and the glory, for ever. Amen." Matthew 6:9–13

(KJV). We can learn from Jesus' example that we are to pray reverently, earnestly, and humbly with all praise to our holy God.

WHAT DO WE PRAY—Known as the Model Prayer, Jesus gives us instruction for what we are to pray, whether in a group or by ourselves. First, He tells us to pray to our Heavenly Father, worshipping Him in all humility. We are to praise Him by acknowledging that we desire His will to be done in our lives here on earth, just like His will is done in heaven. We can then ask Him to meet our needs and to forgive us as we seek to forgive others. We should ask for His protection and deliverance from the evil one. Finally, we should end our prayer just as we began it, lifting Him in praise and glorifying His name.

WHEN DO WE PRAY—Prayer should be as automatic as breathing. 1 Thessalonians 5:16–18 (NASB) instructs us to "Rejoice always; **pray without ceasing**; in everything give thanks; for this is God's will for you in Christ Jesus." Praying without ceasing means to allow your prayer life to become a dialogue with the Lord each day. Prayer does not demand a formal salutation nor does it need to end with Amen. Conversations with God can happen as soon as you wake up, while you get ready for the day, in the car—anytime, anywhere. He is delighted when you acknowledge His presence and His protection, eager to show you more as you seek Him more.

WHY DO WE PRAY—Philippians 4:6–7 (NASB) tells us: "Be anxious for nothing, but in everything by prayer and supplication with thanksgiving let your requests be made known to God. And the peace of God, which surpasses all comprehension, will guard your hearts and your minds in Christ Jesus." If we can gain the peace of God through prayer, the question, then, is why don't we pray? You have access to God and His infinite wisdom and power. Involve the Lord in everything that concerns you, and experience the unfathomable riches of God's wisdom and peace through Christ Jesus.

Reflections:

_____

_____

PRAYER

"Ask, and it shall be given to you; seek and you shall find; knock, and it shall be opened to you. For everyone who asks receives, and he who seeks finds, and to him who knocks it shall be opened ... If you then, being evil, know how to give good gifts to your children, how much more shall your Father who is in heaven give what is good to those who ask Him!" Matthew 7:7, 8, 11 (NASB)

I want you to come to me with everything—all of your hopes and dreams. My desire is that you seek my will as you make decisions, and that you are honest with me concerning any doubts you may have. After all, I already know what you ask and why you ask it. Even you, who are not yet perfected and have sin in your life, know how to give good gifts to your children. How much more then will I, the Lord God, give that which is good to you if only you will ask? Have confidence that I want to give you every good gift at the proper time.

PRAYER

"But as for me, I will watch expectantly for the LORD; I will wait for the God of my salvation. My God will hear me." Micah 7:7 (NASB)

How confident are you that I hear your prayers? Does my hearing depend on your faith in my hearing? Absolutely not! But, your **confidence** in my hearing does depend on your faith in me. So be like Micah, and watch and wait expectantly for me, because I am the God of your salvation. Then you will see and know when your prayers are answered, whether the answer is yes, no or wait. Seek me, ask for discernment, and wait for my reply.

PRAYER

"You ask and do not receive, because you ask with wrong motives, so that you may spend it on your pleasures." James 4:3 (NASB)

I want you to come to me with the desires of your heart, but make sure your motives are pure. Ask yourself if the request will hurt anyone; will it diminish your witness; will it distract you from my purpose for you? If it is simply for your pleasure, your motive is wrong. I have blessed you in countless ways—be thankful, always remembering that I inhabit the praise of my people. Keep your requests open for things of eternal significance, such as the purity of your heart and mind, the filling of the Holy Spirit in you each day, the request for another's healing of mind, body or soul, protection, solace for the one who grieves. Above all, for those whom you love, ask that they desire a relationship with me.

POWER

"Now to Him who is able to do exceedingly abundantly beyond all that we ask or think, according to the power that works within us, to Him be the glory in the church and in Christ Jesus to all generations forever and ever. Amen." Ephesians 3:20–21 (NASB)

Do you have my power working within you? My glory through Christ Jesus is shown by your witness to your generation. I am able to do so much more than you can imagine—as described in My Word—"exceedingly abundantly beyond all that you ask or think." Don't depend on your own ideas and actions, but rely on me to show you far beyond your limited scope of solutions. My Power in you will give you a glimpse into your potential as you walk with me and include me in your decisions. Be a part of My Glory to all generations!

POWER

"And He has said to me, 'My grace is sufficient for you, for power is perfected in weakness.' Most gladly, therefore, I will rather boast about my weaknesses, that the power of Christ may dwell in me. Therefore, I am well content with weaknesses, with insults, with distresses, with persecutions, with difficulties, for Christ's sake; for when I am weak, then I am strong." 2 Corinthians 12:9–10 (NASB)

I have unlimited grace to give you. When you are weak—either physically, emotionally or intellectually—I am strong. My ability to meet you at the point of your need will strengthen your faith as you experience the incredible power and force of your Father's love. Just as Paul was content to be abused, persecuted and ultimately slain, the next time you feel inadequate and weak, consider it an opportunity for the world to see me at work in you. Call on My Name and absorb My Power in times of need. When you are weak, become strong in me!

POWER

"For God has not given us a spirit of timidity, but of power and love and discipline." 2 Timothy 1:7 (NASB)

When you are afraid, be assured that your fear is not from me. Fear immobilizes you, causes panic, exhaustion, loss of focus, and hopelessness. When you are attacked by this tool of the enemy, recognize it and renounce him! Remember that I have given you the tools you need: My Love, My Power and My Discipline. Claim them in the Mighty Name of Jesus.

WISDOM

"Behold, Thou dost desire truth in the innermost being, and in the hidden part Thou wilt make me know wisdom." Psalm 51:6 (NASB)

You must first be truthful with yourself, and then you must be truthful with me. My wisdom will not come if you share only partial truths about your concern. There will be unrest, frustration and anxiety until you come clean and reveal everything to me, the Omnipotent One. When I give you my wisdom, it will be perfect for the moment.

ENCOURAGEMENT

D o you have someone in your life who is a champion of encouragement to you? I hope so. In my life, there are two women who stand tall in matters of encouragement. The first, I am happy to say, is my mother. She has always been my great encourager. No matter what I may say or do that might discourage another mother, my mom finds the silver lining in all my efforts. It is as if she refuses to focus on my weaknesses, but rather my strengths. What a great role model she has been!

The second woman is a dear friend who has been with the Lord for a number of years. Her name is Tommie Sue. We met when she moved here from Houston with her husband, Dan, who joined our ministerial staff. A few of us helped her unpack and set up her kitchen in a home just a block from our church. What struck me about Tommie Sue was her generous spirit and her smile. We became fast friends and the next fall she taught the first Prestonwood Injoy Women's Bible study in my home.

She introduced me to Psalm 37:4 (NASB): "Delight yourself in the Lord, and He will give you the desires of your heart." She set such a good example of doing just that, as I watched her set her sights on the Lord in everything. She encouraged me all the time; sometimes with words, but most often with her actions. Her coffers were full with a husband she adored and three daughters who exemplified the love and encouragement she gave so freely.

I thought of Tommie Sue today as I began refinishing a mantel I purchased recently. As I applied the stripping agent and began scraping away all the layers of paint and varnish, the years seemed to fade away, as I remembered the day God gave Tommie Sue one of the desires of her heart—this mantel. She was so excited with her big smile and those bright eyes shining, as she exclaimed, "Suzy, just look what Dan has given me!" Did I mention that back then, she was the only one who called me Suzy besides my mom? What a blessing to have this mantel as a reminder of a dear friend who impacted my life more than she ever knew.

I am convinced God places people in our lives to encourage us—to make us more determined, hopeful and confident. Thank God for the encourager in your life. And if you don't think you have one, think again … "This is my command—be strong and courageous! Do not be afraid or discouraged. For the Lord your God is with you wherever you go." Joshua 1:9 (NLT)

Reflections:

_____

_____

ENCOURAGEMENT

"The Lord God is my strength, and He has made my feet like hinds' feet, and makes me walk on my high places." Habakkuk 3:19 (NASB)

Am I your strength? Make it your practice to come to me for encouragement and boldness in your walk. I will lift you up and give you sure-footed confidence to accomplish all I have planned for you to do. Find your purpose—pray and seek—and then rely on me to give you the strength to pursue and conquer it. Remember that what I command you to do, I will enable you to do.

ENCOURAGEMENT

"Older women likewise are to be reverent in their behavior, not malicious gossips, nor enslaved to much wine, teaching what is good, that they may encourage the young women to love their husbands, to love their children, to be sensible, pure, workers at home, kind, being subject to their own husbands, that the word of God may not be dishonored."
Titus 2:3–5 (NASB)

This instruction I give is for all women, young or old; beyond that, it is good advice to both male and female. I desire for you to revere me in your behavior. Be addicted to My Spirit rather than wine or strong drink, which leads to loose tongues. Don't allow yourself to gossip and tear down the character of another. It is a form of judging, and that does not please me. Teach what is good to those younger than you, investing in their lives. Encourage friends to love their spouse and be subject to them, to love their children, and to be pure, hard workers and kind. You honor My Word every time you do these things.

ENCOURAGEMENT

"Instruct them to do good, to be rich in good works, to be generous and ready to share, storing up for themselves the treasure of a good foundation for the future, so that they may take hold of that which is life indeed." 1 Timothy 6:18–19 (NASB)

I am pleased when you think of ways to bless others. A phone call at just the right time, a meal shared with someone in need, a promise of prayer to a hurting friend, a financial gift to help the less fortunate, time with a child, love expressed through smiles and hugs, and sharing My Word to build someone's faith. Be ready at all times, asking me to point you to one who needs to know someone cares. Experience the treasures of life lived in love.

SALVATION

'The word is near you, in your mouth and in your heart'—"that is, the word of faith which we are preaching, that if you confess with your mouth Jesus as Lord, and believe in your heart that God raised Him from the dead, you shall be saved; for with the heart man believes, resulting in righteousness, and with the mouth he confesses, resulting in salvation." Romans 10:8–10 (NASB)

I have given you instructions for salvation using both your heart and mouth, so that you can be confident in it. If you know that Jesus died for *your* sins and believe in your heart that I raised Him from the dead, you will be saved. You achieve righteousness by believing in Him. Salvation is yours when you confess with your mouth Jesus is Lord. Share what is in your heart—let others know about your confidence in Christ.

PROTECTION

"He who dwells in the shelter of the Most High will abide in the shadow of the Almighty." Psalm 91:1 (NASB)

I Am the LORD your God, the Most High, the Almighty! When you depend upon me for your protection and shelter from the storms of life, you dwell with me. The shadow of my love covers you during controversy, threats, attacks from the adversary and suffering. You have nothing to fear when you abide in me – I have you covered.

STEWARDSHIP

"Therefore be careful how you walk, not as unwise men, but as wise, making the most of your time, because the days are evil. So then do not be foolish, but understand what the will of the Lord is."
Ephesians 5:15–17 (NASB)

Each person has the same amount of time in their day. Why do some people accomplish more than others? Don't be foolish as some who go about each day unaware of the traps of evil, self-centeredness, greed, laziness, and lack of purpose. These selfish pursuits waste precious time and dishonor me. Rather, be wise and make the most of your time. Work diligently at your task for the day. Find ways to bless someone else if you have time that is uncommitted. When you seek my will and submit to my way, your time will be blessed.

STEWARDSHIP

"Will a man rob God? Yet you are robbing me! But you say, 'how have we robbed Thee?' In tithes and offerings. You are cursed with a curse, for you are robbing me, the whole nation of you! Bring the whole tithe into the storehouse, so that there may be food in my house, and test Me now in this," says the LORD of hosts, "if I will not open for you the windows of heaven, and pour out for you a blessing until it overflows." Malachi 3:8–10 (NASB)

In the days before Christ was born, the tithe of ten percent was brought to the storehouse of the temple in the form of grain, crops, and livestock. Today, your tithe is still required and should be given to your house of worship to maintain the buildings, pay the pastor and staff, and share in spreading the gospel. Since everything you have is from me, including your ability to get wealth, do not let anything have priority over the gifts you return for my work. When you give in obedience, you are sharing in Kingdom work and I will pour out upon you blessings to overflowing!

Week Forty

CHOSEN

W e form our opinions based, in part, on our own experience. Whenever I think of being chosen in the human experience, I think of the process of adoption. My first experience with it came when our daughter was unmarried and pregnant. After much agony in prayer and family discussion, she made the courageous decision to nurture the baby in her womb and seek adoptive parents. It was a very difficult decision, but one she never regretted. In the process, two choices were made. First, our daughter chose the couple she felt would give her son a loving home with a mother and a father. Secondly, this couple chose him to be their son. He was chosen.

The second experience came when another family member, also unmarried and pregnant, realized she could not take care of a second child on her own. One day soon after I found out about the pregnancy, I asked for prayer for my family concerning this unexpected pregnancy during a round-table Bible study session. One of my good friends at the table reminded me that her daughter was still searching for a child to adopt. A few months later, my niece handed this couple in their late 40's a beautiful baby boy … a bitter sweet moment, yet covered in prayer and confidence that the child had been given in love to a capable and loving couple who had prayed for years for such a time as this. He was also chosen.

You have been chosen as well. In John 15:16 (MSG) Jesus states "You didn't choose me, remember; *I chose you*, and put you in the world to bear fruit, fruit that won't spoil. As fruit bearers, whatever you ask the Father in relation to me, he gives you." This means that whatever we ask in Jesus' name and for His kingdom will be done in His way, His time.

Ephesians 1:3–6 (MSG) exclaims "How blessed is God! And what a blessing he is! He's the Father of our Master, Jesus Christ, and takes us to the high places of blessing in him. Long before he laid down earth's foundations, he had us in mind, had settled on us as the focus of his love, to be made whole and holy by his love. Long, long ago he decided to *adopt* us into his family through Jesus Christ."

Romans 8:29–34 (NLT) punctuates God's choice. "For God knew his people in advance, and he chose them to become like his Son, so that his Son would be the firstborn among many brothers and sisters. And having chosen them, he called them to come to him. And having called them, he gave them right standing with himself. And having given them right standing, he gave them his glory. What shall we say about such wonderful things? If God is for us, who can ever be against us? Since he did not spare even his own Son but gave him up for us all, won't he also give us everything else? Who dares accuse us whom God has chosen for his own? No one—for God himself has given us right standing with himself. Who then will condemn us? No one—for Christ Jesus died for us and was raised to life for us, and he is sitting in the place of honor at God's right hand, pleading for us."

It is both humbling and overwhelming to think of the nature and plan of God's love for us. As you reflect on being one of the Chosen, how can you say thanks?

Reflections:

_____

_____

CHOSEN

"For whom He foreknew, He also predestined to become conformed to the image of His Son, that He might be the firstborn among many brethren; and whom He predestined, these He also called; and whom He called, these He also justified; and whom He justified, these He also glorified." Romans 8:29–30 (NASB)

Before you were born, I knew you and planned your destiny to become like My Son. Because you were predestined, you were called; and because I called you, I have justified you through Christ's death to be glorified with Him for eternity. I have plans for your life—seek My Son to begin your calling on earth. And then, after being justified here on earth through your faith in Him, you will have the magnificent reward of being glorified with Him forever!

CHOSEN

"There is neither Jew nor Greek, there is neither slave nor free man, there is neither male nor female; for you are all one in Christ Jesus. And if you belong to Christ, then you are Abraham's offspring, heirs according to promise." Galatians 3:28–29 (NASB)

When you begin to compare yourself to others, remember that you are one in Christ. This means that you are not below or above your fellow Christians, but equal. Yes, equal to all believers, past, present and future. That list includes Abraham—because you are Christ's, then you will inherit the promise made to Abraham. <u>You are one of the chosen people</u>, so celebrate the knowledge that you were once lost and now found, wandering and now bound for the Promised Land.

CHOSEN

"For he is not a Jew who is one outwardly; neither is circumcision that which is outward in the flesh. But he is a Jew who is one inwardly; and circumcision is that which is of the heart, by the Spirit, not by the letter; and his praise is not from men, but from God." Romans 2:28–29 (NASB)

I want you to understand that being one of the chosen has more to do with your faith and trust in me than with your natural birthright. Rather than the futility of attempting to keep the law, you now have the New Covenant of Christ who by His Grace saves you from the punishment of death and hell. It is not the circumcision of the body, but circumcision of the heart that gives you hope and unity in Christ. Because your heart has been transplanted into this Garden of Amazing Grace, invite others to join who have no hope.

CHOSEN

"Blessed be the God and father of our Lord Jesus Christ, who has blessed us with every spiritual blessing in the heavenly places in Christ, just as He chose us in Him before the foundation of the world, that we should be holy and blameless before Him. In love He predestined us to adoption as sons through Jesus Christ to Himself, according to the kind intention of His will." Ephesians 1:3–5 (NASB)

Before you chose me, I chose you. When there was nothing formed, before the foundation of the world, you were chosen to be holy and blameless before me through the loving sacrifice of My Son. You who have Christ as your Lord were predestined to be my adopted children. Let this blessing of spiritual knowledge guide you today as you remember you were chosen to be a Child of the King!

FAITH

"And He said to them … 'For truly I say to you, if you have faith as a mustard seed, you shall say to this mountain, 'Move from here to there,' and it shall move; and nothing shall be impossible to you. [But this kind does not go out except by prayer and fasting.'"] Matthew 17:20–21 (NASB)

How big is your request today? Does it seem impossible to accomplish? There are many prayers I wish to answer, but I want to see the level of commitment in faith of the one making the request. If what you ask is beyond the scope of human help, then you must believe that I can give you the request you make. This kind of faith takes earnest prayer and fasting, committing yourself in the name of My Son Jesus who can do the impossible.

FAITH

"But My righteous one shall live by faith; and if he shrinks back, my soul has no pleasure in him. But we are not of those who shrink back to destruction, but of those who have faith to the preserving of the soul."
Hebrews 10:38–39 (NASB)

I am not pleased when my children shrink back from the faith which has rescued them from death and destruction. If you have been made righteous through faith in My Son Christ, then continue in your faith. Don't allow anyone or anything to distract you from the truth you have in Christ. **There is nothing the evil one enjoys more than causing fear and doubt in the righteous.** Rebuke him by exercising your faith, reading and believing the promises in My Word. When testing comes, you will stand strong and your soul will be preserved.

CHOSEN

"And so, as those who have been chosen of God, holy and beloved, put on a heart of compassion, kindness, humility, gentleness and patience; bearing with one another, and forgiving each other, whoever has a complaint against anyone; just as the Lord forgave you so also should you. And beyond all these things put on love, which is the perfect bond of unity." Colossians 3:12–14 (NASB)

You are chosen. Nothing in this world is random or by chance. I have chosen you, beloved, to be holy. Just as your Lord Jesus Christ forgave you, you must reflect this forgiveness with others. Be kind and compassionate, gentle and patient. Bear the burdens of those you know with humility and a forbearing spirit. Beyond all of this, wear love like a fragrance and draw others to the unifying Spirit of Christ.

Week Forty-One

WORRY

"And which of you by worrying can add a single hour to his life's span?"
Luke 12:25 (NASB)

Worry / Anxiety—Both of these words evoke a sense of unrest about something important to us. And so the scripture tells us it can't add time to our life ... in fact, it takes time from us. Think about what is bothering you at this very moment. Whether it's a relationship that has gone awry, a financial problem, or any other event in your life that has caused your heart to beat a little faster when you think of it, time is passing that cannot be retrieved.

For example, in the process of building our third home, my husband and I know to expect a certain number of problems and the anxiety that goes with them. As those issues arise, it is easy to jump from A to Z and imagine that what is now will always be. To further complicate the problem, we have no control over when and how the problem will be resolved. We can only communicate with the builder and trust him to fix it.

Except, that is not at all the only thing we can do. We can also communicate with the Father … about our house, our children, our grandchildren, our health, the state of our nation, our finances, our faith … and the list goes on. We have the awesome privilege to go to Him with our problems. 1 Peter 5:6–7 (NASB) tells us "Therefore humble yourselves under the mighty hand of God, that He may exalt you at the proper time, **casting all your <u>anxiety</u> on Him, because He cares for you**."

We must practice taking our cares to Him because it does not come naturally. When I was a young Christian, I thought God only wanted me to bring Him the really big problems. After all, He was busy running the world. He couldn't possibly care about the little things. But after the experiences of raising children and grandchildren, all the while trying to maintain a healthy relationship with my husband, nurturing extended family and friends, and most importantly, growing in my faith through studying His Word, my view of who God is has changed.

You see, our view of God determines how we relate to Him. The measure of our faith in Him to both care and guide us in all things is directly proportionate to our knowledge of who He is. The more we learn of Him through His Word, the more we realize just how much we can trust Him. Jeremiah 32:17 (NIV): "Ah Sovereign Lord, you have made the heavens and the earth by your great power and outstretched arm. Nothing is too hard for you!" When we really "get" that, it dramatically changes our ability to "let go and let God."

"Be anxious for nothing, but in everything by prayer and supplication with thanksgiving let your requests be made known to God. And the peace of God, which surpasses all comprehension, shall guard your hearts and your minds in Christ Jesus." Philippians 4:6–7 (NASB)

Reflections:

_____

_____

WORRY

"But seek first His kingdom and His righteousness; and all these things shall be added to you. Therefore do not be anxious for tomorrow; for tomorrow will care for itself. Each day has enough trouble of its own."
Matthew 6:33–34 (NASB)

There are many causes for anxiety in your world. Today's headlines may cause you to worry about your nation, the economy, your leaders, your freedoms. Maybe you need to have a discussion with a loved one that is going to be difficult. If you are a student, it may be one of your courses that is causing concern. Natural disasters, health crises, international terrorism, and escalating crime continue to threaten your way of life. What is the antidote to all of this anxiety? Seek me to take your burdens and the cares of this world. I know your individual needs, and I will supply them as you trust in me. Choose Christ and nothing will ever separate us!

WORRY

"Humble yourselves, therefore, under the mighty hand of God, that He may exalt you at the proper time, casting all your anxiety upon Him, because He cares for you." 1 Peter 5:6–7 (NASB)

I know you have anxiety, as the world grows more evil each day. I warn you in My Word that these days will be difficult, with men loving darkness rather than light because their deeds are evil. But you have the Light of Christ in you. Use it to dispel the dark recesses of worry, discouragement, and fear. Come humbly before me, casting all your anxiety upon me. This is my will—for comfort and guidance now, and for exaltation on that Day.

SALVATION

"For there is one God, and one mediator also between God and men, the man Christ Jesus, who gave Himself as a ransom for all, the testimony borne at the proper time." 1 Timothy 2:5–6 (NASB)

I am the One True God. At the proper time of my choosing, I gave you My Son Jesus Christ to be a ransom for your soul. He lived a sinless life and died in complete dependence upon me, His Heavenly Father. No other god throughout history has proven his love for mankind by giving his life for all who would believe. His death was witnessed by many, and more importantly, His resurrection from the dead, to prove His Power to overcome sin with new life and life eternal. He now sits at my right hand to mediate for you. This is Our Gift to you, that you might have access to divine wisdom and power—and the faith to gain eternal life.

SUFFERING

"Therefore we do not lose heart, but though our outer man is decaying, yet our inner man is being renewed day by day. For momentary, light affliction is producing for us an eternal weight of glory far beyond all comparison, while we look not at the things which are seen, but at the things which are not seen; for the things which are seen are temporal, but the things which are not seen are eternal." 2 Corinthians 4:16–18 (NASB)

Be glad and rejoice in your knowledge that there is much more to life than what you see. Though you know your outer body is decaying, you understand that your soul is being renewed daily, never giving way to death and decay. How much hope and confidence this should give you as you feast on the Bread of Life! So do not lose heart with the temporary afflictions you suffer, for they are grounding you for eternal Glory which will surpass everything your mind can conceive.

PRAISE

"But as for me, I will hope continually, and will praise Thee yet more and more. My mouth shall tell of Thy righteousness, and of Thy salvation all day long." Psalm 71:14–15a (NASB)

My desire for you is that you would put all of your hope and trust in me. Tell others of the unsurpassable love you have found in My Gift of Jesus Christ and the Holy Spirit. Tell them of the assurance you have of your salvation because My Word has promised that if you believe in your heart that Jesus is the Son of God, and that He died for your sins, you will be saved from the punishment of sin which is death. Tell them that your desire to praise the One you love is because He first loved you.

PRAISE

"O LORD, our LORD, how majestic is Thy name in all the earth, Who hast displayed Thy splendor above the heavens!" Psalm 8:1 (NASB)

I made the heavens and the earth for you to enjoy, and to give you a glimpse of what the new heaven and the new earth will be like. When you see the majestic mountains reach into the clouds, when a waterfall crashes onto thousand-year-old rocks, when the aquamarine ocean surf swells and curls, when a sapphire sky radiates the warmth of spring, when a beautiful voice sends you into rapture, when a child's smile warms your heart—this is but a small representation of the splendor I have created for you above the heavens. Amazing things are in your future!

PRAISE

"For a day in Thy courts is better than a thousand outside. I would rather stand at the threshold of the house of my God, than dwell in the tents of wickedness. For the LORD God is a sun and shield; the LORD gives grace and glory; no good thing does He withhold from those who walk uprightly." Psalm 84:10–11 (NASB)

If you have tasted of My Grace, then you will agree with the psalmist that one day with me is better than 1,000 without me. But for those who do not believe that My Son came to save the lost, this truth may seem foolish. When sin has captured their senses, they are more comfortable with like-minded people. They have not experienced my guidance and protection, nor my grace and glory. How I long for all to come to me in faith and obedience. I want all to experience the wealth of their reward for trusting me and walking in My Way.

REPENTANCE

I n the New Testament, the English word **repentance** is translated from the Greek word *metanoia,* which is a compound word: *meta* (different or beyond) and *noeo* (to think or perceive). *Metanoia* therefore means to think differently, think again or perceive beyond. It is in essence a transformative change of mind or heart. *Easton's Bible Dictionary*

You may have heard repentance defined as a turning away from the object of temptation and going 180 degrees in the opposite direction. In order to accomplish such a bold move, you really do have to think differently, think again and perceive beyond. Let's take those concepts one by one.

- <u>Think Differently</u>—Once you succumb to temptation and the deed is done, you must now live with your decision to sin. Sin is seductive and intoxicating. It is easy to temporarily lose all of your good sense, but once you yield to the temptation the problem multiplies. It is now more difficult than ever to turn yourself around—to think differently. But that is what you must do. The temptation began in your brain and that is where it must be fought in order to achieve repentance.

- <u>Think Again</u>—Repentance is an act of the will that involves not only realizing you were wrong, but thinking again and again about all aspects of the sin and how to navigate through the murky waters of temptation so that repentance of that sin does not have to be repeated.
- <u>Perceive Beyond</u>—The road to repentance involves the realization that your wrong turn could have been avoided if you had only thought about the consequences. You must have a clear perception of the far-reaching consequences beyond the initial regret. How will it affect not only you, but your family, your mental and physical health, your financial future, your character, your reputation, etc.?

Most importantly, consider how your sin will affect your relationship with the Lord. Guilt can become a huge barrier to rekindling your faith and spiritual life. Remember that it is not God who moves away, but you. When you decide to make the 180 degree turn, you will not only move from the sin, you will also move towards God. Because we are doing exactly what God desires for us when we repent, He always moves toward us even as we make the decision to turn. Visualize this beautiful moment of grace next time you make that important turn.

Remember this verse when you need a renewed sense of God's grace: "The Lord is not slow in keeping his promise, as some understand slowness. Instead he is patient with you, not wanting anyone to perish, but everyone to come to repentance." II Peter 3:9 (NIV)

Reflections:

_____

_____

REPENTANCE

"Yet even now," declares the LORD, "return to Me with all your heart, and with fasting, weeping and mourning; and rend your heart and not your garments". Joel 2:12,13a (NASB)

In the days before I sent My Son, it was customary for Israelites to tear their garments when sin and death occurred. Then and now, my desire is that your heart be broken in contrition, not your clothes. Fast, weep, and mourn when you venture into the wilderness of doubt, discouragement, temptation and sin. Put nothing ahead of our relationship—return to me.

REPENTANCE

"Wake up, and strengthen the things that remain, which were about to die; for I have not found your deeds completed in the sight of My God. Remember therefore what you have received and heard; and keep it and repent. If therefore, you will not wake up, I will come like a thief, and you will not know at what hour I will come upon you … He who overcomes shall thus be clothed in white garments; and I will not erase his name from the book of life, and I will confess his name before My Father, and before His angels." Revelation 3:2, 3, 5 (NASB)

It is time to wake up and strengthen your resolve to be about my business. Remember that repentance and obedience please me, and are vital for keeping my commandments until Jesus comes. If you refuse to finish well in your Christian walk, Jesus will come like a thief, but you won't know when. If you replace your human desires with obedience to me, you will be clothed in white garments as an Overcomer, and your name will not be erased from the Book of Life. Then Jesus will confess your name before me and the angels.

Repentance

"Since then we have a great high priest who has passed through the heavens, Jesus the Son of God, let us hold fast our confession. For we do not have a high priest who cannot sympathize with our weaknesses, but one who has been tempted in all things as we are, yet without sin. Let us therefore draw near with confidence to the throne of grace, that we may receive mercy and may find grace to help in time of need."
Hebrews 4:14–16 (NASB)

My Son Jesus came to earth and lived without sin. I sent Him to reveal who I AM in human form, and to sacrifice Himself through an excruciating death on a cross for the sins of all mankind. He did not stay buried, but arose from the grave and passed through the heavens to prepare a place for all those who believe in Him. Because He was tempted here on earth and can sympathize with your weaknesses, you can come directly to Him with confidence—any time, for any reason, in any situation—to receive mercy and grace.

THE LAW

NINTH COMMANDMENT

"You shall not bear false witness against your neighbor." Exodus 20:16
(NASB)

Does lying come easy to you? Do not speak untruthfully about yourself or
anyone else. Have you ever been hurt or angered by the lies told about you?
Keep that in mind the next time you are tempted to be critical of someone's
character. Rather than tearing a person down, build them up using truth as
your cornerstone. If you speak the truth in love, you are keeping my command.
You will gain peace through a clear conscience and the knowledge that you
have been obedient to me.

JUDGMENT

"How long will you lie down, O sluggard? When will you arise from your sleep? A little sleep, a little slumber, a little folding of the hands to rest—and your poverty will come in like a vagabond, and your need like an armed man." Proverbs 6:9–11 (NASB)

Let me teach and judge those who are lazy—those who would rather sleep than work honestly for their food and shelter. Poverty comes to many through no fault of their own, and to some because they have chosen to let others care for them. Poverty changes people and can cause them to commit acts of desperation. You are to help those in need as I have taught you, because in so doing, you show My Love. I will decide when and to whom discipline must come, to open their eyes to the truth. Just do your part to spread love and compassion, and I will take care of the rest.

JUDGMENT

"And inasmuch as it is appointed for men to die once and after this comes judgment, so Christ also, having been offered once to bear the sins of many, shall appear a second time for salvation without reference to sin, to those who eagerly await Him." Hebrews 9:27–28 (NASB)

You who eagerly await Christ, because of your knowledge and acceptance of His free gift of salvation, will see Him face to face. When He comes again, there will be no mention of sin, and there will be no judgment for those in Christ. He bore the sins of many, abandoning His own will, so that you might spend all of eternity with Him. He beckons all to trust in Him, and waits patiently until that last soul surrenders to His unspeakable love.

JUDGMENT

"Therefore do not go on passing judgment before the time, but wait until the Lord comes who will both bring to light the things hidden in the darkness and disclose the motives of men's hearts; and then each man's praise will come to him from God." 1 Corinthians 4:5 (NASB)

It is tempting to pass judgment when you see disobedient and callous hearts thriving in sinful behavior. But I want you to restrain yourself and wait until I judge them. For anything that has been done in darkness, as well as that which is known, will be judged according to motive as well as result. You will be praised for your obedience when you refrain from the temptation of judgment.

Week Forty-Three
OBEDIENCE

When the word obedience is mentioned, my natural inclination is to link it with *dis*obedience and the resultant punishment. A child learns obedience either through reward or punishment. At the age of four, when I painted the neighbor's brand new washing machine bright red, a reward was the last thing on my mom's mind. Though it was my first burst of creativity, the neighbor didn't quite see it that way. Alas, punishment was the tool to help me understand that there are consequences for disobedience.

You may remember in the movie *Forrest Gump*, there were several instances where Forrest took seriously the words of his mom or Lieutenant Dan ... or his girlfriend, Jenny, when she yelled, "Run, Forrest, Run!" He was a simple-minded character who found it easy to comply. Obedience was in his nature.

But what about those of us with a complex nature, living in a complex world? We seem to resist obedience if it doesn't suit our immediate agenda. Though most of us attempt to be good citizens by voting, driving safely, keeping our yards and houses well groomed, paying our taxes, recycling, etc., we each have our areas of weakness which cause us to resist conformity. It may be inconsequential, but if our resistance breaks a law, there is a price to pay.

Unlike obeying the laws of man, obedience towards God is not mandatory. We have a choice. In the Bible, God has given us a full historical account of His people, the Israelites, who wandered away and then returned to His Way—over and over. Moses was given the Ten Commandments, The Law, to instruct them in how to live. There were so many rules attached to these initial Ten, it was impossible to remember them all, much less keep them!

When Jesus Christ was born, lived a sinless life and then died for our sins, the Law of the Old Testament was replaced by the new Covenant of Grace. We live under grace because Christ took on our sin, innocent though He was, and rose victoriously from an agonizing death on a shameful and cruel cross, so that we could share eternity with Him.

God's Word is a complete reference book on how to live victoriously through faith and trust in Jesus Christ. We are given instructions for obedience and we are given warnings concerning disobedience. As you live life and grow in your faith, you begin to realize that His commandments are not for your punishment, but to prevent you from making decisions that will harm you.

"Trust in the Lord with all thine heart; and lean not unto thine own understanding. In all thy ways acknowledge him, and he shall direct thy paths. Be not wise in thine own eyes; fear the Lord, and depart from evil." (KJV) Proverbs 3:5–7

Reflections:

_____

_____

OBEDIENCE

"He who has My commandments and keeps them, he it is who loves Me; and he who loves Me shall be loved by Me, and I will love him, and will disclose Myself to him." John 14:21 (NASB)

I gave the Ten Commandments to Moses on two stone tablets. Prove your love to me by knowing and striving to keep my commandments. Pay attention to my commands and every instruction throughout scripture—they have been given to you for guidance and protection. Remember, a rule written in stone is more than a suggestion; it is a command! As you demonstrate your love for me through obedience, I will reveal more of myself to you. That is a promise.

OBEDIENCE

"Children, obey your parents in the Lord, for this is right. Honor your father and mother (which is the first commandment with a promise), that it may be well with you, and that you may live long on the earth. And, fathers, do not provoke your children to anger; but bring them up in the discipline and instruction of the Lord." Ephesians 6:1–3 (NASB)

I have a promise for those of you who obey your parents: if you practice honor and respect for your parents, I promise to give you a long and well-lived life. Could a rebellious life that dishonors the godly teachings of parents come to an early and disastrous end? Yes, because I have commanded you to obey them. And parents, likewise, raise your children to be disciplined and to love Me. Don't provoke their anger, but provide godly wisdom and counsel seasoned with love.

OBEDIENCE

"For we are His workmanship, created in Christ Jesus for good works, which God prepared beforehand, that we should walk in them." Ephesians 2:10 (NASB)

Do you understand why good works are important? I have created you in my image, so that as you follow the teachings of My Son Jesus, you will want to feed the sick, care for the widows and orphans, help the poor and lonely, and share the good news of a fulfilled life in Christ, both here and for eternity. These good works do not get you into heaven, but your actions demonstrate your love for me as you show love to others.

OBEDIENCE

"Light is sown like seed for the righteous, and gladness for the upright in heart. Be glad in the LORD, you righteous ones; and give thanks to His holy name." Psalm 97:11–12 (NASB)

You are counted righteous if you have Christ in your heart. For the righteous, I will continue to give light for carrying out my purpose. The more you seek my righteousness, the more of it you will find. There is much joy for you as you endeavor to live life my way. Be glad that you have a relationship with me, and give thanks that your holy and omnipotent Creator woos you to Himself with incomparable love.

OBEDIENCE

"Nevertheless, the firm foundation of God stands, having this seal, 'The Lord knows those who are His', and 'Let everyone who names the name of the Lord abstain from wickedness.'" 2 Timothy 2:19 (NASB)

Are you confident that I know you as my child? Where is my seal on you, my mark of authentication? If you are mine, and you call me Lord, then verify your allegiance to me by abstaining from the wicked ways of the world. You demonstrate your faith and your relationship with me through your actions.

DISOBEDIENCE

"But my people did not listen to my voice; and Israel did not obey Me. So I gave them over to the stubbornness of their heart, to walk in their own devices." Psalm 81:11–12

Let the lessons learned by the people of Israel be a constant reminder to you. My Word and My Way are to teach you to honor your maker, keep you from harm and guide you to live life with Godly wisdom. But Israel refused to listen; over and over they thought they knew better than the One who had 1) released them from Egyptian bondage, 2) protected them by parting the Red Sea, 3) took care of all their needs in the desert, and 4) gave them hope of a Promised Land. So, I let their stubbornness rule them, walking in their own way. Hard lessons were learned as they were denied entry into this land flowing with milk and honey. Years later, their descendants were allowed to enter as they put their trust in me. The Author and Finisher of your faith knows best—trust me.

FAITH

"Then He said to Thomas, 'Reach here your finger, and see my hands; and reach here your hand, and put it into my side, and be not unbelieving, but believing.' Thomas answered and said to Him, 'My Lord and my God!' Jesus said to him, 'Because you have seen me, have you believed? Blessed are they who did not see, and yet believed.'" John 20:27–29 (NASB)

Thomas was blessed when My Son Jesus allowed him to touch His hand where the nail had been driven, and put his hand where the sword had pierced Jesus' side. Thomas proclaimed My Son to be "his Lord and his God." Though Jesus knew Thomas needed proof to truly believe, He admonished him by reminding him that there would be many who would believe without this proof. Blessed are you today when you believe without touching the Master's hand, but rather by trusting My Word and being filled with My Spirit.

Week Forty-Four

WORD OF GOD

WORD OF GOD—The Bible, so called because the writers of its several books were God's organs in communicating his will to men. It is his "word" because he speaks to us in its sacred pages. Whatever the inspired writers here declare to be true and binding upon us, God declares to be true and binding. This word is infallible, because (it was) written under the guidance of the Holy Spirit, and therefore free from all error of fact or doctrine or precept. *Easton's Bible Dictionary.*

In order to gain knowledge of God through the Bible, you must first accept the above premise. People question the validity of the Bible as God's Word: 1) because it was written over a long period of time, 2) because so many different people wrote it, and 3) because there have been many translations and versions. If you accept the fact that God created the universe and everything in it, then it is reasonable to assume that He can cross all barriers of space, time, and understanding to elicit the outcome of His Word, accurately disseminated by mere man.

"It would be absurd," writes Richard Watson,[8] the first and some would claim the greatest Methodist theologian after Wesley, "to think that he who has given us the power of communicating ideas to each other should have no means of communicating with us immediately from himself."

[9]"The Bible is a glorious display of God's gracious adaptation of himself to all sorts and conditions of people in all ages of history and in the various stages of human development ... In making his will and purpose known to them, God came down to their level, knowing that it was impossible for them to rise up to his. 'For my thoughts are not your thoughts, neither are your ways my ways,' declares the Lord. Isaiah 55:8 (NASB)"

Finally, a profound description of the Word of God is found *where else?* God's Word:

> **"For the word of God is living and active and sharper than any two-edged sword, and piercing as far as the division of soul and spirit, of both joints and marrow, and able to judge the thoughts and intentions of the heart. And there is no creature hidden from His sight, but all things are open and laid bare to the eyes of Him with whom we have to do." Hebrews 4:12–13 (NASB)**

Reflections:

---

8   [1]Richard Watson, *Theological Institutes.* (New York: Carlton and Phillips, 1856), 1:71.
9   William R. Cannon, *Asbury Bible Commentary,* General Introduction

WORD OF GOD

"All Scripture is God-breathed and is useful for teaching, rebuking, correcting and training in righteousness, so that the servant of God may be thoroughly equipped for every good work." 2 Timothy 3:16–17 (NIV)

The thoughts and ideas in My Holy Scripture were breathed into the writers by me. From these Scriptures you are convicted of your sin, corrected in wrong thinking and instructed in right living. You are given insight and strength for developing habits and skills needed to become My Follower. From this you will develop the courage and will to live out My Precepts. You will learn to share and teach My Word. All of this will conform you to the kind of man or woman I want you to be. Study My Word and be inspired.

WORD OF GOD

"If you abide in My Word, then you are truly disciples of Mine; and you shall know the truth, and the truth shall make you free." John 8:31b–32 (NASB)

You do well today to abide in My Word; not just the reading of it, but allowing it to pervade your being. As you draw near to me, you will learn to love me. You will find that I know you best, and I have only your best in mind as you learn from My Word. If you do this, you are truly mine, and you will know Truth and this Truth will make you free.

WORD OF GOD

"Thy word I have treasured in my heart, that I may not sin against Thee."
Psalm 119:11 (NASB)

How much of My Word have you committed to memory? It is good to read and study it; it is better to learn it and treat it as a treasure of your heart. When trials and temptations come, use My Word as your sword of the Spirit; this spiritual armor is your best defense against discouragement and defeat. Repeating My Word as a prayer will give you the courage to withstand the schemes of the evil one and arm you with My Power. The gates of hell shall not prevail!

WORD OF GOD

"All flesh is like grass, and all its glory like the flower of grass. The grass withers, and the flower falls off, but the word of the LORD abides forever." 1 Peter 1:24–25a (NASB)

I made you with flesh and blood that will one day wither and die, just like blades of grass and flower petals. The things of the world will not last, but My Word abides forever. Look to that which is imperishable, for in it you will find living, lasting Truth.

DISCIPLINE

"All discipline for the moment seems not to be joyful, but sorrowful; yet to those who have been trained by it, afterwards it yields the peaceful fruit of righteousness." Hebrews 12:11 (NASB)

Have you ever recognized a time of sorrow or frustration in your life to be a consequence of sin? When you have been rebellious or careless in your actions, not taking into account how your actions would affect your loved ones, have you been surprised when an unhappy outcome resulted? I am patient because I want to give you the opportunity to turn back to me on your own. But my discipline is swift and sure when I know it is necessary for your repentance. It is never pleasant to receive discipline, but when you come to terms with my purpose, you will turn from the sin and enjoy My Presence and Peace as you pursue righteousness.

DISCIPLINE

"For those whom the LORD loves He disciplines, and He scourges every son whom He receives. It is for discipline that you endure; God deals with you as with sons; for what son is there whom his father does not discipline? But if you are without discipline, of which all have become partakers, then you are illegitimate children and not sons." Hebrews 12:6–8 (NASB)

I love you. When your actions are rebellious and your sin nature takes over, I teach you through discipline, just as you teach your children when they disobey. You must realize that even discipline is a language of love. Be thankful when you are corrected, knowing that if you were not my child, there would likewise be no discipline, for I discipline those I love. And this discipline brings about endurance as you learn that obedience offers peace to you and pleasure to your Heavenly Father.

SALVATION

"And I will pour out on the house of David and on the inhabitants of Jerusalem, the Spirit of grace and of supplication, so that they will look on Me whom they have pierced; and they will mourn for Him, as one mourns for an only son, and they will weep bitterly over Him, like the bitter weeping over a first-born." Zechariah 12:10 (NASB)

It was prophesied that Jerusalem would mourn bitterly when Jesus was nailed to a cross with a crown of thorns, and a sword pierced through his side. The crowd mocked Him with a sign that read, "King of the Jews." I poured out a Spirit of grace on the Jews, as they sought my forgiveness. They mourned and wept like one weeps over the loss of a first-born child. How much they misunderstood. Their sorrow and repentance was warranted for their behavior and motive; yet in their aggressive hunger for His death, they were ironically fulfilling my divine plan to raise Him from the grave three days later, victorious over sin and death!

Week Forty-Five

GLORY

The Glory of God is described in the Old Testament by Ezekiel and Solomon, and in the New Testament by John. All of their descriptions are in the superlative—bright light, shimmering, brilliant, like fire, golden, splendor, majestic. The Jews used the term "Shekinah" to describe the glory of God.

Though it has been many years since I heard a song entitled "Shekinah" by Cynthia Clawson, I will never forget the vivid vision provoked by her enthusiastic and worshipful rendition. I had never thought much about God's Glory until that night, but was almost hypnotized by the sheer force of imagery produced as the bright lights enveloped the entire stage. Between the strength and conviction of her voice and the bright lights, I was ready for the Rapture!

Ezekiel 1 (NASB) tells of Ezekiel's vision of the Glory of God when he was by the river Chebar among the exiles. Here God charged Ezekiel to boldly prophesy to the people of Israel. He saw the heavens open, and similar to John's vision in Revelation, Ezekiel saw four living beings with wings that gleamed like burnished bronze. In their midst was burning fire and above their heads was an expanse like the gleam of crystal, from which the voice of the Almighty came.

You may remember that King David got to plan the new temple in Jerusalem, but it was his son, Solomon, who was given the privilege of building it. To summarize 2 Chronicles 6–7 (NASB), at the dedication of the temple, Solomon climbed atop a huge bronze platform before the altar of the LORD in the presence of all the assembly of Israel. He knelt and spread his hands towards heaven and offered a comprehensive prayer for Israel and God's blessing upon them. When he finished praying, fire came down from heaven and consumed the burnt offering and sacrifices, and "the glory of the LORD filled the house." The priests could not enter because of God's glory, so all of the assembly and priests bowed down to the pavement with their faces to the ground and praised the LORD.

Revelation 21 & 22 (MSG) describe in detail "The City of Light," the Holy Jerusalem resplendent in the bright glory of God. It shimmers like a precious gem, the streets made of pure gold that is translucent as glass with jasper walls which are garnished with every precious gem imaginable. The Lord God and the Lamb are the Temple, and the City does not need the sun or moon for light because <u>God's Glory is its light</u> and the Lamb is its lamp! Its gates made of pearl will never be shut and there won't be any night. The Water-of-Life River will flow crystal bright from the Throne of God and the Lamb, right down the middle of the street. There will be a Tree of Life planted on each side of the River, producing twelve kinds of fruit, a ripe fruit each month. The leaves of the Tree are for healing the nations. Never again will anything be cursed.

Just think, the most beautiful scene in this world will pale in comparison to the Shekinah Glory of God we will witness in the New Jerusalem. For now, I hope to never look at the majestic brilliance of a sunset without thinking of God's Glory that awaits all who trust in Him.

Reflections:

GLORY

"But we all, with unveiled face beholding as in a mirror the glory of the Lord, are being transformed into the same image from glory to glory, just as from the Lord, the Spirit." 2 Corinthians 3:18 (NASB)

When My Son Jesus died on the cross, forgiving your sins, I sent the Holy Spirit to dwell with you until He comes again. Just as Moses wore a veil to cover his shining face after being in the Glory of My Presence, you (with unveiled face) are being transformed into my likeness through the Holy Spirit in you. Yes, My Glory remains in me, but has also been manifested in Jesus who has given you the Holy Spirit. You are becoming more like me as you live out My Word and worship me. As you ask My Spirit to fill you and guide you, My Glory will be revealed in you. Do you see? **From *My* Glory to *Holy Spirit* Glory *in you*.**

Holy Spirit

"Now we have received, not the spirit of the world, but the Spirit who is from God, that we might know the things freely given to us by God, which things we also speak, not in words taught by human wisdom, but in those taught by the Spirit, combining spiritual thoughts with spiritual words. But a natural man does not accept the things of the Spirit of God; for they are foolishness to him, and he cannot understand them, because they are spiritually appraised." 1 Corinthians 2:12–14 (NASB)

Do not be frustrated by your efforts of sharing a spiritual moment that falls on deaf ears. When the reaction from others is either to ignore or mock, realize that they may not be tuned in to My Spirit. Unbelievers certainly are not, and even believers may have tuned me out. What is profound to you is foolishness to them. But rejoice in this gift of the Spirit that I have given you, so that you can know and speak truths which are spiritually discerned. Ask me for opportunities to share with those who are seeking to fill the spiritual void in their life. Prepare to share!

HOLY SPIRIT

"Moreover, I will give you a new heart and put a new spirit within you; and I will remove the heart of stone from your flesh and give you a heart of flesh." Ezekiel 36:26 (NASB)

Is your heart broken today? Has this brokenness caused feelings of emptiness, resentment, jealousy, rebellion, depression, sadness or hopelessness? If you are my child, come to me and lay your burdens at my feet. If you want to trust me for the first time, ask me now to forgive you and cleanse you and make you whole. In either circumstance, I alone can remove the hard layer of resistance and give you a brand new heart, softened and infused with my love.

HOLY SPIRIT

"He said to them, 'It is not for you to know times or epochs which the Father has fixed by His own authority; but you shall receive power when the Holy Spirit has come upon you; and you shall be My witnesses both in Jerusalem, and in all Judea and Samaria, and even to the remotest part of the earth.'" Acts 1:7–8 (NASB)

What is your experience with the Holy Spirit? If you do not have the Spirit of Christ in you, you must first trust Him by faith to save you from your sins. He died on the cross for you, to give you an eternal home with Him and an abundant life on earth through His gift of the Holy Spirit. This Spirit of God will then empower you to live victoriously. You will find courage and strength even on your darkest day because of Christ's Spirit in you. Trust Christ as Savior and Lord, and begin this new Spirit-filled life today.

TRUST

"I will extol Thee, O LORD, for Thou has lifted me up, and hast not let my enemies rejoice over me. O LORD my God, I cried to Thee for help, and Thou didst heal me." Psalm 30:1–2 (NASB)

I am the LORD and I hear your cries for help; I know the burdens you carry. If you trust me, know that I have all wisdom and understanding. I can heal anyone, anywhere, anytime—though sometimes physical healing is not the only healing needed. Because I know all situations and souls surrounding your request, my answer is not always going to fit within your time frame or in the exact manner you wish it to be answered. Trust me to know what is best for you. Whether my healing comes to you here on earth or in heaven, know that the brilliance and splendor of heaven will far surpass your best day on earth.

TRUST

"Come to me, all who are weary and heavy-laden, and I will give you rest. Take my yoke upon you, and learn from me, for I am gentle and humble in heart; and you shall find rest for your souls. For my yoke is easy, and my load is light." Matthew 11:28–30 (NASB)

Are you weary today? I know that the burdens you carry are heavy, and yet you continue to trudge around day after day trying to hold them in place. When you confide in a friend, you may feel better temporarily, but eventually the burdens return. I am the only One who can take your burdens and effect physical, emotional and spiritual changes in your heart. When you come to the place where you can do nothing, it is the perfect place to lay your burdens down at my feet. Let me deal with each burden at the right time, in the right way. Lay your burdens down.

SALVATION

"Who is the liar but the one who denies that Jesus is the Christ? This is the antichrist, the one who denies the Father and the Son. Whoever denies the Son does not have the Father; the one who confesses the Son has the Father also." 1 John 2:22–23 (NASB)

Do not be misinformed. If you think you can have a relationship with me, but deny the saving grace of My Son, Jesus, you lie to yourself. You cannot separate us. I tell you that the antichrist is the supreme master of deceit and lies, denying both My Son and me, because he wants you to follow him. You are mine only if you confess My Son as the One and Only Christ who died so that you might live with us for all eternity. Confess your sins today, ask for the saving grace of Christ, and enjoy fellowship with us through the Holy Spirit now and forever.

Week Forty-Six

DIRECTION

W hile embroiled in an important decision over the last few days, my mind wandered to "wouldn't it be nice if we each had our own little fairy to whisper the right choice in our ear when we deliberate the pros and cons of an issue?" I consider myself a decision maker, but there are times I wish I had a ready expert to make the decision for me. Sometimes, the answer really is just that simple—hire an expert!

We are such complex beings, and whether male or female, most of the time, we would rather do things our way. Stubborn may be too harsh a word, but we do have our opinions. When we need some direction, however, we usually stew a little until the answer becomes clear, whether through an epiphany, laborious research or through that expert I mentioned earlier.

Even experts need experts, since none of us knows it all … which brings us to the point of this precept called direction. What seems more manageable to you: 100 experts for 100 different problems or one expert for all problems? I think most would agree that the logistics alone for involving 100 experts would become hard to handle. Conversely, what about the ability to call on One Expert for all our needs, both the practical and the spiritual?

Proverbs 3:4–6 (TLB) advises, "If you want favor with both God and man, and a reputation for good judgment and common sense, then <u>trust the Lord completely</u>; **don't ever trust yourself**. In everything you do, put God first, and he will direct you and crown your efforts with success."

One might argue that to never trust ones' self shows a lack of confidence, and after all, aren't we supposed to be confident as Christians? Well, yes, that is exactly the point of the advice. Since we human beings are not infallible, our judgment is going to fail from time to time. However, if we use our Infinitely Infallible God to direct our path, our efforts are going to be "crowned with success." That's the kind of Christian confidence I highly recommend.

It takes a great deal of faith to give it all to God, to let Him guide you to the right choice for a school, a business decision or even a piece of furniture. It does not matter what you question. He knows it all and He owns it all. When I remember to quit stewing and get praying, it is amazing how quickly the answer comes … and without fail I ask myself, "now, why didn't I do that sooner?"

Let us strive to seek God's direction more, so that we can become like the psalmist:

"I will bless the Lord who counsels me; he gives me wisdom in the night. He tells me what to do." Psalm 16:7 (TLB)

Reflections:

_____

_____

DIRECTION

"Thy word is a lamp to my feet, and a light to my path ... Thou are my hiding place and my shield." Psalm 119:105, 114 (NASB)

Peace, protection and direction—these I freely give to all who seek me. When you are troubled by things of this world and you need protection from the storms of life, come to me. When you are confused and don't know which way to go, find the answers in My Word. When the pressures of life cause anxiety and worry, bring it all to me. If you want the kind of peace that passes all understanding, find it by laying everything at my feet.

DIRECTION

"The plans of the heart belong to man, but the answer of the tongue is from the LORD. All the ways of a man are clean in his own sight, but the LORD weighs the motives. Commit your works to the LORD, and your plans will be established." Proverbs 16:1–3

There is but one way to be confident that your plans will come to fruition. If you commit your ideas and actions to me, and constantly seek my guidance, you will see your plans established. It is possible to set a worthy goal, but carry it out in a way that displeases me. Keep in mind that I see not only results, but observe your motives along the way. Do not deceive yourself. When you commit to follow my guidance, be honest and pure in your objectives, and I will bless your efforts.

DIRECTION

"For if you cry for discernment, lift your voice for understanding; if you seek her as silver, and search for her as for hidden treasures; then you will discern the fear of the LORD, and discover the knowledge of God."
Proverbs 2:3–5 (NASB)

Have you ever been so distraught over your circumstances, so helpless, that you literally cried out in a loud voice to me? I hear you before you speak, but I want to know how serious you are in discerning my will. Will you allow pride to prevent you from crying out to me? May it never be! The kind of understanding you need is not found in books. It is truly hidden treasure. Seek it with all of your being. Discover amazing knowledge, deep and hidden, that only I can give.

THE LAW

TENTH COMMANDMENT

"You shall not covet your neighbor's house; you shall not covet your neighbor's wife or his male servant or his female servant or his ox or his donkey or anything that belongs to your neighbor." Exodus 20:17 (NASB)

Do you ever wish you had a house or a boat or car like that of a friend? When you see them enjoying their possessions, do you long for more? Or maybe you would be happy with less than they have, but just more than you have? Beware of allowing your mind to go down this path. Wishful thinking can devolve into discontent and bitterness. Remember that I know you intimately, and some of what you want would be harmful for you. Rather, be content and thankful for what you have. Prefer peace over prosperity.

STEWARDSHIP

"For what does it profit a man to gain the whole world, and forfeit his soul?" Mark 8:36 (NASB)

Profit: the difference between the amount paid and the real cost of a good or service. In your life, has there been something you were willing to pay almost anything for, only to learn too late that its true value was far less? Was it a person, possession, or something less tangible such as honor or a title? This is why I tell you not to love the things of this world. They are fleeting, and too often, what you want comes at too great a cost. Rather, invest yourself in knowing and loving the Son of God who paid the ultimate price—at no cost to you—so that you could share in the incredible gain (profit) of Eternal Life.

SALVATION

"For by grace you have been saved through faith; and that not of yourselves, it is the gift of God; not as a result of works, that no one should boast." Ephesians 2:8–9 (NASB)

A priceless, one-of-a-kind Gift was bought with a price you could not pay, by a Person you have never seen. You have been given the free gift of salvation by faith through My Son Jesus Christ. His blood sacrifice for all mankind has taken away your sins, and given you the promise of eternal life. There is nothing you can do to earn it—Christ has done it all for you—you just need to accept His Amazing Gift of Grace.

WITNESS

"And He said to them, 'Go into all the world and preach the gospel to all creation. He who has believed and has been baptized shall be saved; but he who has disbelieved shall be condemned.'" Mark 16:15–16 (NASB)

My desire is for all to come to the saving knowledge of My Son Jesus Christ and follow His example in baptism. Help pave the way for the unsaved across the world. If you can go, then go across the street or across the globe to share what Christ has done for you and how faith in Him has changed you. If you can't go, then give so that others can go. Above all, pray that none would be condemned, but that the world would come to know that Christ loved them enough to die on the cross for their sins to give them hope here on earth and eternal life with Him.

END TIMES – ESCHATOLOGY

END TIMES—Eschatology refers to Christian doctrine including the subjects of death, the second coming of Jesus Christ, the resurrection of the dead, the last judgment, heaven and hell. *Dictionary of Bible Themes*

<u>OVERVIEW OF END TIMES:</u>

"For you yourselves know full well that the day of the Lord will come just like a thief in the night." 1 Thessalonians 5:2 (NASB).

The above verse speaks of the day Jesus Christ will come again to collect all who have believed and trusted in Him as their Savior. But what precedes this great day?

"Let no one in any way deceive you, for it (the day of the Lord) will not come unless the apostasy comes first, and the man of lawlessness is revealed, the son of destruction (the antichrist), who opposes and exalts himself above every so-called god or object of worship, so that he takes his seat in the temple of God, displaying himself as being God." 2 Thessalonians 2:3–4 (NASB)

"Beloved, do not believe every spirit, but test the spirits to see whether they are from God, because many false prophets have gone out into the world. By this you know the Spirit of God: every spirit that confesses that Jesus Christ has come in the flesh is from God; and every spirit that does not confess Jesus is not from God; this is the spirit of the antichrist, of which you have heard that it is coming, and now it is already in the world." 1 John 4:1–3 (NASB)

"For false Christs and false prophets will arise and will show great signs and wonders, so as to mislead, if possible, even the elect…for just as the lightning comes from the east and flashes even to the west, so will the coming of the Son of Man be…but of that day and hour no one knows, not even the angels of heaven, nor the Son, but the Father alone. For the coming of the Son of Man will be just like the days of Noah…eating and drinking, marrying and giving in marriage, until the day that Noah entered the ark, and they did not understand…so will the coming of the Son of Man be. Then there will be two men in the field; one will be taken and one will be left. Two women will be grinding at the mill; one will be taken and one will be left. Therefore be on the alert for you do not know which day your Lord is coming." Matthew 24:24…42 (NASB)

To summarize the above verses, we need to understand that there are spirits of the antichrist alive in the world right now. Apostasy (departure from Christianity) has already begun. When the Antichrist finally shows himself, he will proclaim that he is God and will sit on the throne in the temple of Jerusalem.

Some believe that The Rapture of the Church (when all Christians will meet Jesus in the air) will happen before the seven-year Tribulation begins, while others believe it will happen either at the end of 3-1/2 years or at the end of The Tribulation. What we know for certain is that no one except The Father knows when The Second Coming of Jesus will be. So, we wait and hope for that day when there will be no more sorrow or pain or death, and we will be in the presence of The Lord for eternity. Heaven is described as a magnificent, beautiful place in Revelation. Read it again and become expectant for that day of perfection when we ride with Jesus in the final battle, and then stand in the light of God's Glory when we meet Him face to face.

Reflections:

_____

_____

END TIMES

"And he (the antichrist) causes all, the small and the great, and the rich and the poor, and the free men and the slaves, to be given a mark on their right hand, or on their forehead, and he provides that no one should be able to buy or to sell, except the one who has the mark, either the name of the beast or the number of his name. Here is wisdom. Let him who has understanding calculate the number of the beast, for the number is that of a man, and his number is six hundred and sixty-six." Revelation 13:16–18 (NASB)

In the last days, the Antichrist will have control over the economy of the world. No one will be exempt from his law. Everyone, even those rich and powerful, will be subject to him and given a mark either on their right hand or on their forehead. This beast will have a name and his number is 666. No one will be able to buy or sell if he doesn't have the beast's name or number on his hand or forehead. This revelation will come to pass, so be sure you are ready—not with the mark of the beast, but with My Salvation. To all who believe in the risen Lord Jesus Christ who was and is and is to come, stand firm against the beast and gain eternal life.

END TIMES

"And I saw heaven opened; and behold, a white horse, and He who sat upon it is called Faithful and True; and in righteousness He judges and wages war." Revelation 19:11 (NASB)

There is a battle raging in the air and on the earth between the spirits of darkness and the Holy Spirit. Though the time is not yet come, there will be a day when My Son Jesus will descend from heaven on a white horse. His name is Faithful and True, and He will come to wage war against those who have chosen to side with the evil one. He will judge them, and with His armies of believers, He will strike them down. Make sure you are on His side!

END TIMES

"But realize this, that in the last days difficult times will come. For men will be lovers of self, lovers of money, boastful, arrogant, revilers, disobedient to parents, ungrateful, unholy, unloving, irreconcilable, malicious gossips, without self-control, brutal, haters of good, treacherous, reckless, conceited, lovers of pleasure rather than lovers of God; holding to a form of godliness, although they have denied its power; and avoid such men as these." 2 Timothy 3:1–5 (NASB)

Do these descriptions fit the times in which you are living? When My Word warns you to avoid such men as these, take it seriously. Look at each word to make sure these words do not describe you. I know you fall short, but I also know your heart—whether you are working on your weaknesses or making excuses for your behavior. Finally, and most crucially, do you hold to a form of godliness, while denying My Power? This Power is available to you through My Holy Spirit. Claim it and be filled each day with the inspiration and confidence to achieve great things for My Kingdom.

END TIMES

"And then they will see the Son of Man coming in clouds with great power and glory, and then He will send forth the angels, and will gather together His elect from the four winds, from the farthest end of the earth, to the farthest end of heaven." Mark 13:26–27 (NASB)

I want you to visualize the Son of Man, Christ Jesus, coming with great power and glory in the clouds. Imagine Him dressed in white with My Glory radiating from Him. If you have been born into the Kingdom through faith in the suffering of His death to the forgiveness of your sins, and the power of His resurrection to eternal life with Him, then you are among the *elect*. He will send His angels to gather the *elect* (including you) from the farthest end of earth to the farthest end of heaven. It will be the most exciting, awe-filled moment of your life as you reign with Him!

HOLY SPIRIT

"Not that we are adequate in ourselves to consider anything as coming from ourselves, but our adequacy is from God, who also made us adequate as servants of a new covenant, not of the letter, but of the Spirit; for the letter kills, but the Spirit gives life." 2 Corinthians 3:5–6 (NASB)

Be constantly aware that all skills, knowledge and wisdom you possess are from me. You would have nothing unless I ordained it for you. I have given you both the law and the Holy Spirit. Consciousness of your sin (the law) kills, but the new covenant of the Holy Spirit (My Spirit in you) renews and perpetuates your life for all eternity. Take hold of this Spirit in you and let others see the victory over sin and death that you have gained through the sacrificial death, burial and resurrection of My Son Jesus Christ.

HOLY SPIRIT

"For who has known the mind of the LORD, that he should instruct Him? But we have the mind of Christ." 1 Corinthians 2:16 (NASB)

I have given you My Son Jesus who came in human form to show you My Ways. When you trust Him to be your Savior, you receive not the spirit of the world, but the Spirit of Christ who is my gift to you. As you study My Word, the Holy Spirit will develop and transform your thoughts to have the mind of Christ. Relinquish the wisdom of the world—for as you learn more of Christ, you learn more of me.

HOLY SPIRIT

"Not by might nor by power, but by My Spirit," 'says the LORD of hosts.' Zechariah 4:6b (NASB)

The things I want to accomplish in you will not be done by your independent efforts. It is My Spirit in you which will bring about My Purpose. Therefore, seek me with your whole heart, so that which is known only to me will be revealed to you as you diligently seek me. My Spirit will help you overcome all obstacles as you trust in me. I will overwhelm you with love and purpose and victory!

Week Forty-Eight
PRIDE

Pride is provocative. It may come in the form of pleasure over an accomplishment or pride in our children or grandchildren. Or maybe it lurks in the seemingly innocent attitude of self-sufficiency. Unfortunately, any prideful attitude that causes resentment and disapproval from others will likely discolor our Christian walk and our relationship with the Lord.

Asaph was an outstanding musician during King David's reign who was appointed minister of music in the Temple (1 Chronicle 15:19; 16:5). He wrote twelve of the Psalms, one of which mentions this kind of damaging pride. Psalm 73:2–8 (NLT) states "But as for me, I almost lost my footing. My feet were slipping, and I was almost gone. For I envied the *proud* when I saw them prosper despite their wickedness. They seem to live such painless lives; their bodies are so healthy and strong. They don't have troubles like other people; they're not plagued with problems like everyone else. They wear *pride* like a jeweled necklace and clothe themselves with cruelty. These fat cats have everything their hearts could ever wish for! They scoff and speak only evil; in their *pride* they seek to crush others."

Asaph resolves this 73rd Psalm in verses 27–28 with "Those who desert Him will perish, for you destroy those who abandon you. But as for me, how good it is to be near God! I have made the Sovereign LORD my shelter, and I will tell everyone about the wonderful things you do." Asaph realized that he was wrong to envy the proud because they were far from God. We must seek to recognize pride by continually seeking God's way.

You may remember Hezekiah, King of Judah and descendent of David. He reopened the doors of the Temple in the very first month of his reign at the age of 25. He organized all the Levites to begin the process of purifying and repairing the Temple (2 Chronicles 29). Even this man known as "Good King Hezekiah" who was faithful to God fell prey to a different kind of pride when he became deathly ill. 2 Chronicles 32:24–26 (NLT) states "He prayed to the Lord, who healed him and gave him a miraculous sign. But Hezekiah did not respond appropriately to the kindness shown him, and he became proud. So the Lord's anger came against him and against Judah and Jerusalem. Then Hezekiah humbled himself and repented of his pride, as did the people of Jerusalem. So the Lord's anger did not fall on them during Hezekiah's lifetime."

The Warnings: Proverbs (NLT)

Pride leads to disgrace, but with humility comes wisdom. (11:2)

Pride leads to conflict; those who take advice are wise. (13:10)

Pride goes before destruction, and haughtiness before a fall. (16:18)

Pride ends in humiliation, while humility brings honor. (29:23)

The Antidote:

"For the world offers only a craving for physical pleasures, a craving for everything we see, and pride in our achievements and possessions. These are not from the Father, but are from this world. And this world is fading away, along with everything that people crave. **But anyone who does what pleases God will live forever.**" 1 John 2:16–17 (NLT)

Reflections:

_____

_____

PRIDE

"The arrogance of your heart has deceived you, you who live in the clefts of the rock, in the loftiness of your dwelling place, who say in your heart, 'Who will bring me down to earth?' Though you build high like the eagle, though you set your nest among the stars, from there I will bring you down, declares the Lord." Obadiah 1:3–4 (NASB)

Do not be deceived by your heart. The arrogant proudly go about their day thinking that because they are rich and powerful, they cannot be brought down. I want you to know that if you ascend to the heights of earthly stature, but do it without my blessing, I will bring you down. Nothing of any lasting value can be sustained unless I bless it. Make sure your goals are aligned with my purpose for you.

PRIDE

"Pride goes before destruction, and a haughty spirit before stumbling."
Proverbs 16:18 (NASB)

Pride is like a cancer which grows undetected until it suddenly erupts with a vengeance. Just as cancerous cells overtake healthy cells, pride can infect otherwise honorable attributes. Think of the gifts you have been given— talents and abilities, physical attributes, character traits, possessions—I have blessed you so that you might bless others. Be careful to remember that I am the Giver of all good gifts. Use your gifts with a thankful heart and humility so that you will not stumble.

REPENTANCE

"While I was fainting away, I remembered the LORD; and my prayer came to Thee, into Thy holy temple. Those who regard vain idols forsake their faithfulness, but I will sacrifice to Thee with the voice of thanksgiving. That which I have vowed I will pay. Salvation is from the LORD." Jonah 2:7–9 (NASB)

Have you been rebellious like Jonah, running to things which you know are not my will for you? Remember that I will allow you to run, but I will never give up wooing you back to me. Jonah remembered me in his suffering, and he knew I had heard him. He understood that he had forsaken his faith for a time, but was ready to turn back to me with thanksgiving. He knew his salvation was from the Lord. If you are wandering away from me today, stop and seek me. Repent and receive mercy from the One True God.

Repentance

"For the sorrow that is according to the will of God produces a repentance without regret, leading to salvation; but the sorrow of the world produces death." 2 Corinthians 7:10 (NASB)

If you are honest with yourself, you have regrets. It is impossible to live life without sin, so these regrets have a way of pulling you into defeat and despondency, ultimately leading to the death of your spirit. But it is possible to have sorrow for your sins according to the will of God, producing repentance that leads to salvation. The antidote to regret is confession. Confess your sins, turn from them, and your sorrow will turn into song.

SPEECH

"For everyone who exalts himself shall be humbled, and he who humbles himself shall be exalted." Luke 14:11 (NASB)

What thoughts do you have when someone brags? Do you quickly analyze their motivation, and pass judgment—or do you understand their weakness and give them the encouragement they seek? Do not try to humble the one who raises himself up; that is my work. And when you witness true humility, learn from it because humility is honorable and beautiful in my sight. The humble man has the mind of Christ, and is able to recognize his own limitations by knowing the One without limitations who humbled Himself as the Sacrifice for all.

UNBELIEF

"The fool has said in his heart, 'There is no God.' They are corrupt, and have committed abominable injustice; there is no one who does good. God has looked down from heaven upon the sons of men, to see if there is anyone who understands, who seeks after God." Psalm 53:1–2 (NASB)

When I look down on you, I see not your outward appearance but your heart. I see your yearnings and the ebb and flow of your Godly desires. I know you are not perfect in yourself, but you are perfect in Christ if you believe He has made you a new creature. The fool believes there is no God, and goes about his day fulfilling every ungodly desire, refusing to accept that Judgment Day will come for him. But you, dear seeker, you have sought me out in My Word today. You are blessed for continuing to grow in your knowledge and assurance of my love through My Son Jesus Christ.

WISDOM

"Oh, the depth of the riches both of the wisdom and knowledge of God! How unsearchable are His judgments and unfathomable His ways! For who has known the mind of the LORD, or who became His counselor? Or who has first given to Him that it might be paid back to him again? For from Him and through Him and to Him are all things. To Him be the glory forever. Amen." Romans 11:33–36 (NASB)

Do you desire to know me better, to understand My Ways and My Judgments? For the one who has not put any time and effort into searching for Kingdom riches, the task may seem as simple as making the decision to search. But for those who know me in any small or great way, they understand that searching for My Wisdom and Knowledge must become a daily obsession in order to glean Truth. No man has ever known me fully because all things come *from, through* and *to* me. Therefore, seek me with humility and diligence—blessings abound for those who do!

Week Forty-Nine
LOYALTY

Considering all of your relationships, who commands the highest level of loyalty? Is it your spouse, your children, a parent, a friend? Who do you defend at all costs, not necessarily because they are always right, but because they have somehow earned your devotion over a period of time? Can you explain how they captured your heart? Was it something they said or did? Or is it simply the passage of time and all the seemingly small moments that have bonded your lives together?

When loyalty is mentioned, I think of Ruth and her beautiful promise of commitment to her mother-in-law, Naomi. Ruth 1:16–17 (NASB) states "Do not urge me to leave you or turn back from following you; for where you go, I will go, and where you lodge, I will lodge. Your people shall be my people, and your God, my God. Where you die, I will die, and there I will be buried. Thus may the Lord do to me, and worse, if anything but death parts you and me." At Naomi's bidding, Ruth had the chance to go back to her homeland after her husband died, find a new mate and start a new life. Instead, she chose to go home with her grief-stricken, widowed mother-in-law who had lost both of her sons. What an uncommon act of love and loyalty.

When it comes to The Lord, we know His loyalty is matchless. David writes "Your unfailing love, O Lord, is as vast as the heavens; your faithfulness reaches beyond the clouds. Your righteousness is like the mighty mountains, your justice like the ocean depths. You care for people and animals alike, O Lord. How precious is your unfailing love, O God! All humanity finds shelter in the shadow of your wings. You feed them from the abundance of your own house, letting them drink from your river of delights. For you are the fountain of life, the light by which we see." Psalm 36:5–9 (NLT)

But what about our loyalty to Him? He who has given so richly to us—do we shout our praise and adoration for His unfailing love? Proverbs 3:3–7 (MSG) cautions us in a vivid word picture: "Don't lose your grip on Love and Loyalty. Tie them around your neck; carve their initials on your heart. Earn a reputation for living well in God's eyes and the eyes of the people. Trust God from the bottom of your heart; don't try to figure out everything on your own. Listen for God's voice in everything you do, everywhere you go; he's the one who will keep you on track. Don't assume you know it all. Run to God! Run from evil!"

Let us sing and shout the words of David, **"You thrill me, Lord, with all you have done for me! I sing for joy because of what you have done."** Psalm 92:4 (NLT).

Reflections:

_____

_____

LOYALTY

"For what shall a man give in exchange for his soul? For whoever is ashamed of me and my words in this adulterous and sinful generation, the Son of Man will also be ashamed of him when He comes in the glory of His Father with the holy angels." Mark 8:37–38 (NASB)

When you feel shame, your natural tendency is to ignore the shame by not speaking of it. Now, think of this in relation to me. When you are afraid to speak of me and My Word to those who might slander you or even hate you, have you not put the sinful world ahead of your desire to please me? Do not be afraid to be my witness in this sinful and adulterous world you live in, so that when the Son of Man comes in My Glory with the holy angels, He will be proud to call you His faithful and courageous servant.

LOYALTY

"Then those who feared the LORD spoke to one another, and the LORD gave attention and heard it, and a book of remembrance was written before Him for those who fear the LORD and who esteem His name. 'And they will be mine,' says the LORD of hosts, 'on the day that I prepare my own possession, and I will spare them as a man spares his own son who serves him.' So you will again distinguish between the righteous and the wicked, between one who serves God and one who does not serve Him." Malachi 3:16–18 (NASB)

Like men of old, will you pledge to fear me and honor My Name? Will you claim to be mine even to those who deny my existence? Will you stand up for My Word and keep My Name holy? Then I will spare you as a man spares his own son. And your name will be in the Book of Remembrance naming those who fear me and esteem My Holy Name. And all will know those who serve me and those who do not.

PRAISE

"This is the day which the LORD has made; let us rejoice and be glad in it!" Psalm 118:24 (NASB)

Start your day with this pronouncement: "Thank you, God! You have made a brand new day for me to enjoy. I rejoice in the possibilities laid before me as I begin yet another day in the Light of your Love!" It is good to begin each day with thanksgiving and gladness in your heart. Be optimistic and enthusiastic as you think of the opportunities you have—to make life better for your family, to cheer up a friend, to learn something new, to commune with me and to light up the world with my love—this is your day to shine!

REPENTANCE

"Repent therefore and return, that your sins may be wiped away, in order that times of refreshing may come from the presence of the Lord."
Acts 3:19 (NASB)

How do you feel when you know you have been disobedient to My Word? Do you try to ignore me by being busy, by putting anything and everything ahead of me? Do you run from me, all the while knowing that you cannot? These empty actions can only bring suffering, anxiety, and emptiness. Return to me; give me your burdened heart by relinquishing all sin and the guilt that accompanies it, and you will experience a time of refreshing that comes only in My Presence.

LOVE

"But love your enemies, and do good, and lend, expecting nothing in return; and your reward will be great, and you will be sons of the Most High; for He Himself is kind to ungrateful and evil men. Be merciful, just as your Father is merciful. And do not judge and you will not be judged; and do not condemn, and you will not be condemned; pardon, and you will be pardoned." Luke 6:35–37

Look for opportunities today to demonstrate My Kind of Love. Search your heart for ways to love the unloving; love those with whom you do not see eye to eye. Follow my example and be kind even to those who are ungrateful. When you give your time or money, expect nothing in return. Your reward will be great because you follow My Way. Just as I am merciful to those who do not deserve mercy, practice mercy with others, remembering My Mercy to you. Do not judge and condemn others in your own mind, but pardon them just as you want to be pardoned. Let me take care of the sins of others; your opportunity is Love.

REPENTANCE

"Let the wicked forsake his way, and the unrighteous man his thoughts; and let him return to the LORD, and He will have compassion on him; and to our God, for He will abundantly pardon. 'For my thoughts are not your thoughts, neither are your ways my ways,' declares the LORD."
Isaiah 55:7–9 (NASB)

What sin has you in its grasp? Does this sin of thought or action demand more and more of your time? Does it keep you from me? Remember that you do not think as I do, nor act as I act. My ways are perfect and I am filled with compassion. There is no resentment in me, nor retribution, when you come humbly before me to ask my forgiveness. Give me your burden of sin. Return to me. No relationship on earth is more important than ours.

REPENTANCE

"Repent and turn away from all your transgressions, so that iniquity may not become a stumbling block to you. Cast away from you all your transgressions which you have committed, and make yourselves a new heart and a new spirit! For why will you die, O house of Israel? For I have no pleasure in the death of anyone who dies", declares the Lord God. "Therefore, repent and live". Ezekiel 18:30b–32 (NASB)

I long for you to repent and turn from your evil thoughts and ways. Get rid of the stumbling block! Many distractions are pleasurable for a time, but they will inevitably leave you empty. Make an intentional U-turn away from the sin which separates you from me, and receive a new heart and a new spirit. I have no pleasure in the death of anyone, so why continue to die? Repent and live!

Week Fifty

ASSURANCE

T he assurance we have in the Triune God—Father God, Jesus Christ Son of God and the Holy Spirit of God—begins with faith. Paul writes in Hebrews 11:1 (NASB) "Now faith is the assurance of things hoped for, the conviction of things not seen." To have *conviction* about God requires a certain amount of personal experience and knowledge of God.

For instance, the sun gives us confidence in its ability to provide warmth and light, food for plants through photosynthesis, direction as the sun moves across the sky during the day, and a frame of reference for time in a 24-hour period. Because these basic elements are witnessed each day, our experience and varying degrees of knowledge concerning the sun give us confidence that the sun will set this evening and rise again in the morning. We know it happened yesterday, and we hope it will happen again every day, though we have yet to see tomorrow's sun.

So if faith is the beginning of our quest for assurance, how do we go about building our faith? If you have ever read books or attended seminars on success, one of the oft-repeated tenets of success-building is to attach yourself to "rising stars" in your industry. You learn what to do and what not to do by observing their habits and the way they make decisions. It is the same with your faith. Observe people of great faith and probe the reasons for their faith.

The best place to learn about these "Hall of Famers" is to make a list from Hebrews 11. Then take some time to read each story and why each person stood tall on this list of people of great faith. Men such as Abel, Enoch (who did not see death because he was "pleasing to God"), Noah, Abraham, Isaac, Jacob, Joseph, Moses, Rahab, Esther, and David all achieved recognition — because of their faith.

Moving forward to the great men of faith in the New Testament, you will learn how Jesus' disciples trusted Him even though they didn't understand all He said. Some noteworthy apostles were Matthew, Mark, Luke, John, Peter, Paul, and James. After Jesus ascended, the Holy Spirit was given to all who sought deeper knowledge and understanding of God's power through Jesus Christ.

If we are truly seeking God, He will give each of us assurance of His love for us through the sacrifice of His Son, Jesus, and His gift of the Holy Spirit when Jesus ascended to heaven. His desire to be an active participant in the growth of our faith is so that we might own an unshakable conviction in who He is.

"Now to Him who is able to keep you from stumbling, and to make you stand in the presence of His glory blameless with great joy, to the only God our Savior, through Jesus Christ our Lord, be glory, majesty, dominion and authority, before all time and now and forever. Amen." Jude 1:24–25 (NASB)

Reflections:

ASSURANCE

"And my God shall supply all your needs according to His riches in glory in Christ Jesus." Philippians 4:19 (NASB)

I am God, but am I your God? As you surrender your life to me fully, I will supply all your needs. The riches I give to you cannot be gained by human means, for I fulfill the needs of your soul, the needs met only through My Son Christ Jesus. As you trust in this Gift of Grace, enjoy the confidence of knowing He cared for you before you even knew Him.

ASSURANCE

"If we say that we have fellowship with Him and yet walk in the darkness, we lie and do not practice the truth; but if we walk in the light as He Himself is in the light, we have fellowship with one another and the blood of Jesus His Son cleanses us from all sin." 1 John 1:6–7 (NASB)

What does it mean to have fellowship with me? Do you enjoy being in My Presence and communing with me in the Spirit? Are you walking in My Light by offering all of your life to me in obedience? The good news for you is that I am available and ready to be with you any time—day or night—no appointment necessary. My desire is that you seek me daily, whether you cry with suffering or shout for joy. As you share your day with me, moments large and small, and confess your sins daily, the blood of Jesus will cleanse you, giving you peace and the assurance that you can rely on me for everything.

ASSURANCE

"And this is the confidence which we have before Him, that, if we ask anything according to His will, He hears us. And if we know that He hears us in whatever we ask, we know that we have the requests which we have asked from him." 1 John 5:14–15 (NASB)

This is my promise for answered prayer. When you pray, are you confident that I hear you? Are you confident that I can do what you ask? Here is the secret to confident prayer: you must ask your request *according to My Will.* If you believe that I am God, and that I know all situations surrounding your request, then ask whatever you will 1) believing that I can grant the request, 2) accepting My Wisdom to know what is best, and 3) trusting me even when the answer doesn't come in the form you expect. My decisions are always right and always on time—ask and trust.

SALVATION

"And for this reason He is the mediator of a new covenant, in order that since a death has taken place for the redemption of the transgressions that were committed under the first covenant, those who have been called may receive the promise of the eternal inheritance. For where a covenant is, there must of necessity be the death of the one who made it. For a covenant is valid only when men are dead, for it is never in force while the one who made it lives." Hebrews 9:15–17 (NASB)

I have given you My Son Jesus Christ, the Mediator of a New Covenant; that you who have been called may receive the promise of your eternal inheritance. In order for there to be a new covenant, there had to be death of the One who made the covenant. Christ's death on the cross was the validation of the covenant, and His resurrection, the evidence of the power in Him to grant eternal life to those who have their hope in Him.

PROTECTION

"I will lift up my eyes to the mountains; from whence shall my help come? My help comes from the LORD, who made heaven and earth. He will not allow your foot to slip; He who keeps you will not slumber." Psalm 121:1–3 (NASB)

When you need help, where do you turn? Do you call a family member or friend? Do you run to me first, or do you save me for times of extreme crisis? I want your automatic response to be like the psalmist, lifting your eyes and your heart to me, Creator of heaven and earth. It does not matter the type of trouble or the time you call, I will never be too busy or too tired to help you. Your act of trust will be rewarded with my love and protection over <u>you</u>, one of my best creations!

DISCIPLINE

"Let your roots grow down into him and draw up nourishment from him. See that you go on growing in the Lord, and become strong and vigorous in the truth you were taught. Let your lives overflow with joy and thanksgiving for all he has done." Colossians 2:7 (TLB)

This is my desire for you—that you grow in your knowledge of Christ. And, just like a mighty oak which grows not only upward and outward for all the world to see, but has roots that grow deep and hidden in the earth, I want your hidden roots to grow strong in the enriched soil of time spent with me. When you study My Word and learn of Christ's earthly ministry, internalize His amazing love and grace—His abandonment of His own comfort and safety for the salvation of the whole world. What joy, exultation, and humble adoration should be yours as you contemplate the unfathomable riches of His love!

PROTECTION

"How great is Thy goodness, which Thou has stored up for those who fear Thee, which Thou hast wrought for those who take refuge in Thee, before the sons of men! Thou dost hide them in the secret place of Thy presence from the conspiracies of man; Thou dost keep them secretly in a shelter from the strife of tongues." Psalm 31:19–20 (NASB)

Come to me and let me show you the goodness which I have stored up for all who fear me and take refuge in me. When you feel unjustly accused or conspired against, take heart knowing that My Son has experienced all of this and more. If He who was without sin came to me for comfort and protection, then be confident His example is right for you as well. Place your trust in the secret shelter of My Presence, where the plans and conspiracies of mere man have no power to destroy what I love and protect.

Week Fifty-One
ATTITUDE

<u>Charles R. Swindoll</u>: **Attitudes**[10]

"The longer I live, the more I realize the importance of choosing the right attitude in life. Attitude is more important than facts. It is more important than your past; more important than your education or your financial situation; more important than your circumstances, your successes, or your failures; more important than what other people think or say or do. It is more important than your appearance, your giftedness, or your skills. It will make or break a company. It will cause a church to soar or sink. It will make the difference between a happy home or a miserable home. You have a choice each day regarding the attitude you will embrace.

Life is like a violin. You can focus on the broken strings that dangle, or you can play your life's melody on the one that remains. You cannot change the years that have passed, nor can you change the daily tick of the clock. You cannot change the pace of your march toward your death. You cannot change

---

10   Charles R. Swindoll, *Attitude* quote, Charles R. Swindoll, Inc. © 1982. All rights reserved. Permission to use 2015.

the decisions or reactions of other people. And you certainly cannot change the inevitable. Those are strings that dangle! What you can do is play on the one string that remains—your attitude.

I am convinced that life is 10 percent what happens to me and 90 percent how I react to it. The same is true for you."

Lou Holtz: "Ability is what you're capable of doing. Motivation determines what you do. **Attitude** determines how well you do it."

Winston Churchill: "**Attitude** is a little thing that makes a big difference."

Zig Ziglar: "Your **attitude**, not your aptitude, will determine your altitude"

The above quotes from four well-known individuals define what "attitude" is and isn't, what it affects, what it does, its importance. Chuck Swindoll's description has been widely used in sermons, and in homes across America to lead teens to a better understanding of their potential if they will saturate their objectives with some of Chuck's Godly wisdom.

Most people desire to have a good attitude. The question then becomes "how does one implement a good attitude?" Though attitude is easily recognizable and can be labeled "good" or "bad" in a heartbeat, we need to know how to turn a selfish attitude into one that is pleasing to God. Ephesians 4:21–24 (NLT) gives us good instruction: "Since you have heard about Jesus and have learned the truth that comes from him, throw off your old sinful nature and your former way of life, which is corrupted by lust and deception. Instead, let the Spirit renew your thoughts and attitudes. Put on your new nature, created to be like God—truly righteous and holy."

Paul's beautiful description of Christ's attitude in Philippians 2:5–11 (NIV) states: "You must have the same attitude that Christ Jesus had. Though he was God, he did not think of equality with God as something to cling to. Instead, he gave up his divine privileges; he took the humble position of a slave and was born as a human being. When he appeared in human form, he humbled himself in obedience to God and died a criminal's death on a cross. Therefore, God elevated him to the place of highest honor and gave him the name above all other names, that at the name of Jesus every knee should bow, and every tongue declare that Jesus Christ is Lord, to the glory of God the Father."

Reflections:

_____

_____

ATTITUDE

"Do not rejoice when your enemy falls, and do not let your heart be glad when he stumbles; lest the LORD see it and be displeased, and He turn away His anger from him." Proverbs 24:17–18 (NASB)

How do you feel when someone you dislike makes a mistake? It may be a friend or neighbor, or it may be a politician whose views you oppose. Seek me and know my thoughts, lest you be guilty of enjoying their fall. This attitude displeases me and could cause my anger to turn from their offense to yours. I will take care of sin and its consequences, while you work hard to keep yourself upright.

ATTITUDE

"Whatever you do, do your work heartily, as for the Lord rather than for men; knowing that from the Lord you will receive the reward of the inheritance. It is the Lord Christ whom you serve." Colossians 3:23–24 (NASB)

Are you looking forward to today and the work you have to do? If the answer is no, then try a different approach. Keep in mind that I have allowed you not only the circumstances of each day, but also the opportunity to see it as your effort to please me, as you please those for whom you work, whether it is for your family or your employer. No matter what the task, do it with me in mind and notice the difference in your attitude. Not only will you enjoy your work more, but those around you will, too, as your new attitude rubs off on them. When pleasing me becomes your ultimate goal in everything, your eternal reward is sure, and your earthly results a bonus.

SALVATION

"For a child will be born to us, a son will be given to us; and the government will rest on His shoulders; and His name will be called Wonderful Counselor, Mighty God, Eternal Father, Prince of Peace."
Isaiah 9:6 (NASB)

How could Isaiah have known a Child would be born that would rule the world? He called him Wonderful Counselor to indicate that His counsel would be beyond the mind of natural man. He called him Mighty God because He would have victory over all the evil in the world. He called him Eternal Father because He would care for his own like a father, and live in eternity with all who would accept His free gift of eternal life. And he called him Prince of Peace because He brings peace and tranquility to all who believe. One day He will rule the whole world in peace—and the prophecy will be complete.

LOVE

"Who shall separate us from the love of Christ? Shall tribulation, or distress, or persecution, or famine, or nakedness, or peril, or sword? ... For I am convinced that neither death, nor life, nor angels, nor principalities, nor things present, nor things to come, nor powers, nor height, nor depth, nor any other created thing, shall be able to separate us from the love of God, which is in Christ Jesus our Lord."
Romans 8:35, 38–39 (NASB)

I have given you My Son Jesus Christ. He loved you enough to pay the ultimate price of death on a cross in order for you to have victory over both sin and death. Nothing can separate you from our love ... not death, not life, not angels, not principalities, not things present, not things future, not powers, not height, not depth, not any other created thing ... <u>nothing</u> can separate you from our love.

PRAYER

"Truly, truly, I say to you, he who believes in me, the works that I do shall he do also; and greater works than these shall he do; because I go to the Father. And whatever you ask in my name, that will I do, that the Father may be glorified in the Son. If you ask me anything in my name, I will do it." John 14:12–14 (NASB)

Jesus said that if you believe in Him, you can do the same and even greater works than He did when He was alive. Do you truly believe that you could turn water into wine, heal the sick, skillfully debate the opposition, and walk on water? Understand that there are two qualifiers: 1) you must ask in the name of My Son Jesus, and 2) I must be glorified. Believe in me, trust me; and then, when the need arises, test this promise in the name of Jesus, always desiring for my will to be accomplished and My Name to be glorified.

PRAYER

"Beloved, if our heart does not condemn us, we have confidence before God; and whatever we ask we receive from Him, because we keep His commandments and do the things that are pleasing in His sight." 1 John 3:21–22 (NASB)

Have you experienced the joy and peace of keeping my commandments and doing that which pleases me? There is a confidence you display because you know you are on the path I have purposed for you. But what happens to this confidence when you go your own way and ignore my teachings? Does your guilt alienate you from the rich relationship you otherwise have with me? Your own heart condemns you, but I wait patiently for you to return to me. Stay focused on my purpose for you today; ask for help and I will provide it.

LOVE

"If I speak with the tongues of men and of angels, but do not have love, I have become a noisy gong or a clanging cymbal." 1 Corinthians 13:1 (NASB)

You can have the gift of eloquent speech, but it amounts to noise if it is not seasoned with love. Whether you are talking to a large gathering or a single soul, pray for discernment, both for you and the listener. You must consider the listeners' viewpoint, or how will the listener receive what you say? And when you are confronted without warning, ask me to help you focus on listening and responding in love. Words laced with love pave the path to understanding.

Week Fifty-Two
HEAVEN

H eaven—The place of the everlasting blessedness of the righteous; the abode of departed spirits. Christ called it His Father's house, paradise, the eternal kingdom, a place prepared for all who believe.
Easton's Bible Dictionary

In order to give even a minimal overview of heaven, we must begin with the "why" of heaven—why do we need heaven and what is its purpose. Then we can observe through the eyes of the apostle John the vision he was given about heaven—where it is, who will be there, what it looks like, etc. Full books have been written on the subject, but our purpose is to get a glimpse of it, and whet our appetites for what lies ahead!

> "For God so loved the world that He gave His only begotten Son, that whoever believes in Him shall not perish, but have eternal life. For God did not send the Son into the world to judge the world, but that the world might be saved through Him." John 3:16–17(NASB)

Jesus explains "I am the living bread that came down out of *heaven*; if anyone eats of this bread, he will live forever; and the bread also which I will give for the life of the world is My flesh." John 6:51 (NASB)

"To him who overcomes, I will grant to eat of the tree of life, which is in the Paradise of God." Revelation 2:7b (NASB)

Heaven ... is it a place or a state of mind? John 14:2, 3, 6 (NASB) describes it as a definite place. "In My Father's house are many dwelling <u>places</u>; if it were not so, I would have told you; for I go to prepare a <u>place</u> for you. If I go and prepare a <u>place</u> for you, I will come again and receive you to Myself, that where I am, there you may be also ... I am the way, and the truth, and the life; no one comes to the Father but through Me."

There is much symbolism in Revelation, but the most significant is that of the Trinity—Father, Son, and Holy Spirit—versus the 'False Trinity'—Dragon (Satan), Beast (antichrist), and False Prophet (satanic spirit). Hope is given to those who worship God and the Lamb, Jesus Christ. Doom is warned for followers of the beast who is the antichrist; he will dominate and seduce followers, ultimately leading them to the second death through the false prophet, the deceiving satanic spirit.

Revelation is a book of prophecy concerning the end of the earth as we know it, and "The Coming of the Lord" ['coming' is *Parousia (pah-roo-SEE-ah)* in the Greek language].[11] This prophecy was given through visions to John the apostle while he was imprisoned on the Isle of Patmos during a time of great pressure on Christians to deny their faith and bow to emperor worship. We are taken with John on a visual mind journey up to heaven.

The first scene is of the Lord clothed in a white robe girded with a golden sash standing amidst seven golden candlesticks which represent the seven churches. His hair is white, eyes like a flame of fire, His feet glow like burnished bronze, and He is holding seven stars in His right hand which represent the angels of the seven churches. Out of His mouth comes a sharp two-edged sword, His face is

---

11   *Children of the Day*, A Woman's Bible Study, Beth Moore, 2014, p. 109

like the sun and his voice like the sound of many waters. He tells John to write to the seven churches, giving direction regarding their actions and attitudes.

The throne of God is described as clear jasper with an emerald rainbow around it. God is surrounded by 24 elders and four living creatures full of eyes in front and back rising from a sea of crystal. They look like a lion, a calf, a man, and an eagle, each having six wings and continually saying night and day, "Holy, Holy, Holy is the Lord God, the Almighty, who was and who is to come."

Next, a Lamb standing as if slain between the throne and 24 elders takes a book with seven seals from the right hand of God. The creatures and elders fall down before the Lamb singing a new song: "Worthy are You to take the book and to break its seals; for You were slain, and purchased for God with Your blood men from every tribe and tongue and people and nation. You have made them to be a kingdom and priests to our God; and they will reign upon the earth." Myriads of angels say with a loud voice, "Worthy is the Lamb that was slain to receive power and riches and wisdom and might and honor and glory and blessing."

The Lamb breaks the seven seals one by one, each of which has significance towards the destruction of the earth and its inhabitants, those who follow God and those who succumb to the deception of Satan. War, famine, death, misery of the saints, earthquakes and finally, fire is thrown down to earth causing peals of thunder, flashes of lightning and an earthquake. Chapters 4-19 of Revelation describe this seven-year period known as The Tribulation. The angels then prepare to blow their trumpets ...

FIRST TRUMPET: Hail and fire mixed with blood burns 1/3 of earth, trees, and grass

SECOND TRUMPET: A burning mountain is thrown into the sea, turning 1/3 of sea to blood, killing 1/3 of sea creatures, and destroying 1/3 of ships

THIRD TRUMPET: Great burning star "Wormwood" falls on 1/3 of rivers and springs causing 1/3 of water to become bitter and kill many men

FOURTH TRUMPET: 1/3 of sun, moon, and stars are darkened, so 1/3 of sunlight for day and 1/3 of moonlight for night is taken away

FIFTH TRUMPET: Bottomless pit is opened and locusts are allowed to torment (but not kill) all men for five months. They sting like scorpions; men will seek death and will not find it.

SIXTH TRUMPET: Four angels at the river Euphrates lead 200 million horsemen to kill 1/3 of mankind with the mouths of their horses that have heads like lions, burning fire, smoke, and brimstone. The remaining 2/3 of mankind will not repent.

Before the *seventh trumpet* sounds, there is an interlude with two segments:

1. John is told to eat the book which will taste sweet as honey, but will become bitter in his stomach. He is told to prophesy again concerning many people and nations, tongues, and kings.

2. Authority is given to two witnesses to prophesy for 1260 days. They are given power to defend themselves by turning water into blood and issuing plagues. After the 1260 days, the beast comes out of the abyss and kills them, leaving their bodies in the street for 3-1/2 days. Afterwards, the breath of God blows into them and they stand causing great fear among the people. God calls them to heaven in a cloud and an earthquake kills 7000. The rest are terrified and give glory to God in heaven.

SEVENTH TRUMPET: When this trumpet sounds, the voices in heaven declare: "The kingdom of the world has become the kingdom of our Lord and of His Christ; and He will reign forever and ever." The mystery of God will be finished.

Seven angels then pour out seven bowls of the wrath of God on the earth as follows:

FIRST BOWL: Malignant sores on those who worship the beast and his image

SECOND BOWL: Sea becomes blood and kills everything in the sea

THIRD BOWL: Rivers and springs become blood to avenge the blood of the saints and prophets

FOURTH BOWL: Pours on the sun to scorch men with its intense heat

FIFTH BOWL: Darkness pours on the throne of the beast, and people gnaw their tongues because of the pain and sores

SIXTH BOWL: Pours on the river Euphrates, drying it up to prepare the way for the kings from the east

Before the **seventh bowl** is poured out, John sees three unclean spirits like frogs coming out of the dragon, beast, and false prophet (remember, this is symbolic of the false trinity). These demonic spirits perform signs to draw kings from all over the world to come to a place called Har-Magedon (Armageddon) for the great war of the God Almighty.

SEVENTH BOWL: When this bowl is poured into the air, a loud voice from the temple proclaims, "IT IS DONE." There are flashes of lightning, peals of thunder and an earthquake mightier than any since man came to live on the earth. Huge hailstones weighing 100 pounds each fall, killing multitudes. Islands and mountains are no more. Cities of the nation fall and the great city is split in three parts.

John sees the heavens open and the Lord, called Faithful and True, rides a white horse. His eyes are flaming and many diadems adorn his head. His robe drips blood and His name is called The Word of God. Armies clothed in white linen follow Him on white horses. There is a sharp sword in His mouth to strike down nations. King of Kings and Lord of Lords is written on His thigh and robe.

The beast and the false prophet are thrown alive into the lake of fire burning with brimstone. An angel comes down and throws the dragon into the abyss for 1000 years, after which he will be released for a short time.

At the end of the 1000 years, Satan (dragon) is released to deceive the nations and gather them together for war. They surround the camp of saints and the beloved city, but fire comes down from heaven and devours them all. Satan is then thrown into the lake of fire with the beast and the false prophet to be tormented day and night forever.

Heaven is referred to as the New Jerusalem. The first earth, heaven, and seas have passed away. The new holy city comes down from heaven with the glory of God. It is brilliant like jasper and has a great high wall with 12 gates and 12 angels; the names of the 12 tribes of Israel are written on the gates, 3 gates on each side. The walls have 12 foundation stones, each named for one of the 12 apostles.

The city is 1500 miles high, wide and long, the walls being 72 yards thick. The walls are jasper and the city is pure gold like glass. Foundation stones are of every precious stone—jasper, sapphire, chalcedony, emerald, sardonyx, sardius, chrysolite, beryl, topaz, chrysoprase, jacinth, and amethyst. Each of the 12 gates is a single pearl and the streets are pure gold like transparent glass.

A crystal clear river of the water of life flows from the throne of God and the Lamb down the middle of the street. A tree of life is on either side, bearing a different fruit each month of the year. The leaves of the tree are for healing the nation. Those with His name on their foreheads see God's face and serve Him.

There is no temple in it because the Lord God and the Lamb are its temple. No need for the sun or moon, for the glory of God illumines it and the lamp is the Lamb. The gates are never locked and it is always day. Nothing unclean can enter, but only those whose names are written in the Lamb's book of life.

The angel tells John not to seal up the words of the prophecy of the book because the time is near. "Let the one who does wrong still do wrong; and the one who is filthy still be filthy; and let the one who is righteous still practice righteousness; and the one who is holy, still keep himself holy.

Jesus proclaims, "Behold, I am coming quickly, and My reward is with Me, to render to every man according to what he has done. I am the Alpha and the Omega, the first and the last, the beginning and the end. I, Jesus, have sent

My angel to testify to you these things for the churches. I am the root and the descendant of David, the bright and morning star."

A New Heaven and Earth ... "The Lord is not slow about His promise, as some count slowness, but is patient toward you, not wishing for any to perish but for all to come to repentance. But the day of the Lord will come like a thief, in which the heavens will pass away with a roar and the elements will be destroyed with intense heat, and the earth and its works will be burned up." 2 Peter 3:9–10 (NASB)

The Lord is coming soon to take those who have trusted Him to this new heaven, where He will wipe away all tears. Are you ready? You don't want to miss this Parousia!

Reflections:

_____

_____

HEAVEN

"Behold, I tell you a mystery; we shall not all sleep, but we shall all be changed, in a moment, in the twinkling of an eye, at the last trumpet; for the trumpet will sound, and the dead will be raised imperishable, and we shall be changed. For this perishable must put on the imperishable, and this mortal must put on immortality. But when this perishable will have put on the imperishable, and this mortal will have put on immortality, then will come about the saying that is written, 'Death is swallowed up in victory. O Death, where is your victory? O Death, where is your sting?'" 1 Corinthians 15:51–55 (NASB)

This mystery of Christ's Second Coming is going to change everything. If you have asked Christ to save you from sin and death, then this pronouncement is the beginning of the reward for your faithfulness. When the last trumpet sounds announcing Christ coming through the clouds to receive all believers, you will be changed from mortal to immortal in the twinkling of an eye. Whether you have already passed from this life, or you are still living at the time of His coming, you will be changed. Death *will be* swallowed up in victory!

SALVATION

"And the angel said to them, 'Do not be afraid; for behold, I bring you good news of a great joy which shall be for all the people; for today in the city of David there has been born for you a Savior, who is Christ the Lord. And this will be a sign for you: you will find a baby wrapped in cloths, and lying in a manger.' And suddenly there appeared with the angel a multitude of the heavenly host praising God and saying, 'Glory to God in the highest, and on earth peace among men with whom He is pleased.'" Luke 2:10–14 (NASB)

I used an angel to tell of the greatest and most joyous event in human history. He announced the birth of the Savior, My Son Jesus Christ. He gave them a sign to identify Him—that He would be wrapped in cloths and lying in a manger. And then, in the most beautiful coronation ever seen or heard, a multitude of my heavenly host appeared with praises of "Glory to God in the highest, and on earth peace among men with whom He is pleased." Glorify His Name today as you remember His immaculate conception, birth in a lowly stable, life and ministry and miracles, suffering and death on a cruel cross, and then victory over sin and the grave. Exalt Him as you look forward to the celebration of a lifetime when you see Him face to face!

HEAVEN

"For the Lord Himself will descend from heaven with a shout, with the voice of the archangel, and with the trumpet of God; and the dead in Christ shall rise first. Then we who are alive and remain shall be caught up together with them in the clouds to meet the Lord in the air, and thus we shall always be with the Lord." 1 Thessalonians 4:16–17 (NASB)

This is the reward for your faithfulness and perseverance. One day my trumpet will sound, and you will hear the voice of the archangel announcing Jesus Christ. He will descend from heaven in the clouds, and those believers who have already been buried will rise first. Then all of you who are alive when He comes will be caught up together with them to meet the Lord in the air. There will be no more separation, but an eternity to enjoy being in the presence of the One who has all knowledge, wisdom, power, and love!

HEAVEN

"And He shall wipe away every tear from their eyes; and there shall no longer be any death; there shall no longer be any mourning, or crying, or pain; the first things have passed away." And He who sits on the throne said, "Behold, I am making all things new." And He said, "Write, for these words are faithful and true." And He said to me, "It is done. I am the Alpha and the Omega, the beginning and the end. I will give to the one who thirsts from the spring of the water of life without cost." Revelation 21:4–6 (NASB)

I am the Alpha and the Omega, the beginning and the end. There was nothing but void before I formed the earth and the heavens and all that is within. When the end of this world comes, the first heaven and earth will pass away in a consuming fire. I will make a new heaven and a new earth, and there will be no more suffering, no more tears and mourning, and there will be no more death. I am making all things new. For all who have thirsted and partaken of the Living Water of Christ, there will be singing and rejoicing for this free gift of eternal life. Paradise will be incomplete without you—make sure your thirst is quenched with the Living Water of Christ.

SALVATION

"Enter by the narrow gate; for the gate is wide, and the way is broad that leads to destruction, and many are those who enter by it. For the gate is small, and the way is narrow that leads to life, and few are those who find it." Matthew 7:13–14 (NASB)

Think about the differences in the wide gate versus the narrow gate. The wide gate lets many people pass at the same time, while the narrow gate admits only one at a time. The wide gate allows people of any belief system to pass, but the narrow gate is for those who are willing to worship and obey the Lord Jesus Christ with their whole heart. The wide gate costs nothing and gives passage to ultimate destruction. The narrow gate cost My Son Jesus everything and gives you passage into eternal life. Choose this day the Narrow Way for an eternity with your Savior and Lord.

SPEECH

"Thus says the LORD, 'Let not a wise man boast of his wisdom, and let not the mighty man boast of his might, let not a rich man boast of his riches; but let him who boasts boast of this, that he understands and knows Me, that I am the LORD who exercises lovingkindness, justice, and righteousness on earth; for I delight in these things,' declares the LORD." Jeremiah 9:23–24 (NASB)

I, the LORD, have given you everything you have, and have allowed you to be all that you are. Any wisdom, power, might or riches you possess are from me. Rather than falling into the temptation of pride and boasting about what you have or what you have done, let your boasting be about one thing only: that you know and understand me. Boast all day long that I am your LORD, full of lovingkindness, exercising both justice and righteousness on the earth. I delight in you who treasure your relationship with me enough to tell others that all you are and all you have are because of me.

PRAISE

"And as He was now approaching, near the descent of the Mount of Olives, the whole multitude of the disciples began to praise God joyfully with a loud voice for all the miracles which they had seen, saying, 'Blessed is the King who comes in the name of the LORD; peace in heaven and glory in the highest!' And some of the Pharisees in the multitude said to Him, 'Teacher, rebuke your disciples.' And He answered and said, 'I tell you, if these become silent, the stones will cry out!'" Luke 19:37–40 (NASB)

Imagine the boldness and excitement and utter lack of self-control the disciples experienced as they joyfully exclaimed My Son Jesus as King, and shouted for peace in heaven and glory in the highest! He came in My Name, the LORD God Almighty; and yet the multitudes did not recognize Him even after witnessing all of the miracles done in My Name. When they demanded silence from Jesus's followers, Jesus let them know that even if He were to silence them and everyone around them, the stones would cry out! Nothing would stop His Name from being proclaimed as the Son of God and the King of Kings!

PRAISE

"Now to Him who is able to keep you from stumbling, and to make you stand in the presence of His glory blameless with great joy, to the only God our Savior, through Jesus Christ our Lord, be glory, majesty, dominion and authority, before all time and now and forever. Amen." Jude 1:24-25 (NASB)

It is the last day of this year. I want you to stand blameless before me when the *last day of your life* comes. I have shared my heart with you through scripture and shown you the way to salvation. I have given you the free gift of eternal life at great cost to My Son who suffered and died a painful death that you might have life everlasting. He now sits on the throne at my right hand waiting for that one last soul to trust Him as their Savior and Lord. Invite Him in to have dominion and authority over your life, so that you have the assurance and joy of standing in His Glorious and Majestic Presence!

ABOUT THE AUTHOR

Susan Butler is a new writer who brings years of Bible study and practical Christian experience into focus with this very personal conversation between Almighty God and you!

Growing up in a Bible-believing family in Shreveport, Louisiana, Susan has enjoyed a personal relationship with Christ since she was eight years old. She met C.J. Butler, her husband, while attending Louisiana College. They live in Frisco, Texas and have two grown children and two grandchildren.

Susan developed her skills as an interior designer and owned her own business, Interpretations, Inc., for thirty years. She continued her education in design at The Art Institute in Houston and University of North Texas in Denton. In the midst of raising her family, she was drawn to church activities at Prestonwood Baptist, where she has been a member for over thirty years, participating in Bible fellowship, women's Bible study, choir and various volunteer opportunities.

God began preparing Susan for this journey when she was prompted to gather scriptures which were meaningful to her—not realizing at the time that there was purpose beyond the prompting. Her course was set in 2012 when she was impressed to use those verses to write a 365-day devotional book. She believes God led her to write from His perspective to share His heart in a very personal way using today's vernacular. As she diligently sought the indwelling of the Holy Spirit during each writing session, her desire was that the short, focused messages would be the conduit to elicit a hunger in readers for a closer walk with The LORD.

Below are two verses from which she drew inspiration, strength and power:

"For the word of God is living and active and sharper than any two-edged sword, and piercing as far as the division of soul and spirit, of both joints and marrow, and able to judge the thoughts and intentions of the heart. And there is no creature hidden from His sight, but all things are open and laid bare to the eyes of Him with whom we have to do." Hebrews 4:12–13 (NASB)

"For if you cry for discernment, lift your voice for understanding; if you seek her as silver, and search for her as for hidden treasures, then you will discern the fear of the Lord, and discover the knowledge of God." Proverbs 2:3–5 (NASB):

REFERENCES

The Holy Bible

New American Standard Bible®, marked (NASB), Ryrie Study Bible © 1976, 1978, The Moody Bible Institute of Chicago, The Lockman Foundation,

King James Version marked (KJV), public domain.

New King James Version® marked (NKJV), © 1982, Thomas Nelson.

New International Version®, marked (NIV) © 1973, 1978, 1984, 2011, Biblica, Inc.™ Zondervan. www.zondervan.com

New Living Translation, marked (NLT) © 1996, 2004, 2007, 2013, Tyndale House Foundation.

The Living Bible® marked (TLB) © 1971. Tyndale House Publishers, Inc.

THE MESSAGE © marked (MSG) by Eugene H. Peterson 1993, 1994, 1995, 1996, 2000, 2001, 2002, Tyndale House Publishers, Inc.

The Voice ™ © 2008 by Ecclesia Bible Society.

Bible Gateway, a division of The Zondervan Corporation. https://www.biblegateway.com

Dictionary of Bible Themes

Easton's Bible Dictionary

Books—Periodicals—Bible Studies:

Bisagno, John R., *Love is Something You Do*, www.amazon.com (Love precept)

Byrd, Deborah, *Earth & Sky*, "What is a Blood Moon?" {March 30, 2014} (Unbelief precept)

Cannon, William R., *Asbury Bible Commentary*, General Introduction (Word of God precept)

Fechner, Michael, Founder, H.I.S. BridgeBuilders, mikefechner.com, www.hisbridgebuilders.org (Sowing and Reaping precept)

McClure, Bruce, *Earth & Sky*, "What is a Blood Moon?" {March 30, 2014} (Unbelief precept)

Merriam Webster Dictionary—online App

Moore, Beth, *Children of the Day*, 2014, p. 109 (Heaven precept)

Moore, Beth, *Daniel*, 2006, (Sovereignty precept)

Stager, Lawrence, *Journal of Biblical Archeological Review*, "Child Sacrifice in Carthage: Religious rite or population control?" {1984, January: 31-46} (Sacrifice precept)

Swindoll, Charles R., *Attitude* quote, Charles R. Swindoll, Inc. ©1982 (Attitude precept)

Watson, Richard, *Theological Institutes*, (New York: Carlton and Phillips, 1856), 1:71. (Word of God precept)

WND Faith, ""1st" The Blood Moon, Now The Supermoon", (Unbelief precept)

Wolff, Samuel R., [Joint author with L. Stager above] (Sacrifice precept)

Zola Levitt Ministries, © 2015, www.levitt.com. *The Seven Feasts of Israel*, 6-8. *The Miracle of Passover*, 17. (First Fruits precept)